The Evolution o
Hindu Ethical I

Asian Studies at Hawaii, No. 28

The Evolution of Hindu Ethical Ideals

By S. Cromwell Crawford

Asian Studies Program
University of Hawaii
THE UNIVERSITY PRESS OF HAWAII

Manufactured in the United States of America

Library of Congress Cataloging in Publication Data

Crawford, S. Cromwell.
The evolution of Hindu ethical ideals.

(Asian studies at Hawaii; no. 28)
Bibliography: p.
Includes index.
1. Hindu ethics—History. I. Title. II. Series
DS3.A2A82 no. 28 [BJ122] 950s [294.5'48'09] 81-13114
ISBN 0-8248-0782-0 AACR2

For Suzanne and Christine, my daughters and friends

Contents

Acknowledgments

In writing this book I have received inestimable help from colleagues at the University of Hawaii: K. N. Upadhyaya, Philosophy; J. P. Sharma, History; Lee Siegel, Religion; Walter Maurer and Rama Nath Sharma, Indo-Pacific Languages. The resultant work still leaves room for improvement, but without the expert contributions of my friends I would be less confident of what has been produced.

I am also deeply grateful to Professor Philip Jenner, Chairman (1980) of the Asian Studies Publication Committee, University of Hawaii, for his enthusiastic support, and also to the members of the Committee for their generous acceptance of this work for publication: Alice Dewey, Gayatri Kassebaum, David Kornhauser, and John Stephan.

Abbreviations

Ait. B.	Aitareya Brāhmaṇa
Āpas.	Āpastamba Dharma Sūtra
Āśv. G. S.	Āśvalāyana Gṛhya Sūtra
AV.	Atharva Veda
Baud.	Baudhāyana Dharma Sūtra
BG.	Bhagavadgītā
Bṛh. Up.	Bṛhadāraṇyaka Upaniṣad
BS.	Brahma Sūtra
Chānd. Up.	Chāndogya Upaniṣad
Gaut.	Gautama Dharma Sūtra
JB.	Jaiminīya Brāhmaṇa
Manu	Mānava Dharma Śāstra
Mait. S.	Maitrāyaṇi Saṁhita
Mbh.	Mahābhārata
Muṇḍ. Up.	Muṇḍaka Upaniṣad
MS.	Mīmāṁsā Sūtras
NS.	Nyāya Sūtras
NB.	Nyāya Bhāṣya
Pañc. B.	Pañcaviṁśa Brāhmaṇa
PP.	Padārthadharmasaṃgraha of Praśastapāda
RV.	Ṛg Veda
ŚB.	Śatapatha Brāhmaṇa
SPS.	Sāṁkhyapravacana Sūtra
SK.	Sāṁkhya Kārikā
ŚV.	Ślokavārttika

TS.	Taittirīya Saṁhita
Taitt. Up.	Taittirīya Upaniṣad
VS.	Vaiśeṣika Sūtras
VB.	Vaiśeṣika Bhāṣya
Vas.	Vasiṣṭha Dharma Sūtra
Ved. S.	Vedānta Sūtras
Yāj.	Yājñavalkya Smṛti
YS.	Yoga Sūtras
YB.	Yoga Bhāṣya

Introduction

Hindus call their religion *Sanātana Dharma,* which literally means "Eternal Law." The name should in no wise suggest that the ethical ideals connected with this religion are eternal in the sense of being fixed, static, unchanging substances. To the contrary, Hindu ethics, like the river Ganges, has been in a state of ceaseless flow through the ages, constantly changing its course and currents relative to the hard, intervening realities of Indian history. All of its fundamental presuppositions—*karman, saṁsāra, dharma*—have evolved from streams of thought originating in earliest times. These elements have survived until the present day, not inspite of change but because of change. Thus, under the rubric of eternal, universal law, Hindu ethics combines continuity with dynamic diversity.

The merit of viewing Hindu ethics as a process is that, with the aid of historical tools, we can evaluate later moral developments by judging them in relation to the original intentions of their sources. Many exciting discoveries are made. We find, for instance, that while *jāti* (caste) is a tributary of *varṇa* (class), it has so widely meandered from the psychological insights of the original social scheme that it has become something entirely different.

The evolutionary character of Hindu ethics also gives it a contemporary relevance. Being open to change, its principles can be adapted to contemporary ethical situations. In the critical Résumé, Chapter 4, I have tried to show, for example, how Hinduism's reverential attitude toward Nature can provide modern technological societies with guidelines for an ethics of ecology.

This study will follow the evolution of Hindu ethics through three main periods covering more than twenty-five hundred years. They are the Vedic Period (1500–500 B.C.); the Sūtra and Epic Period (500 B.C.–300 A.D.); and the Darśana Period (to 1100 A.D.). Primary literary sources will be used chiefly. These include: the Vedas, Brāhmaṇas, Upaniṣads, Dharma Sūtras, Dharma Śāstras, Epics, Nyāya, Vaiśeṣika, Sāṁkhya Yoga, Pūrva Mīmāṁsā, and the Vedānta.

Once these sources have been examined there will be no mistake that they are all part of a single tradition and are talking about the same subject, but each views it from a particular stance creating diversity within unity.

Thereafter, the reader will find it difficult to speak generally about "Hindu ethics" without qualifying it with specific textual references. Just as it is unfair and inaccurate to say "the Bible says," or even "the Old Testament says" or "the New Testament says"; it is equally unscientific to speak of *Śruti* ethics or *Smṛti* ethics without locating the particular author. The point is, because of the evolutionary factor in Hindu ethics, changing metaphysics give rise to changing ethics. External circumstances and unusual situations also precipitate shifts in ethical positions.

The next term in the title of this book which requires some explanation is the word "Hinduism." This term is appropriate for later periods of Indian religion which must be distinguished from the earlier period more properly described as Vedic Brahmanism. At the same time, it is equally misleading to draw hard and fast distinctions between the two.

Scholars who claim a generic discontinuity between Brahmanism and Hinduism deny a linear evolution to some of the Indo-Āryan ideas which later blossomed in the Upaniṣads. Not having a sense of their inner evolution, they consider such notions as *saṁsāra, karman,* and *ahiṁsā* as "entirely unknown to pre-Upaniṣadic Vedic religion,"[1] and, therefore, ascribe them to non-Vedic sources. True, belief in *saṁsāra* became full-blown only by the time of the Buddha, but, as Deussen shows, it is possible to trace its gradual evolution from earlier times.[2] *Karman* is not clearly formulated in the Ṛg Veda, but its ethical principles are evident when Ṛgvedic seers recognized suffering as the consequence of previous sin. *Ahiṁsā* has psychological roots going back to the reverence with which primitive man looked upon all of life. The *Vānaprasthas* were the first to give it definite shape. Since *ahiṁsā* was a Vānaprastha ideal, the objection that it could not be Vedic because it conflicts with animal sacrifice, simply does not apply.

In addition to these ideals, several other ethical concepts can be listed to demonstrate the continuity between the early and later periods of Indian religious thought. Worth particular mention are: world order *(ṛta),* truth *(satya),* tolerance, hospitality, duty, and the whole network of values connected with the joint family.

Aside from ethical links, such scholars as L. D. Barnett *(Antiquities of India),* A. A. Macdonell *(India's Past),* A. L. Basham *(The Wonder that was India),* and W. Norman Brown *(Man in the Universe)* have brought to light other aspects of cultural continuity. According to Brown,

> It would be possible to compile a catalogue of many hundreds of cultural items appearing in ancient Indian civilization which are then reborn or at least reappear in constantly changing fashion in succeeding periods during centuries, even millennia.[3]

On the basis of these researches, it seems eminently justifiable to use the word "Hinduism" to cover both the earlier and later periods of Indian religious thought.

The third term in the title which bears clarification is the word "ethics." Technically speaking, Webster defines ethics as "the science that treats of the principles of human morality and duty." Hinduism does not have a science of morals in the fashion of some Aristotelian or Thomistic model. However, it does have a moral philosophy which postulates a *summum bonum* and specifies the proper means for achieving it. This highest ideal is the state of liberation or *mokṣa.* In it a man finds his self-fulfilment and deepest bliss. It is founded on the metaphysical conviction of the oneness of reality which is attainable through direct experience. *Mokṣa* serves as the ultimate standard of right conduct. It measures the value or disvalue of an act by the extent to which it either helps or hinders the attainment of freedom. Actions most distinctively oriented to *mokṣa* are those characterized by truth, nonviolence, sacrifice, and renunciation.

There is no denying the fact that the philosophers were keenly interested in moral conduct, but this did not make them the authors of morality. Habits of life regarding right or wrong conduct were already part of a long-standing tradition. However, as part of their practical teachings, the sages integrated traditional morality into their respective systems in accordance with their own standards of ultimate value. Therefore, in my opinion, it is not correct to say that the philosophers simply "assumed morality." How could they adopt so nondeliberate an attitude toward a discipline which they all recognize as the necessary propaedeutic for enlightenment? They all agree with the Muṇḍaka Upaniṣad: "This Soul, *(Ātman)* is obtainable by truth, by austerity *(tapas).* By proper knowledge *(jñāna),* the student's life of chastity *(brahmacarya),* constantly [practised]."[4]

Śaṅkara is a good illustration of the philosopher who, though recognizing that ethics belongs to the phenomenal world which must be transcended, nevertheless remains true to the Upaniṣadic insistence upon moral qualifications for intuitive knowledge. Śaṅkara does not leave the impression that he is just tagging traditional morality on to his system, but his critical exegesis of the scriptures clearly demonstrates a process of selectivity in keeping with his own metaphysical presuppositions. It is precisely this element of selection which lends variety to the ethics of the different philosophical systems, a phenomenon which we could not have found had all the philosophers merely accepted the traditional morality, lock, stock, and barrel. Even if that were the case, it must be remembered that orthodox morality was by no means monolithic. The philosopher was, therefore, always confronted with at least three options. There was the discipline known as *pravṛtti* or 'active life'; the discipline known as *nivṛtti* or 'quietism'; and the combination of the two in the discipline called *niṣkāmakarman* or 'detached action.'

The ethics of each system of thought will be treated comprehensively on three different levels. On the objective level, we explore the social dimensions of ethics. On the subjective level, we search for personal elements of ethics. And on the transcendental level, we analyse the moral structure of the "life absolute." Because of the close ties between ethics and metaphysics, wherever necessary, there will be a clear-cut elucidation of the philosophical facets in which the ethics is set.

It is possible that the plurality of thought covering so vast an area of time and literature is likely to leave the reader somewhat confused about its unity. For this reason, at the risk of repetition, an extensive summary is provided in the concluding chapter.

Along with the summary there appears a critique of Hindu ethics. In part, this, too, is a résumé of the critical commentary that has been maintained throughout the text. The critical and analytical approach has been dictated by two considerations.

First, I have tried to avoid looking *at* Hindu ethics in the style of a biologist observing an insect under a microscope. "Objectivity" and "detachment" are words with academic appeal, but the values by which people live do not reveal their inner secrets to one who curiously and coldly scrutinizes them from without. There are too many subtle nuances which prove elusive for the scientific approach. This is especially true of Hindu values which, within their internal structure, are vignettes of India's long and changing history. In this context one can say, to know India, try grasping the myriad forms of *dharma,* for in the depths of this single word lies an entire civilization!

At the same time, perusal of several Indian texts dealing with Hindu ethics from *within* has convinced me that the inside view of the religious partisan is too often marred by an extravagant, blind, unreasoning, and arrogant attachment. There are far too many cultural chauvinists endlessly harping on the so-called spiritual ideals of India versus the material ideals of America and the West.

The approach taken in this book is one that steers a course between the Scylla of detachment and the Charybdis of attachment, and in so doing combines the merits of both approaches. Wherever I have made judgments regarding truth and value, they have been based upon a criterion of human authenticity consistent with the Hindu understanding of man. I have also evaluated the system by its inner coherence and by the functional consistency of its major components. However, this critical stance has not prevented me from standing sympathetically within the system and seeing beyond the shadows to the substance.

This "detached-within" approach has been possible for me because, though I am not a Hindu, I was born, educated, and spent twenty-seven continuous years in India. Having learned the language, culture, and religion of the people, as a son of the soil, I can do no less than adopt a scholarly respect for the values of the land.

CHAPTER 1

The Ethics of the Vedic Period

I. Introduction

Our study of Hindu ethics goes back to ancient times with the Āryan invasions of North India which were chronologically parallel to the Hellenic invasions of Greece (*circa* 2000–1000). The Āryans were tall, fair people who spoke an Indo-European language. These pastoral nomads had migrated from the steppes of Eastern Europe, finally making their new home on the upper branches of the Indus River in the northwestern region of India. The culture of these conquering tribes was in sharp contrast to that of the declining Indus civilization.

Not long after their occupation of the land, the Āryans commenced their speculative activities which issued in the formation of the Vedas. The word veda means "knowledge" and is etymologically related to the English words "wit" and "wisdom." The Vedas are divided into three main sections: (1) the Mantras, (2) the Brāhmaṇas, and (3) the Upaniṣads.

(1). The Mantras or hymns are found in four collections called Saṁhitās which are the core of Vedic literature. These are: The Ṛg Veda Saṁhitā; The Yajur Veda Saṁhitā; The Sāma Veda Saṁhitā; and The Atharva Veda Saṁhitā. Professor H. Zimmer observes that "the Vedic hymns are the oldest extant literary and religious monument of the so-called Indo-European family of languages."[1] Many of the theological, ethical and ritualistic elements of the Vedic period are strikingly similar to the Homeric period. The present form of the Mantras was probably fixed *circa* 1500–1000 B.C.

Interpretation of these hymns is often difficult, because they are written in old Sanskrit and represent a very ancient tradition whose meaning is sometimes lost. The problem of interpretation is compounded by the selective character of this collection. Only those hymns which conformed to the ritualistic interests of the compilers were included. This makes the Saṁhitās a partial and one-sided source of information—a factor we shall have to bear in mind when assessing the early Vedic interest in ethics.

(2). The Brāhmaṇas were formed in the centuries immediately following the Saṁhitās (1000–700 B.C.). They are prose writings which attempt to elucidate the meaning and significance of the Saṁhitās, but often misread them. Because they are chiefly preoccupied with the discussion of Vedic sacrifices, modern philosophers unfortunately tend to bypass the Brāhmaṇas.

(3). The age of the Āraṇyakas and Upaniṣads (700–500 B.C.) followed the Brāhmaṇic period. Traditionally, the Upaniṣads are closely associated with Brāhmaṇas, but in spirit they are quite distinct. Whereas the Brāhmaṇas are theological and liturgical, the Upaniṣads are philosophical, and mystical. This is the reason the Upaniṣads are known as the *Jñānakāṇḍa* or knowledge part of the Veda, while the Brāhmaṇas are called the *Karmakāṇḍa* or ritual part. The Upaniṣads provide the foundation for the Vedānta philosophy which, in the opinion of Max Müller, is "a system in which human speculation seems to have reached its very acme."

Together, the Mantras, Brāhmaṇas, and Upaniṣads constitute the three main classifications of the Vedas and are revered as *Śruti* or revealed literature. The reverence attributed to the Vedas ensured their preservation and authenticity to a degree unmatched by other works of antiquity. Speaking of the accuracy of the oral tradition, A. A. Macdonell declared: "The Vedas are still learnt by heart as they were long before the invasion of Alexander, and could now be restored from the lips of religious teachers if every manuscript or printed copy of them were destroyed."[2]

So here, in pristine form, is a body of literature which has guided the spiritual destiny of the Hindus from ancient times and which is no less sacred to this day. Ethically, the chief contribution of these scriptures lies in their evolution of such seminal concepts as: *ṛta* (cosmic order), *varṇa* (class) and *āśrama* (stages of life) *dharmas*, the law of *karman* (moral causation), *saṁsāra* (transmigration), *ahiṁsā* (harmlessness), and *mokṣa* (liberation). The fact that these ancient ethical concepts have survived more than three thousand years of turbulent history indicates their survival value and justifies their contemporary investigation.

II. Ethical Thought in the Mantras

The ancient Indian seers recognized a cosmic order which served as the foundation of their ethics. They called it *ṛta,* a concept which an eminent historian has described as "the highest flight of Ṛg-Vedic thought."[3]

Originally, *Ṛta* was a concept pertaining to the physical universe, denoting the Law of Nature operative in the movement of the planets, the succession of night and day, and the rotation of the seasons. As the principle of order in the universe, it endowed all of the natural phenomena with symmetry and aesthetic form. The beauty and uniformity of heaven and earth were looked upon as proceeding from their unalterable observance of cosmic law.

Gradually, the cosmic sense of *Ṛta* as Natural Law developed into the social sense of *Ṛta* as Moral Law. The nature of this development was crucial for the status of morality. It meant that virtue was given the same immanental position in the social world as law occupied in the physical world. The Moral Law, like the Law of Nature, was intrinsically real, and not relatively real. It endowed the chaotic striving of human nature with ethical form in the same manner as *Ṛta,* cosmically conceived, imposed beauty and order upon physical chaos.

The idea of *Ṛta* as Moral Law became a salient feature of Vedic thought. It is the sense of value based on this idea which accounts for the remarkable unity of thought among the poets. They are all agreed:

> A man should think on wealth, and strive to win it by adoration of the path of Order, Counsel himself with his own mental insight, and grasp still nobler vigour with his spirit.[4]

Exhortations of this kind are numerous. They point to the fact that *Ṛta* was the *summum bonum* around which the whole of Vedic religion and society was modelled. So great was its influence that in later times its principles were perpetuated through the characteristic Hindu concepts of *dharma* and the law of *karman.*

The ethical impact of *Ṛta* on the Vedic mind is seen in the confidence it generated in respect to the goodness of life in this world. All of the events in nature and in history were teleologically understood. Consciousness of *Ṛta* imparted the feeling of being at-home in the world. It offered solace and security. The world was not a place where blind, capricious forces held sway, but was a benevolent habitat in which men could expect to enjoy all of the good things of life—material and spiritual.

To be sure, the Vedas always recognize the reality of evil: but since righteousness is as much part of the cosmic structure as the laws by which the planets move, there is no reason to doubt that "as the sun rises tomorrow, virtue will triumph." Unlike Zoroastrianism where good and evil are on par with one another, there is no trace of moral dualism in Vedic religion. The forces of good are generally represented by Indra (god of the heavens), while the forces of evil are represented by the demon Vṛtra. The battle between the two is fierce, but Indra always prevails. The poet says:

> I will declare the manly deeds of Indra, the first that he achieved, the Thunder-wielder.
> He slew the Dragon, then disclosed the waters, and cleft the channels of the mountain torrents.
>
> He slew the Dragon lying on the mountain: his heavenly bolt of thunder Tvaṣṭar fashioned.
> Like lowing kine in rapid flow descending the waters glided downwards to the ocean.
>
> Impetuous as a bull, he chose the Soma, and in three sacred beakers drank the juices.
> Maghavan grasped the thunder for his weapon, and smote to death this first-born of the dragons.
>
> When, Indra, thou hadst slain the dragon's firstborn, and overcame the charms of the enchanters,
> Then, giving life to Sun and Dawn and Heaven, thou foundest not one foe to stand against thee.
>
> Indra with his own great and deadly thunder smote into pieces Vṛtra, worst of Vṛtras.
> As trunks of trees, what time the axe hath felled them, low on the earth so lies the prostrate Dragon.[5]

The hymns not only present us with a universal standard of morality represented by *Ṛta,* they also lay down certain duties as the concrete manifestation of *Ṛta.* The first set of duties is religious, consisting of prayers and sacrifices to the gods. Without going into the specific nature of these duties, we shall enquire into their bearing on the moral life.

In the opinion of some scholars, Vedic worship is utilitarian and lacking in sincerity.

> We fear the gods whose effects are dangerous to us, and love those that help us in our daily pursuits. We pray to Indra to send down rain, and yet beg him not to send the storm. The sun is implored to impart a gentle warmth, and not force the world into drought and famine by scorching heat. The gods become the sources of material prosperity, and prayers for the goods of the world are very common.[6]

This description of Vedic worship as lacking moral qualities is too one-sided to do justice to the facts. Professor R. C. Majumdar is nearer to the truth when he observes that although the process of Vedic sacrifice was relatively simple, "the theory about it was quite a complex one, as the object and necessity of sacrifice were often regarded from radically different points of view."[7] According to one point of view, sacrifice was a barter between God and man: man offered God food and drink, and God reciprocated by blessing him with material prosperity, many sons, and long life. But sacrifice was also approached in a nonutilitarian manner. There is absolutely no idea of give and take; instead, "sacrifice becomes an act of thanks-giving, mingled with affection and gratitude to the gods for the benefits already received from them, and expected in future."[8]

Worship on this second level was morally structured. Emphasis was placed on the spirit of sacrifice as against its mechanical performance. The poet says: "Utter a powerful speech to Indra which is sweeter than butter or honey."[9] Like Indra, the gods penetrate the depths of men's hearts to find out what are their true motives. Worship which is properly motivated is offered in the spirit of *ṛta* (moral law), *satya* (truth), *śraddhā* (faith), and *tapas* ("kindling of the spiritual fire"). This definition of worship seems to warrant the conclusion that Vedic worship is grounded in the Vedic values.[10]

Having described the moral aspects of Vedic worship from the manward side, let us now enquire into its moral aspects from the godward side. If the characterisation of the gods, who are the chief objects of Vedic worship, is, indeed, a projection of the people's own idealized self-image, theology should offer us some clues about how the people envisioned their own moral possibilities, embodied in the persons of the gods.

A theological investigation of the hymns shows that the Vedic deities "formed a motley group of varied and complex character."[11] These deities were the personification of natural phenomena, as their very names indicate: Sūrya (the sun god), Uṣas (the god of Dawn), Agni (the fire god). In the process of personalizing the agencies of nature, some of the gods continue to be viewed rather physicalistically. Those who are more completely personalized are often attributed human passions and instincts no better than those of the worshippers in whose image they are made. These gods are viewed as "strong rather than good, powerful rather than moral."[12] Worship of such deities naturally tended to be more utilitarian than moral.

Yet, in spite of these moral deficiencies in Vedic theology, the overall picture of the gods is one that testifies to the "strong moral sense of the Vedic Aryans."[13] Their ethical aspirations could not be satisfied by relating to the gods on a materialistic basis. In the final analysis, the ethical aspirations prevail over the utilitarian considerations, and these aspirations are projected in a conceptualization of the gods which is predominantly moral.

The ethicising of the gods began at a very early age. Professor E. W. Hopkins has shown that the Indic tribes, prior to being domiciled between the Indus and Ganges rivers, "had passed beyond the stage of undiluted fear in the presence of unnamed demons and had already invested with a moral quality the 'kind bright' *devas* or spirits of light, which quality differentiated these powers from the *rākshas* or 'injurers that go about by night' and 'rejoice in darkness'."[14] Certainly, there is the element of fear in man's relation to the gods, but this fear rises out of the sense of having violated a divine law and is, therefore, infused with the feeling of moral culpability. The gods are feared because they send disease, but this punishment is not regarded as capricious or accidental. It is the just recompense of moral wrongdoing. The age-old problem of physical evil is thus explained in terms of moral evil.

On the whole, the gods are approached through love rather than fear. The first steps in the development of *bhakti-mārga* (the path of devotion) can be traced to the Vedic attitudes toward the gods. The relationship with Indra affords a good illustration. It is said that when Indra's lightning bolt strikes, "the world is full of fear." But although Indra is feared because he punishes sin, he is loved and admired for his beneficence. The poet sings:

> In perfect unison all yearning hymns of mine that find the light of heaven have sung forth Indra's praise. As wives embrace their lord, the comely bridegroom, so they compass Maghavan about that he may help.[15]

The devotee's love for the *deva* (god) is in the nature of a response to the *deva's* love for the devotee. Agni is particularly praised for his love toward man.

> Agni, thou art our Providence, our Father thou: we are thy brethren and thou art our spring of life.[16]

Such outpourings of love indicate that *karman* (duty) ensued from *bhakti* (devotion). The *bhakti* nature of this relationship between man and God is of great ethical significance. Since motives determine the quality of an act, it makes a world of difference when an act is impelled by love instead of being compelled by fear.

We have shown that the distinction between the *rākṣasas* and the *devas* is such that whereas the former capriciously hurt man and inspired fear, the latter were benefactors of mankind and inspired loving devotion. However, the goodness of the gods does not lie principally in their being good to man, but in being morally good. It is this moral element which absolutely distinguishes the "kind bright" *devas* from the *rākṣasas* who "rejoice in darkness."

The moral character of the gods springs from their association with *Ṛta.* Belief in *Ṛta* had distinctly ethicising effects upon the nature of the gods. Since *Ṛta* was Eternal Law, they were all subject to it. All of the gods are viewed as "strengtheners of the Law" and "furtherers of *Ṛta.*" Agni is addressed as "Ruler of sacrifices, guard of Law eternal, radiant One."[17] Viṣṇu is described as "primeval germ of Order even from his birth."[18] Indra says to one uncertain about his existence, "I exist, O Singer, look upon me here, all that exists I surpass in splendor. The Eternal Law's commandments make me mighty."[19] Like the Warrior god, Bṛhaspati is called "guilt scourger, guilt avenger," "who slays the spoiler and upholds the mighty Law."[20]

Chief among the guardians of *Ṛta* are Varuṇa and Mitra. The poet joyously acknowledges their leadership in the moral realm:

> Those who by Law uphold the Law, Lords of the shining light of Law
> Mitra I call and Varuṇa.[21]

Varuṇa, as the root *(var)* of his name suggests, is the exalted coverer of the universe. His eye is the sun, the sky is his robe, and the storm his breath.[22] As the Universal Monarch, Varuṇa sits in his great heavenly palace, surrounded by his messengers who report on the moral conditions prevailing on earth.[23] Varuṇa is a *dhṛtavrata,* one of steady and consistent resolve. He is just, but there is kindness in his justice.

The intimate relation between Varuṇa and the ethical order is clearly brought out in the following hymn. The first verse refers to *Ṛta* as cosmic order. The last one has reference to the ritual order. The remainder of the hymn is a celebration of *Ṛta* as the ethical order.

1. Wise, verily, are creatures through his greatness who stayed even spacious heaven and earth asunder;
   Who urged the high and mighty sky to motion, the Star of old, and spread the earth before him.
2. With mine own heart I commune on the question how Varuṇa and I may be united.
   What gift of mine will he accept unangered? When may I calmly look and find him gracious?
3. Fain to know this my sin I question others: I seek the wise, O Varuṇa and ask them.
   This one same answer even the sages gave me, Surely this Varuṇa is angry with thee.
4. What, Varuṇa, hath been my chief transgression, that thou wouldst slay the friend who sings thy praises?

Tell me, Unconquerable Lord, and quickly sinless will I approach thee with mine homage.

5. Free us from sins committed by our fathers, from those wherein we have ourselves offended.

   O King, loose, like a thief who feeds the cattle, as from the cord a calf, set free Vasiṣṭha.

6. Not our own will betrayed us, but seduction, thoughtlessness, Varuṇa! wine, dice, or anger.

   The old is near to lead astray the younger: even sleep removeth not all evil-doing.

7. Slavelike may I do service to the Bounteous, serve, free from sin, the God inclined to anger.

   This gentle Lord gives wisdom to the simple: the wiser God leads on the wise to riches.

8. O Lord, Varuṇa, may this laudation come close to thee and lie within thy spirit.

   May it be well with us in rest and labour. Preserve us evermore, ye Gods, with blessings.[24]

It is worth noting that the elements of fear and utility do not enter into the devotee's relationship with Varuṇa. The god-man relationship is conceived purely in moral terms. Hence, sin, which is the disruption of this relationship, is also morally conceived. However, it is fair to state that sin is not consistently perceived through moral categories in the Vedic literature. Often, the sin against Agni is nothing more than an infraction of some liturgical rule. In such cases, ritualistic rectitude is given prominence over ethical rectitude. Sometimes sin is construed physicalistically and is deemed capable of transference from one person to another by means of magic. But whenever the sense of *satya* and *ṛta* prevails, sin is ethicised. Ethically perceived, as in all relationships with Varuṇa and Mitra, sin is *asatya* (untruth), and *anṛta* (injustice). Sinners, therefore, are known as *anṛta* (without *ṛta*), and *asatya* (without truth).

The moral character of man's relationship with Varuṇa is also brought out in the recognition of human freedom. In the hymn just quoted, we note the emergence of a strong sense of individual responsibility within the traditionally corporate structure of collective guilt. The notion of solidarity in sin is not questioned. In all tribal states of society the group, be it family or clan, is the primary responsible unit. However, the Vedic Indian, within this general orientation, is nevertheless struggling toward a morality of individual responsibility. Vasiṣṭha prays: "Free us from sins committed by our fathers,"[25] and thereby raises the question of culpability: Is it right to be held responsible for what others have done, just because they happen to be blood relations? Vasiṣṭha also distinguishes corporate sins from "those wherein we have ourselves offended."[26]

The struggle for individual responsibility is further evidenced in the distinction made between voluntary and involuntary sins:

> Not our own will betrayed us, but seduction, thoughtlessness, Varuṇa! wine, dice or anger.[27]

A third pointer in the direction of asserting individual responsibility is the need for an existential knowledge of oneself. This internal grasp of spiritual truth as the expression of one's personal freedom should serve as a light by which one walks along the moral path. Knowing the sacred mantras by heart is mechanical as compared to a personal knowledge of the Supreme One who dwells in the heart and who sustains all that is through the operation of *Ṛta.*

So far we have seen the correlation between Vedic worship and Vedic values. For the most part, the religious duties satisfied the ethical aspirations of the people. While it was the duty of men to serve the gods, it was the function of the gods, all of whom were ethical personalities, to help the devotees reach the highest goal of union with the Divine.

In addition to these religioethical duties, men also had socioethical duties. Much emphasis was placed on the need for cultivating the virtues of cooperative living. A. C. Bose draws attention to the frequent usage of the prefix *sam (syn*—Greek; *cum*—Latin; com—English) as expressive of an ethic of collective living. He says: "We find a systematic attempt to build up *saṁhṛdaya* (or *sahṛdaya*), literally, concord, that is, the union of hearts, and *saṁjñānam,* unity through common understanding, at all social levels."[28]

We shall now list some of the duties and virtues aimed at bringing about social concord. The most celebrated virtue is *Satya* or Truth. Its social importance is derived from its metaphysical underpinning. Because Ultimate Reality is *Sat* (Truth), it follows that in a world structured by Truth, men should live by the principles of Truth. Again, the gods provide the models. Mitra and Varuṇa are described as "true to Law." By the opposite token, lying is called the "murder of speech." It is utterly reprehensible "when a mortal knowingly . . . injures with double tongue a fellow-mortal."[29] In the hands of Indra, the speaker of untruth becomes "like water which the hollowed hand compresses."[30]

The mark of a truthful man is consistency. Such a man can be depended upon to act with responsible predictability because he follows the unswerving pathway of *Ṛta.* Everything he does is true and ordered. The ideal embodiment of consistency is Varuṇa. As the upholder of *Ṛta,* Varuṇa can always be relied upon to act with justice and compassion. He is therefore known as a *dhṛtavrata*—one whose ways are unchanging.

Another important social duty is *dāna* or offering of gifts. An entire hymn is dedicated to *Dakṣiṇā*—the largess presented by the wealthy nobles to the priests who perform the sacrifical rites. The benefactors are praised for not counting the cost of sacrifice, but giving out of the abundance of their hearts. Great are the rewards of such liberality!

> The liberal die not, never are they ruined: the liberal suffer neither harm nor trouble.
> The light of heaven, the universe about us,—all this doth sacrificial Guerdon give them.[31]

Perhaps this eulogy to *Dakṣiṇā* and other hymns written in the same vein, suffer as a result of their sacerdotal ties. One gets the uneasy feeling that generosity is being praised because the priests are dependent upon the offerings. A more disinterested treatment of the subject is found in a hymn addressed to Liberality.[32] The first verse declares the need for unquestioning philanthropy in the presence of human want. There is no justification for refusing food to the poor and the hungry, even on religious pretexts. To the argument that the hungry are probably being punished by the gods for their sins, the answer is: "The Gods have not ordained hunger to be our death: even to the well-fed man comes death in varied shape."[33]

The hymn also praises Liberality, because it breeds prosperity and success. "The riches of the liberal never waste away."[34] "Success attends him in the shout of battle."[35]

Liberality is further enjoined because of certain prudential considerations. There is no telling what the future holds—today a prince, tomorrow a pauper! The wise will, therefore, try to build up goodwill as insurance against the lean years of their lives—"let the rich satisfy the poor implorer, and bend his eye upon a longer pathway."[36]

The last two considerations seem to place liberality within the framework of an ethic of reciprocity, rather than an ethic of disinterested service to one's fellowman. Actually, the two ideals are not in conflict. Aside from the observable fact that generosity does have its rewards, the hymn writer is realistic enough to know that the spirit of *dāna* varies in quality from person to person. All men ought to be generous, but all men cannot be expected to be generous in the same way.

> The hands are both alike; their labour differs.
> The Yield of sister milch-kine is unequal.
> Twins even differ in their strength and vigour:
> two, even kinsmen, differ in their bounty.[37]

We now turn from the subjective treatment of ethics to its objective treatment, and shall examine the social organization within which the individual was supposed to develop his personal capacities.

In the Ṛgvedic period the four traditional *āśramas* or stages in life were not developed. But even at this period Vedic culture was ahead of its time in respect to the premium it placed upon education. The *Brahmacarya* or Student stage was compulsory for all. The purpose of education was to cultivate in youth a sense of responsible citizenship. Hereditary privileges played no part. Education was free and open. All that the *ṛṣis* (Seers of truths found in the Vedas) expected of the pupil was a dedication to his studies, and an espousal of the celibate life. Sexual continence was not treated as an end in itself, but only as a means to bringing the sexual life under the discipline of *Ṛta.* Support for the centres of learning was underwritten by the community at large and by members of the royalty.

Fathers initiated their children into Vedic studies and taught them family crafts. At the appropriate time, the children moved out into the *āśramas* (hermitages) where they were taught by the *ṛṣis.* These teachers were held in the highest honour. The sage controlled the life of the nation. Wisdom was exalted above both wealth and political power.

Having been imbued with wisdom, self-control, and civic responsibility, the young person was deemed mature enough to start a family of his own. He then became a householder or *gṛhastha.* The family was the basic unit of Āryan society. We shall look at the Ṛgvedic family from the points of view of the family ideal, forms of marriage, and type of family structure.

The ideal of marriage in the Ṛgvedic period is a graceful blending of the biological and spiritual elements. Marriage was more than a contract; it was a sacrament. The sanctity in which society held the institution of marriage is discernible from these verses of the marriage hymn:

> I take thy hand in mine for happy fortune that thou mayst reach old age with me thy husband.
> Gods, Aryaman, Bhaga, Savitar, Purandhi, have given thee to be my household's mistress.
> O Pūṣan, send her on as most auspicious, her who shall be the sharer of my pleasures;
> Her who shall twine her loving arms about me,
> And welcome all my love and mine embraces.
> For thee, with bridal train, they, first, escorted Sūrya to her home.
> Give to the husband in return, Agni, the wife with progeny.
> Agni hath given the bride again with splendour and with ample life.
> Long lived be he who is her lord; a hundred autumns let him live.[38]

Monogamy was the general form of marriage, polygamy being permitted and practised only among the wealthy social classes. The monogamous form of marriage assured a woman her personal prestige. She did not have to suffer the humiliation of playing second fiddle to anyone competing for her husband's interest and affection. Levirate forms of marriage were also common.

While the marriage hymn entreats the groom to accept his bride as a god-given gift, there are rudimentary references to less spiritual methods of establishing a union. These are *rākṣasa* (marriage by forceful abduction of a woman during war), and *prājāpatya* (marriage with the specific purpose of procreation). The Atharva Veda refers also to the *gāndharva* method which is based only on mutual love between the two parties involved.

Regarding the conditions of wedlock, we find that the only prohibitions in the Ṛgvedic period are the ones that forbid marriage between father and daughter and between brother and sister.

The Āryan family was patriarchal and patrilinear, and is even until today. The matriarchal family was nonexistent in Vedic society. The patriarch presided over the joint family constituted by the father, grandfather, sons, and their wives. The Ṛg Veda fosters the ethics of joint family living in mutual love and concord. It likens the home to "a lake with lotus blossoms."[39] The Atharva Veda enjoins the members to "love one another as the cow loves the calf she has borne" and to "be of one mind, following the leader."[40]

Theoretically, the patriarch had absolute control over the property, but in practice adhered to were the rules of equitability. The father was not a dictator, but rather the model of compassion as expressed in this prayer: "Be to us easy of approach, even as a father to his son."[41] Before the specialisation of professional roles, the father served his children as a teacher. Every father was a *ṛṣi* on a small scale.

The patriarchal structure of the family elevated the role of the male over the female; even so, women in the Ṛgvedic period enjoyed more status and freedom than in later periods.

There are several supplications in the Ṛgvedic hymn for the birth of a son.[42] The appreciation of males should not be taken to imply the depreciation of females. "There is no evidence to show that girls were exposed as unwanted babes."[43] To the contrary, a maiden was admired for her beauty and purity, was provided with an education, and was given considerable freedom. The sensitivity of the Vedic poet for female grace is shown in his description of the beauty of Dawn. Pictured as a maiden clad in white, she disperses the powers of darkness and evil, and creates a life of order, regularity, and beauty. "The Fair, the Bright is come with her white offspring; to her the Dark One hath resigned her dwelling."[44]

Like boys, girls were expected to go through the Brahmacarya stage. The importance of female education is shown by the fact that, according to the Atharva Veda, a *brahmacāriṇī* has better prospects for marriage than one who is uneducated. We are reminded that "the custom of *upanayana* of girls prevailed down to the Sūtra period, though it had then become a mere formality in the case of the majority."[45] Some women excelled in learning and were ranked as *ṛṣis.* Viśvavārā, a lady of the family of Ātri is credited with a well-known hymn to Agni.[46] Other cultured women who composed mantras are Apālā, Ghoṣā, Lopāmudrā, Indrāṇī, and Śāśvatī.[47]

Women not only enjoyed educational rights but religious rights as well. They joined their husbands in performing rituals and making sacrifices. Before the Udgātṛs in the Brāhmaṇa period regarded it as their own prerogative, it was customary for a wife to sing the Vedic hymns at the time of sacrifice. It is pointed out that "women performing the Sandhyā or offering sacrifices by themselves, unaccompanied by their husbands, figure as late as the time of the Rāmāyaṇa (11. 20.15)."[48]

The marital rights of a female are evidenced by her having a voice in the selection of her husband. Sometimes this meant the freedom to make the wrong choice. The poet laments: "How many a maid is pleasing to the suitor who fain would marry for her splendid riches."[49] Freedom to choose one's partner means the girl was married at an age of discrimination, following puberty. The Ṛg Veda reflects a society in which both sexes had the opportunity to meet each other prior to marriage.[50] During the *samana* festival, young, unmarried girls had freedom to meet and talk with strangers.

Women also had certain social rights. Wives moved freely in their homes and in society. In the marriage hymn there is the specific injunction: "Go to the householder's mistress and speak as lady to thy gathered people."[51] Women were not confined to hearth and home, nor were they secluded in *purdah,* but participated in public life, and even debated in public assemblies.

Having described the rights and privileges within the home, we must not overlook the essential obligations. The chief domestic virtue was hospitality. The ideal of friendship was not limited to humans, but included nonhuman creatures as well. The Vedic seer prays:

> Strong One! make me strong,
> May all beings look on me with the eye of friend
> May I look on all beings with the eye of friend
> May we look on one another with the eye of friend.[52]

The *āśrama* organization in the early Vedic period stopped with the *Gārhasthya* stage. The *Vānaprasthya* and *Saṁnyāsa* stages had not developed at this time. This does not mean there were no ascetics in the Vedic age. There are references to *munis* and *yatis* who claimed to possess occult powers through penances. "The Munis, girdled with the wind, wear garments soiled of yellow hue. They, following the wind's swift course go where the Gods have gone before. Transported with our Munihood we have pressed on into the winds. You, therefore, mortal men, behold our natural bodies and no more."[53] Such references to Munis in the early Vedic period are rare and unfavourable, which seems to suggest that they were probably legacies of pre-Vedic non-Āryan culture.

Leaving *Āśramadharma,* we now move to a second facet of objective ethics, namely, *Varṇadharma.* This is the ethical pattern for the organization of society. Society was divided into two compartmentalized groups—the Āryans and the Dāsas (Dasyus). The division was racial, cultural, and religious. The tall, fair, conquering Āryans were ethnically distinct from the indigenous inhabitants who were short, flat-nosed, and of dark complexion. Apparently, colour was a preeminent line of demarcation. Furthermore, the Dāsas represented the survivors of the ancient Harappa culture, and, as such, differed from the Āryans in custom and language which impressed the Āryans as very strange and unintelligible. The religious difference was equally sharp. Whereas the Āryan religion was centred around sacrifice to nature gods, the religion of the Dāsas was organized around phallic worship.

Because of these deep-rooted differences, the Āryan tribes united with one another for the purpose of subjugating the indigenous people. Indra, the warrior god, is hailed in many a Ṛgvedic hymn as the one who "smote the Dasyus and gave protection to the Aryan colour."[54] The conquered Dāsas were kept by the Āryans as slaves. Within the social organization the Dāsas were known as the Śūdras. The barriers between the conflicting groups were sometimes removed through the marriage of Āryans with Dāsa mistresses, and when Āryans, caught in intertribal rivalry, would make alliances with Dāsa chieftains.

In addition to these two main divisions in Ṛgvedic society in which the Dāsas constituted a distinct "colour," Āryan society itself was divided into separate classes on the basis of profession. An important question is whether these professional classes in this early period had already hardened into castes. Scholarship has been divided on this issue with Geldner, Oldenberg, Macdonell, and Keith answering affirmatively, and with Zimmer, Weber, and Muir responding negatively. To make up our mind on a subject of such crucial importance for social ethics, we shall have to examine the evidence for ourselves.

The first reference to the fourfold division of Hindu society is found in a Ṛgvedic hymn known as *Puruṣa-sūkta.* The hymn is about the original cosmic sacrifice in which primeval man *(puruṣa)* was offered as a sacrifice to himself by the gods who were his children. In the process of creation it specifically mentions the traditional four castes: Brahmin, Kṣatriya, Vaiśya, and Śūdra.

> When they divided Purusha how many portions did they make?
> What do they call his mouth, his arms? What do they call his thighs and feet?
> The Brāhman was his mouth, of both his arms was the Rājanya made.
> His thighs became the Vaiśya, from his feet the Śūdra was produced.[55]

On the basis of this hymn it should not be concluded that the castes of the later period were already in evidence in the earliest period. The conclusion is not warranted because the hymn was composed several hundred years later than most of the hymns in the Ṛg Veda. Mention of the first three Vedas (vs. 9) is proof that this hymn was composed after this separate classification was made. Furthermore, the theme of the sacrifice of the Supreme Being is only a later religious development not found in other sections of the Ṛg Veda. Following Colebrooke, R. C. Dutt states that this hymn was composed "after the rude versification of the Ṛg Veda had given place to the more sonorous metre of a later age."[56] For these reasons it seems safe to conclude that the *Puruṣa Sūkta* is a late hymn, and, as such, lends no support to the thesis that the castes of the later period were already present in the earliest period.

However, there is an earlier hymn in which the three *varṇas* seem to be acknowledged. It reads:

> Give spirit to our prayer and animate our thoughts; slay ye the Rākṣasas and drive away disease.
> Accordant, of one mind with Sūrya and with Dawn, the presser's Soma, Aśvins! drink.
>
> Strengthen the Ruling Power, strengthen the men of war; slay ye the Rākṣasas and drive away disease.
> Accordant, of one mind with Sūrya and with Dawn, the presser's Soma, Aśvins! drink.
>
> Give strength unto the milch-kine, give the people strength, slay ye the Rākṣasas and drive away disease.
> Accordant, of one mind with Sūrya and with Dawn, the presser's Soma, Aśvins! drink.[57]

This hymn may be taken to suggest that Āryan society in the Ṛgvedic period was divided into three classes, but the statement is by no means clear. Furthermore, it needs pointing out that the social structure in the Ṛg Veda bears little or no resemblance to that of the Dharma Śāstras where ironclad rules govern each caste with respect to its duties, rights, and disabilities. The class system in the Ṛgvedic period was elastic and flexible. As evidence of its freedom and mobility, the following points are worth mentioning.

In the first place, if rigid castes did indeed exist in the Vedic period, surely there would have been stronger literary evidence than is available, especially since the collection of the hymns is vast, and these hymns were written over a period of some six hundred years. "Is it possible to find a single religious work of later times, of one-tenth the dimension of the Ṛg Veda, which is silent on the system?"[58]

Second, the system definitely was not bound by hereditary ties. A single family could represent various occupations. There is a passage in which father, mother, and son are described as physician, corn grinder, and composer of hymns.[59] In another passage a sage implores Indra to make him a ruler, first; a priest, second; and failing these two, he would settle for becoming a rich man.[60] These passages make it apparent that professions were not hereditary even among priestly families. The idea of heredity itself was not given the same esteem it enjoyed in subsequent periods. "Kavaṣa, the son of a slave girl, could become a sage."[61] Only in a single verse—"thou singest at libations like a Brahman's son"[62] is heredity praised. But here, also, it is doubtful whether 'Brahman' stands for a hereditary class or a professional individual.

Third, Vedic society could not have hardened into caste because of the common practice of communal dining and intermarriage. There were no restrictions in regarding food and drink between the classes. All *varṇas* shared a common diet. Similarly, there were no matrimonial restrictions between the various levels of Āryan society. These restrictions were not necessary because of the homogeneity of the diverse groups in respect to race, religion, and culture.

On the basis of this evidence we conclude that the *varṇas* in the early Vedic society were "open classes." "They were not watertight compartments, the membership of which was determined by virtue of heredity only,"[63] but were based on individual capacity and aptitude.

III. Ethical Thought in the Brāhmaṇas

The Brāhmaṇas constitute the second major body of Vedic literature. They are mainly ritual texts, the concluding portions of which are given to philosophic speculations. The Aitareya and Śatapatha Brāmaṇas are the most important ones. The value of this priestly literature as a source of ethics is difficult to determine precisely. The priests show little interest for questions pertaining to the nature of right action; instead, their imagination runs riot with the theory and practice of ritualism.

It is amazing how the simple speculation in the *Puruṣa-sūkta* dealing with the sacrifice of the Supreme Being *(Parama Puruṣa)* expanded into one of the most complex sacrificial systems ever devised by man. Elaborate rituals are given mystical meanings known only to the priests. These ceremonies included domestic rites and great sacrifices. The domestic rituals covered all human events from the cradle to the grave. The forty *saṁskāras* (sacraments) formulated at a later time provide a good indication of the type and number of ceremonies that had to be observed.

The expansion of sacrifice was based on the supposition that it possessed cosmic power. By virtue of this power, all of the orderly processes within the world were maintained. Without sacrifices, the sun would not rise, and chaos would bring the universe to an untimely end.

The gods continue to be recognized as the upholders of the cosmic order, but they are sustained in this function through the energy of regular sacrifices made by the priests. This rendered sacrifice superior to the gods. Faith in the gods is shifted to faith in the sacrifice. Through faith, the sacrifices operated automatically, without any help from the gods.[64] Sacrifice was independent of the gods, but the gods were not independent of sacrifice. Their divine power and majesty were derived from sacrifice. Their triumph over the *asuras* (demons) was made possible through sacrifice.[65] Even their immortality was the result of sacrifice.[66]

Along with the elevation of sacrifice was the rise to unprecedented power of the priests who jealously guarded the entire system as their exclusive domain. The priests served as the mediators between the gods and men and as the distributors of divine favours. Their special training gave them mastery of the obscure language of the ancient Vedic hymns and provided them with the hidden knowledge concerning the meaning and performance of sacrifice. Knowledge was indispensable because a slight error in the ritual could have serious repercussions upon the priest. Errors in sacrifice cost Bhaga his sight[67], Pūṣan had his teeth knocked out[68], Bhāllabeya broke his arm,[69] and Āṣāḍhi Sauśromateya lost his life.[70] The point to note is that the error and its punishment were not related to any moral aspects of sacrifice, but to its magical and mechanical sides.

Thus, the priest had a dangerous task; but this was incidental to the power he could wield through his knowledge of the correct performance of the rituals. These priestly functions elevated him to the position of a divinity on earth. The Śatapatha Brāhmaṇa declares: "Verily there are two kinds of gods; for the gods themselves assuredly are gods, and then the priests who have studied and teach sacred lore are the human gods."[71] Indeed, the human gods were superior to the heavenly deities, because, without the sacrifices of humans, the deities could not fulfil their divine functions. This fact placed the gods in the control of the priests. Even mighty Indra could be dethroned by the offering of a hundred horse sacrifices. The point to be noticed in this context is that the idea of superiority of being is not qualitatively but quantitatively understood. Superiority is tantamount to coercive power generated by magic. The notion of moral superiority does not enter into the picture.

What were the ends sought through the instrumentality of the priests and the sacrificial rituals? In place of the earlier, often devotional relationship, men contract with the gods for mundane blessings—health, wealth, power, and prosperity.[72] Prayers offered for such blessings were essentially magical techniques which ensured the sacrificer whatsoever he desired. In addition to earthly profits, prayers are offered for the rewards of heaven.

Needless to say, the introduction of magic into religion had a deleterious effect upon morality. This can be illustrated from the Brāhmaṇa doctrine of sacrifice; its theology, its doctrine of sin, and its eschatology.

The overall view of sacrifice *(yajña),* as I have briefly shown, treated it as a sort of machinery which, when correctly manipulated, gave the sacrificer mastery over anything or anyone, in heaven or on earth. Often, the ends sought through this means were purely selfish. Sometimes the sacrificial ritual was utilised for criminal purposes. "If the priest so wished, he could by manipulation bring ruin upon the sacrificer's senses, his life, and his earthly possessions."[73] A good example of this criminal use of sacrifice is found in this passage from the Aitareya Brāhmaṇa.

> The silent prayer is the root of the sacrifice. Should a Hotṛ wish to deprive any sacrificer of his standing place, then he must not at his sacrifice repeat the 'silent praise'; the sacrificer then perishes along with his sacrifice which thus has become rootless.[74]

This demonstrates that sacrifice had no ethical basis. A further proof of the unethical way of viewing sacrifice is the disregard for any moral attributes as the necessary qualifications for the sacrificer. The Aitareya Brāhmaṇa states:

> Even if the performing priest is not a Brāhman (in the strictest sense), or even pronounced to be an ill-reputed man, the sacrifice nevertheless goes up to the gods, and becomes not polluted by the contagion with a wicked man (as in this case the performing priest is).[75]

Next, let us examine the extent to which Brahmanical theology is vitiated by these magico-sacrificial ideas. Whereas in the Ṛg Veda the gods are ethical personalities, in the Brāhmaṇas the gods lack moral qualities. Essentially, the gods are selfish. When Agni, Indra, Soma, Makha,

Viṣṇu, and Viśve devāḥ performed a sacrificial session at Kurukṣetra they could think only of themselves:

> May we attain excellence; may we become glorious; may we become eaters of food![76]

Private gain looms uppermost for the gods that they are prepared to compromise all sense of honour to attain it. They make a solemn pact with the *rākṣasas* to share equally in the victory as they solicit their help to fight the *asuras;* but, once victory comes, the gods go back on their word.

Selfishness also incites the gods to jealousy. They are so envious of each other that they cannot occupy the same abode in the spirit of friendship, but must live separately. There is the story of how Viṣṇu, grown proud because of his skill in sacrifice, "was unable to control that (love of) glory of his."[77] Agni, Indra, and other gods, hating him for his pride, bribed the ants to attack him, which they did. The story concludes: "Having gone nigh unto him, they gnawed his bowstring. When it was cut, the ends of the bow, springing asunder, cut off Vishṇu's head."[78]

Not only are the gods jealous of one another; they are also jealous of men. Notwithstanding their intimate relations with men, and their vested interests in the sacrifices which men offer, the gods demonstrate nothing of the closeness and fondness of the worshipper that we encountered in the Ṛg Veda. As noted earlier, this loving relation between god and devotee was of the utmost significance from the ethical point of view, moulding the outlook of the individual and determining whether his life was to be directed by fear or by love. But here, the gods often evince an unmistakable dislike and disgust for men. They inflict them with the six evils of sleep, sluggishness, anger, hunger, love of gambling, and love of women.[79] They are jealous at the prospects of men attaining immortality as they did. To satisfy the god of death who feels he shall be cheated if men became immortal without laying down their corporeal bodies at the time of death, the divine council takes the following action: "Henceforward no one shall be immortal with the body: only when thou shalt have taken that (body) as thy share, he who is to become immortal either through knowledge or through holy work, shall become immortal after separating from the body."[80]

Such acts of unethical behaviour are recounted without the least effort to take any moral exception. However, the lack of moral sensitivity becomes more pronounced with the attribution of sins of a more serious nature to some of the prominent deities.

Like Varuṇa in the Ṛg Veda, Prajāpati occupies the position of chief importance in the Brāhmaṇas, but unlike Varuṇa, Prajāpati is not consistently conceived as an ethical personality. There is the legend which tells of his developing an illicit passion for his daughter. He said: " 'May I pair with her!' thus (thinking) he united with her."[81] Though the ideal image of Prajāpati is marred by his committing incest, the legend goes on to say that such an act was "a sin in the eyes of the gods," who solicit Rudra to punish him.

Indra is another example of the deethicising process within the personalities of the gods. He breaks his word with Namuci; is guilty of the slaying of Viśvarūpa; and makes love to Ahalyā by deceptively taking her husband's form.

Thus, the unethical way of viewing the divine in the Brāhmaṇas provides theological evidence for the breakdown of the ethical norms by which earlier generations had conducted their lives. In the Ṛg Veda, all of the gods were upholders of *Ṛta* and were the ideal representatives of moral excellence. In the Brāhmaṇas, excellence is ritualistic excellence. The gods are pictured as saying, in the course of divine worship: "Whoever of us, through austerity, fervour, faith, sacrifice, and oblations, shall first compass the end of sacrifice, he shall be the most excellent of us."[82]

In keeping with this norm, human excellence is also ritualistically conceived.[83] Faith is not reliance upon the goodness of the gods, but reliance upon the power of sacrifice.[84] Similarly, truth, as the following verse attests, is the correct performance of sacrificial ritual.

> The gods laid down together their favourite forms and desirable powers, and said, "Thereby he shall be away from us, he shall be scattered to the winds, whosoever shall transgress this (covenant) of ours!" And even how the gods do not transgress that (covenant), for how would they fare, were they to transgress it?—they would speak untruth, and verily there is one law which the gods do keep, namely, the truth. It is through this that their conquest, their glory is unassailable: and so, forsooth, is his conquest, his glory unassailable whosoever, knowing this, speaks the truth. Now, the Tānūnaptra is really that same (covenant of the gods).[85]

Since goodness is ritualistic goodness, it is not surprising that sin and guilt are also unethically conceived. Sin is mechanically understood: "all slaying, even of demons such as Vṛtra, brings the taint of bloodshed, whether justified or not, the fault of the sacrifice passes to him who blames it, as does a third of the sin initiated to anyone who speaks ill of them."[86] Sin was like a virus, a foreign body, to which one could unwittingly fall prey. The pollutant nature of sin is illustrated by the fact that, through the incantations of a presiding priest, it could be magically transferred from the individual paying for the rite to the enemy upon whom he wishes it to be inflicted.

The punishment for sin is meted out by Varuṇa, but the major cause for punishment is ritualistic error. The cure for sin is as external to the individual as the sin itself. Untruth is a pollutant from which the sinner can be freed by the following means:

> He bathes. For impure, indeed, is man: he is foul within, in that he speaks untruth;—and water is pure: he thinks, "May I be consecrated, after becoming pure";—and water is cleansing: he thinks, "May I become consecrated after being cleansed!" This is the reason why he bathes.[87]

Another method by which the sinner purifies himself from the impurities of untruth is by the "pure" sacred grass.

> He then purifies him with a cleanser (pavitra, strainer) of sacred grass; for impure, indeed, is man:—he is foul within in that he speaks untruth;—and sacred grass is pure: 'Having become pure, I shall be consecrated,' thus he thinks;—and the stalks of sacred grass are a means of cleansing,—'Having become cleansed, I shall be consecrated,' thus he thinks; and therefore he purifies him with a cleanser of sacred grass.[88]

An examination of the eschatological ideas of the Brāhmaṇas adds testimony to the independence of ethical criteria in relation to the destiny of man. A fascinating illustration of this point is a legend which reflects the popular eschatological outlook of this period in respect to the punishment in store for the guilty when they get to the next world.

To cure his son Varuṇa of his pride, Bhṛgu sends him in every direction to get a view of the state in which men suffer. Going eastward, and thence southward, he beheld men dismembering men, and saying: "Thus, indeed these dealt with us in yonder world, and so we now deal with thee in return."[89] Varuṇa asks if there is any atonement for this, and is told that his father knows.

Coming to the west, Varuṇa sees men sitting still, being devoured by men sitting still. In response to his horror at this sight, he is told again, "Thus, indeed, these have dealt with us in yonder world, and so we now deal with them in return."[90] He is also told that his father knows the atonement for this.

In the north, the boy hears the cries of men while being consumed by other men. He raises the same horrified question, and is given the same reply about the reason for this carnage and the way of atonement.

The final vision occurs at one of the intermediate spaces. Here he sees two beautiful women standing on either side of a black man with yellow eyes who holds a staff. Terror stricken, Varuṇa returns home, a good deal humbler than when he set out. The father, noticing his chastened state, provides this explanation of the visions.

> As to those men whom thou sawest in the eastern region being dismembered by men hewing off their limbs one by one, and saying, "This to thee this to me!" they were the trees: when one puts firewood from the trees on (the fire) he subdues the trees, and conquers the world of trees.
>
> And as to those men whom thou sawest in the southern region being dismembered by men cutting up their limbs one by one, and saying "This to thee, this to me!" they were the cattle; when one makes offering with milk he subdues the cattle, and conquers the world of cattle.
>
> And as to those men thou sawest in the western region who, whilst sitting still, were being eaten by men sitting still, they were the herbs: when one illumines (the Agnihotra milk) with a straw, he subdues the herbs, and conquers the world of herbs.
>
> And as to those men thou sawest in the northern region who, whilst crying aloud, were being eaten by men crying aloud, they were the waters: when one pours water to (the Agnihotra milk), he subdues the waters, and conquers the world of waters.
>
> And as to those two women whom thou sawest, one beautiful and one over-beautiful—the beautiful one is Belief: when one offers the first libation (of the Agnihotra) he subdues Belief and conquers Belief; and the over-beautiful one is Unbelief: when one offers the second libation, he subdues Unbelief and conquers Unbelief.
>
> And as to the black man with yellow eyes, who was standing between them with a staff in his hand, he was Wrath: when, having poured water into the spoon, one pours (the libation into the fire), he subdues Wrath, and conquers Wrath; and, verily, whosoever, knowing this, offers the Agnihotra, thereby conquers everything, and subdues everything.[91]

Thus, the lesson learned is that by making due offerings one is spared the torments of the future: "Man is born into the world made (by him)." That is to say, in the future world a man receives the reward or punishment for the deeds done in this present life, but the deeds are not so much moral deeds, ethically conceived, as ritualistic deeds, sacerdotally conceived.

The preceding examination of some of the doctrines of sacrifice, sin, theology, and eschatology, shows the pervasive manner in which good and evil have been deethicised. Ritualistic rectitude has been upheld as the norm of goodness, and ethical ideas have been correspondingly neglected.

There is danger at this point to conclude prematurely that ethical ideas have disappeared in the period of the Brāhmaṇas. To avoid this danger it must first be recognized that the ritualism of the Brāhmaṇas was only one aspect of religion during this period. Second, even in aristocratic circles, ritualism could not completely suppress the older moral ideals or prevent new ones from being born. Third, ethical implications were contained in apparently unethical parables and symbolism. As instances, the earlier story of Viṣṇu's pride and the manner in which the ants brought about his decapitation may imply that "Pride goes before a fall." Even the loftiest god can be humbled by the tiniest of creatures when corrupted by pride. And the story of Prajāpati's incest may also be taken to indicate that passion can degrade even a Prajāpati, and that divinity notwithstanding, passion pays a price.

To bring out the ethical elements of the Brāhmaṇas we must mention the conception of man's duties known as the "triad of obligations" or *ṛṇatraya.* The first of these duties is the old idea that sacrifice is something that man owes to the gods. Magical and mystical developments overshadowed, but did not totally eclipse this notion of sacrifice as a *ṛṇa* or debt. The second duty should highlight the fact that the Vedic ideal did not start and stop with the ideal of sacrifice. It also inculcated a sense of indebtedness to the seers for the cultural heritage they had bequeathed to subsequent generations. This debt was paid by transmitting to posterity the tradition one had been fortunate to receive. The third duty expands the ideal further by making one realize his indebtedness to the race, along with the obligation to establish one's own family and bring many sons into the world. Thus, the ideal of *ṛṇatraya* is a comprehensive ideal, not only including man's duty to the gods through sacrifice, but also the perpetuation of the race, and the cultural heritage which it embodies. The individual who fulfils *all* of these obligations is a good man. He is good because he is not only concerned about what he gets out of life, but what he puts into life. Our own assessment of the specific nature of these duties will certainly differ, but there is no gainsaying the sense of responsibility from which they spring. Life is both a gift and a duty, and it is best lived when one tries to establish harmonious relations with one's total environment.

Among the virtues productive of harmony were: honour to parents, hospitality, truth-speaking, self-restraint, austerity, and kindness to animals. Factors regarded as disruptive of harmony were: intoxicants, usury, gambling, women, sloth, hunger, theft, adultery, and murder.

Even though sin was predominantly conceived in ritualistic terms, there is the notion that responsibility is contingent upon volition. One passage describes a sacrificer and his wife having a ritual bath for the purpose of cleansing themselves of impurities. When their ablutions are completed it is said: "even as a snake casts its skin, so does he cast away all sin—there is not in him even as much sin as there is in a toothless child."[92] The reference to the newborn child attests to the belief that sin presupposes a voluntaristic basis. The volitional nature of sin occurs in the following passage which attributes guilt to Soma for having entertained thoughts of oppression toward the priesthood:

> Now as to why he purifies the Soma by means of a strainer *(pavitra)*. When Soma had oppressed his own family-priest Bṛhaspati, he restored to him (his property); and on his restoring it, he (Bṛhaspati) became reconciled to him. Still there was guilt remaining, if only for having contemplated oppressing the priesthood.[93]

While citing these passages it must be admitted that they are rare, and therefore "we have no reason to suppose that there was recognized any general doctrine of the necessity of volition to create responsibility."[94]

Let us now turn to the theological thinking of this time to see whether there are any exceptions from the unethical way of regarding the divine as noticed earlier.

Prajāpati occupies a place of twofold preeminence in the Brāhmaṇas: he is the lord of Creation, and he is also an ethical authority. In the latter role he serves as the ruler and arbiter of ethics and as the dispenser of divine laws. The significance of this role for the perpetuation of ethical ideals is correctly stated by E. W. Hopkins:

> For a thousand years or more it sufficed, if a rule of conduct or law enunciated, to make the statement "thus said Prajapati" (Lord of Creation) and it was as if a Mohameddan said "so spoke the Prophet"; it was no longer a disputable point. He is the Father-god, "we are his children," as the sacred texts proclaim over and over, and his word is law.[95]

This role of Prajāpati is in keeping with the earlier idea of the gods as preservers of the cosmic and moral order. Continuity with the earlier view is also seen in the special characterization of the gods as truth. Passages such as this one come to mind:

> Now, twofold indeed is this (universe)—there is no third—the truth and the untruth: the gods are the truth and men are the untruth.[96]

Since the gods are truth, they serve as ethical models for man:

> Let him then only speak what is true; for this vow indeed the gods do keep, that they speak the truth; and for this reason they are glorious: glorious therefore is he who knowing this, speaks the truth.[97]

Thus, with certain qualifications, it can be shown that there is a place for ethics within the system of the Brāhmaṇas. This fact may be inconsistent with the logic of the sacrificial system in which sacrifice functions mechanically, is superior to the gods, and automatically removes sin.

Nevertheless, the influence of magic in religion "could not do away with the ethical consciousness already awakened, nor did it entirely suppress the idea that morality was an expression of spiritual worth divinely planted in man."[98]

Our discussion so far has centered around man's religious duties with only passing allusions to his social duties. We shall now focus on the latter. During this time, religion and social life were so intermixed that one could hardly be distinguished from the other. In large measure, life expressed itself through religious ceremonials.

The primary social duty toward a child belonging to the three twice-born castes was to provide him with an education. Generally, this took place at age twelve. Education in the Vedic schools was comprehensive. In keeping with its literal meaning of 'drawing out', education covered "the development of all the faculties of man and included within its purview the totality of interests which make up life and not merely a section thereof, viz. the interests of intellectual life. It was education not merely in the contents of the sacred lore but also in the methods of living and self-culture according to the ideals embodied therein."[99]

The chief end of education was to impart an existential awareness of the Absolute.[100] This knowledge could be received through the performance of rituals,[101] but the more excellent way was through the study of the sacred texts. Such study was true "sacrifice to the Brahman."

> The sacrifice to the Brahman is one's own (daily) study (of the Veda). The juhū-spoon of this same sacrifice to the Brahman is speech, its *upabhrit* the mind, its *dhruva* the eye, its *sruva* mental power, its purifactory bath truth, its conclusion heaven. And, verily, however great the world he gains by giving away (to the priests) this earth replete with wealth, thrice that and more —an imperishable world does he gain, and whosoever, knowing this, studies day by day his lesson (of the Veda); therefore let him study his daily lesson.[102]

The empirical effects of studying the scriptures are pointed out. The student becomes "ready-minded, and independent of others, and day by day he acquires wealth. He sleeps peacefully; he is the best physician for himself; and (peculiar) to him are the restraint of the senses, delight in the one thing, growth of intelligence, fame, and the (task of) perfecting the people."[103]

To acquire this education, one had to enroll formally as the pupil of a teacher. There were instances of the father serving as teacher,[104] but, in the Brāhmaṇic age, because of the growth of the ritual literature and the need for special persons to understand its intricacies, "education came to be recognized as a special function of society."[105] A father, therefore, made every effort to secure the services of a famous teacher for his son.

Teachers usually were men of commanding character and intellect. The students loved and respected them as they did their own fathers.[106]

> As indicated in the propitiatory verse beginning with *Sahanavavatu,* which is uttered at the beginning of each day's study, the teacher and his pupil were united by a common aim of preserving and propagating the sacred learning and showing its worth in their life and conduct. Sometimes, the *antevāsins* living in the house of the teacher preferred, and were permitted, to continue that life throughout, because it was so agreeable (Chhand., ii, 23, 2).[107]

The period of studentship normally lasted about twelve years. Moral discipline was considered indispensable to scholarly growth. It is said:

> He who enters on a Brahmacharin's life, indeed enters on a long sacrificial session: the log he puts on the fire in entering thereon is the opening (offering), and that which (he puts on the fire) when he is about to bathe is the concluding (offering); and what (logs) there are between these, are just his (logs) of the sacrificial session.[108]

Related to the internal discipline was the external discipline. The practice of begging for alms was aimed at engendering humility within the student.[109] Other duties, such as tending the sacrificial fires[110] and caring for the teacher's house and cattle,[111] taught him the meaning of responsibility and stewardship.

All such disciplines, external and internal, were intended to cultivate those mental and moral qualities which were the prerequisites for the knowledge of Brahman.[112] In most cases this knowledge only dawned at the end of one's lifetime, which meant that the disciplines of the Brahmacārin were continued beyond the formal stage of the student's life.

The academic aspects of education ranged over several branches of knowledge, ethics, arts, and sciences, chief of which were the three Vedas. Vedic study was known as *Svādhyāya.* Through lively discourses and discussions, the student was made to become involved with his subject in a personal way.

The chief flaw in this educational system was the fact that it was not open to all castes. Śūdras had no right to education. Instead of being based on ability and aptitude, caste was the criterion for admission. On the surface, it was creditable to the system that it related education functionally to the future professions of the students; but since these future professions were dictated by caste, its professional orientation lost something of its pragmatic worth. Thus, according to the system, the Brahmins were the only ones entitled to a full-fledged education. The Kṣatriyas and Vaiśyas received part of their education in the Vedas, but mostly in arts and skills they would require for their future professions. Since the job description of the Śūdras did not warrant a specialized education, they were completely excluded from the system. Only in certain exceptional cases were the Śūdras granted the privilege of education.

The next set of social duties pertained to the family. In addition to his ritual duties, the householder was expected to be truthful in speech; study the Vedas; exercise liberality to high and low; preserve health; multiply economic assets; and treat all members of the household, including guests, as if they were gods!

My interest in the following paragraphs is to survey the impact of ritual morality within two important areas of family life, namely, the status of matrimony, and the status of women.

In the Ṛgvedic period, outside the prohibition of marriage between father and daughter and between brother and sister, no other restrictions were imposed. In the Brāhmaṇic period, this concern for banning wedlock between close relatives is continued with further prohibitions. Strictures are placed against marriage less than four degrees removed from the parents.[113] There are no specific taboos against marriage within the *gotra* (clan), but marriage outside the *gotra* are the more common rule, especially toward the end of the Brāhmaṇa period. The reasoning involved in these conditions of marriage is ethically sound because it does justice to the social, psychological, and especially the biological factors involved in the marriages within one's gens. Differences in heredity are good because they elicit new characteristics in the offspring, and because they neutralise the weaknesses of husband and wife, which otherwise would be compounded.

A less restrictive issue than consanguinity in marriage was the issue of intercaste marriage. Strict separation of castes apparently did not prevent the overt or covert intermixture of blood on a wide scale. It was legal for a Brahmin to take a bride from any of the four classes, though union with a Śūdra incurred social displeasure. Offsprings of these marriages obtained their father's rank, but it was becoming increasingly difficult for the son of a Śūdra woman to be so recognized, as the case of Kavaṣa Ailuṣa and Vasta would indicate. The first party was only admitted to sacrifice because the gods had treated him with favour;[114] the second had to demonstrate his Brahmin blood by walking on live coals without getting burnt.[115]

Covert sexual relations with Śūdra girls were not rare.[116] Children of these unions took their mother's rank; separate castes for these mixtures only emerged in the subsequent period.

Illicit sexual intercourse made the correct establishment of paternity into something of a problem. So freely was sex indulged in that an injunction appears in the Taittirīya Saṁhita calling for sexual restraint on holy occasions:

> Let not a man, after preparing the altar for the sacred fire, approach a Śūdra woman, because in doing so he would be discharging seed into an improper place. Let no man, after a second time preparing the fire-altar, approach another man's wife.[117]

The responsibility for this lowering of sexual standards was placed on women. It is taken for granted: "women are irregular in their conduct." Infidelity on the part of a wife did not forbid her from taking part in sacred rites; she was only obliged to confess her guilt so that unfaithfulness might not be compounded by dishonesty.[118]

These references would suggest that, though the Brahmin caste made great spiritual pretensions, their sexual life did not always measure up to these claims. A sordid example of priestly morality was Yavakri who sexually seduced every woman he fancied, even though cohabitation would entail the death of his paramour. Finally, he paid with his life for his illicit pleasures at the hands of a gandharva.

The close of the Vedic period witnessed the rise of puritanical movements which tried to stamp out the practice of polyandry. Exceptions were made in the case of *niyoga* or the custom of impregnating the wife of an impotent or dead man so that his family may be preserved. Whereas in the Law Books *niyoga* was accepted as a dispassionate duty, in the present period "Niyoga was only a restricted form of polyandry freely indulged in by the parties with as much display of passion and zest as the consciousness of performing a duty."[119]

Next, we must consider the effects of religious ceremonialism upon the status of women. Keith views the situation bleakly. He laments:

> The final proof of the brutal morality of the priest can be adduced in the position assigned to women: woman in India has always suffered much from all religions, but by none has she been so thoroughly despised as by the Brahmans of the period of the Brahmanas.[120]

The survey that follows should corroborate Keith's indictment. There is no doubt that as the Āryan tribes settled in India, the status of women did diminish. But, even so, the situation was not as bleak as Keith describes it.

First, let us examine the factors which contributed to the degradation of womanhood. We begin with the emergence in Vedic belief of an eschatological belief that the spirits of the dead survive in another world, and that it is the duty of sons to help the deceased attain the blessings of heaven through the regular offering of oblations. Failure to make these offerings results in the ancestral spirits roaming restlessly on earth or suffering in hell. This belief, along with its attendant ritualism, invested sons with the highest importance because only through a son's oblation could a deceased father attain salvation. Herein lay the ritualistic superiority of a son over a daughter. The Aitareya Brāhmaṇa makes clear the preference:

> The father, who looks upon the face of his son, born living unto him, discharges his debt in him . . . the son is to him a rescuing boat . . . in him ye have the blameless world of heaven. The daughter is a sorrow, while the son is light in the highest regions of heaven to his father.[121]

An early indication of this preferential attitude toward sons is found in the Atharva Veda where prayers and rituals are performed for the replacement of a daughter by a son in the mother's womb.[122]

The second factor reducing woman to the level of a fourth-class citizen was ceremonial impurity. The Śatapatha Brāhmaṇa classifies woman with the Śūdra, the dog, and the crow as objects of untruth and impurity.[123] Āryan women were probably classified in this way because non-Āryan females of low social background were incorporated into Āryan families as wives or concubines, and the ceremonial uncleanness of the latter seems to have been wiped off on women in general.

The nature of this ritual impurity seems to have had sexual implications. The Śatapatha Brāhmaṇa gives directions for the wife of the sacrificer to be gird with a cord *(yoktra)*, and the reason for this is:

> Impure indeed is that part of woman which is below the navel; and therewith she will be facing the sacrificial butter: that part of her he thereby conceals with the cord, and only with the pure upper part of her body she then faces the sacrificial butter. This is the reason why he girds the wife.[124]

In the course of the sacrifice the wife occupies an inferior position—"the wife is truly the hinder part of the sacrifice."[125] "Even if many women are together and there is but a small boy, he takes precedence of them all."[126]

A third factor affecting woman's place was specialisation. The growth of specialisation meant that her role was domestically and biologically defined. Her real purpose in life was to produce children, especially sons. "The wife as Patni in her capacity of partnership with the lord husband (Pati) recedes into the background, and the idea of Jaya, for bearing children for the husband, becomes more prominent."[127] In the Vājapeya ceremony it is said that the sacrificer's wife "is one half of his own self."[128] This is not a statement of equalitarianism, but a simple biological truth that without a wife a man cannot beget progeny! The wife still performed certain ceremonial roles, especially when these were related to her biological functions, but, in the main, the priest usurped the role she played in religious ceremonies.[129]

The fourth factor responsible for the depreciation of womanhood was the spread of a polygamous spirit. Polygamy was practised within limits in the Ṛgvedic period, but the growth of aristocratic powers and privileges led to the heightening of polygamous tendencies as the elite class of men took unto themselves the women of the conquered race. From ritualistic descriptions in the Brāhmaṇas we gather that it was common for a king to have four wives. If the fourth wife were of low caste, being the daughter of a messenger or a courier, she would only be present at the sacrifice, without taking part in the ceremony.[130] Outside royal and aristocratic circles, the practice of polygamy was less evident, but was apparently widespread enough to take its toll of women's respect and prestige.

The cumulative effect of these four factors placed womanhood in a despicable position. She was looked upon as a temptress, deserving of care because of her female functions, but not deserving of any rights. The Maitrāyaṇī Saṁhitā is most brutal in its assessment: "Woman is Nirriti" (the personification of Evil). She represents untruth in human society, and is classified with dice and drink.[131] She is even inferior to a bad man.[132] The Śatapatha Brāhmaṇa contains the story of the wooing of Vāc in which Vāc yielded to the allurements of song and dance, rather than the recitation of the Vedas. This is taken to explain why "women are given to vain things," and why they readily fancy "him who dances and sings."[133]

Because of these weaknesses, women are forbidden to attend assemblies.[134] They are required to eat meals after their husbands have dined—a husband "should not eat food in the presence of his wife."[135] They must be subservient, never giving their husbands any backchat. They have no right to own any property; they do not even have any rights over themselves![136]

Keith was correct: Indian women have suffered much from all religions, but they have been most brutalised by the Brahmins of the period of the Brāhmaṇas. However, Keith fails to recognise that in spite of the derogatory descriptions and denials of basic rights, women did have something to invest them with the dignity of ethical personalities.

In the first place, it would be unjust to the Brāhmaṇas to fail to appreciate the fact that they do not encourage criminal treatment of female children as practised by other rituals. "The exposure of female children which has been asserted to be mentioned in the Brāhmaṇas is a mere error."[137] Female children were also protected against marriage prior to puberty.

Second, a woman's religious rights were curtailed by the priests, but she still had the privilege of reading the sacred scriptures and performing certain sacrifices along with her husband. In the Vājapeya sacrifice, the husband, climbing the ladder, says: "Wife, let us ascend to heaven."[138] In the two great sacrificial feasts celebrated by royalty, the *Aśvamedha* (horse sacrifice), and *Rājsūya,* the chief queen, played a pivotal role.

Third, though polygamy was on the incline, and polyandry was on the decline, the custom of *niyoga* somewhat equalised sexual liberties. Besides, women's sexual needs were recognized by the acceptance of widow marriage.[139]

Fourth, there was some equity in the punishment for marital infidelity: "the ethical rules for women were the same as those for men, and the same leniency was shown to women as to men."[140]

Summarizing this section, we can do no better than repeat the assessment of Shakuntala Rao Shastri:

> Taken all in all, the Brahmanas reflect a transitional stage in the position of women; owing to the growth of rituals and the development of social institutions, the scope of a woman's life was gradually becoming limited. She is the partner in religious sacrifices of a man and, though the object of a woman's life is fast getting circumscribed by the unusual importance attached to a son, still woman was not merely an object of pleasure but the colleague in the religious life of a man.[141]

We have so far surveyed the duties pertaining to two *āśramas:* the *Brahmacarya* and the *Gārhasthya.* The full *āśrama* theory along with the *Vānaprasthya* and *Saṁnyāsa* stages was only developed in the period of the later Upaniṣads;[142] but in the period of the Brāhmaṇas there was already movement in that direction. The effect of this movement was that of moral leaven within society in general and the priestly class in particular. As Dutt states it:

> The rigid discipline of both mind and body, the ideal of plain living and high thinking, the austere practices and constant meditation upon the Creator and His Creation, the Soul and the Life after Death, so forcibly and frequently enjoined upon in the Upanishads, cannot but have a very ennobling influence upon the moral atmosphere of the time.[143]

The *āśrama* ideal thus generated a moral counterforce to the ethical chaos brought about by the introduction of magic into religion.

We turn now from the *āśrama* duties to the *varṇa* duties. Dr. S. Radhakrishnan has stated: "The institution of caste is not the invention of an unscrupulous priesthood, but a natural evolution conditioned by the times."[144] Without discounting the evolutionary aspects of caste, this statement appears to lack historical cogency when examined in the context of the Brāhmaṇas which cover the period during which caste was solidified. The system might have been evolving on its own momentum, but the priesthood precipitated this evolution, sometimes using immoral and unjust means to ensconce themselves as the overlords of Āryans and non-Āryans alike. Never in the history of the human race have men so presumptuously arrogated unto themselves positions superior to the gods.

The religious justification for caste is based upon the divine origin of this system as recorded in the *Puruṣa-sūkta.* Although the Puruṣa hymn is found in the Ṛg Veda, chronologically it belongs to the period of the Brāhmaṇas. By attributing a divine origin to caste, the original social institution was elevated to the position of a religious institution, and its laws were thereby considered immutable. According to Brāhmaṇic interpretation of the hymn, the purpose of this divine creation was to make caste a stabilising factor in society. It was ordained in order that there might be no "confusion of castes," and that society be maintained in "the proper order."[145] Social stability was achieved, indeed by caste, but this was done at the cost of ethical considerations. We shall now study the consolidation of caste in the age of the Brāhmaṇas and shall indicate the manner in which it obstructed the principled development of morality.

We first study the priestly caste. Motivated by guild spirit and class jealousy, the Brahmins made their order inaccessible by closing the canon of Vedic hymns, thus barring poets of lesser ranks from aspiring to the priestly profession. As a further deterrent, they complicated the theoretical and practical aspects of sacrifice with such hair-splitting minutiae that only a specialist from their own learned ranks could understand and execute the sacerdotal duties.

The Brahmins not only consolidated their superiority by protecting their office against nonpriestly aspirants, they also protected the purity of their blood against Śūdra incursions. The new politics of coexistence meant that Śūdras, treated now as subjects and not as slaves, had increased contact with the Āryans. This posed the problem of maintaining the purity of Āryan blood. To meet the emergency, a policy of social exclusiveness was adopted. Although the original intent of this new social policy was to exclude intercourse with the Śūdra, its effects were more encompassing, thus raising social barriers between the Āryans themselves.

This illustrates one way in which the tactics used to separate Āryans from non-Āryans also separated Āryans from Āryans. Ethnic exclusiveness bred social exclusiveness. The latter tendency was accelerated by the introduction of special rites prescribing different forms of religious and social behaviour deemed appropriate for each separate caste. Judged in isolation, these rules seemed merely decorative, but their cumulative effect was socially destructive. They helped create a climate in which each caste was reminded, in a myriad minuscule manners, of the place it occupied in the hierarchical order of society. The rationale for some of these distinctions was purportedly ethical, but its underlying concept of sin had no basis in ethics. For instance, Śatapatha Brāhmaṇa lays down specifications for the sepulchral mound according to caste distinctions, and to make sure the rules are strictly observed, the issue of sin is raised.

> Let him not make it (the sepulchral mound) too large, lest he make the (deceased's) sin large. For the Kshatriya he may make it as high as a man with upstretched arms, for a Brahmaṇa reaching up to the mouth, for a woman up to the hips, for a Vaiśya up to the thighs, for a Sūdra up to the knee; for suchlike is their vigour.[146]

All of these meaningless distinctions solidified the caste system and intoxicated the Brahmins with delusions of godliness. The Śatapatha Brāhmaṇa declares: "The Brahman descended from a Rishi indeed is all deities."[147] If divinity were the norm of impartial justice, the Brahmins may be respected as the embodiments of the moral order; instead, the Brahmins interpreted their divine status to mean that law served them—they did not have to serve the law. In a strictly ethical sense, there was no law, only laws, hierarchically conceived. For example, the Taittirīya Saṁhitā prescribes: "If there be a dispute between a Brahman and a non-Brahman, the king should support the Brahman; if one opposes the Brahman, he opposes himself; therefore one should not oppose a Brahman."[148] This is only one among several other preferential laws in which the idea of law as justice is entirely absent.

Violations of these laws were threatened with punishments which were grossly unrelated to and disproportionate with the nature of the offence. One guilty of spitting upon a Brahmin was sentenced, in the afterlife, to sitting "in the middle of a stream running with blood, devouring hair."

The second step in the hierarchy was occupied by the Kṣatriyas—the protectors of the people. For them, the hardening of caste distinctions meant that their participation in priestly activities had to be terminated. Without Brahmin priests, they could not take part in sacrifices, because, it is said, "the gods do not eat the food offered by a king who has no priest."[149] However, even though the Kṣatriyas were forbidden from entering the priestly ranks and were not permitted to compose the sacred hymns, many of them channeled their religious insights and aspirations in the direction of metaphysical speculations.

The case of Janaka of Videha is a good illustration of how certain members of the kingly class were not only patrons of learning, but themselves contributed to its expansion. In a theological disputation with three Brahmin sages, Janaka asked them a question related to the Agnihotra which none of them could answer correctly. Then, with true philosophical acumen he himself explained the answer for which he received the highest praise of the sage Yājñavalkya.[150]

A second area in which the authority of the Kṣatriyas was limited was control of priestly appointments. "The Purohitas or family priests were practically irremovable, which only added to the vested rights of the Brahman priests."[151] The relation between the king and his Purohita is looked upon as indissoluble as the bonds between a married couple.[152] Once installed, the king was to honour his Purohita with the same obedience that is owed by a student to his teacher, a son to his father, and a servant to his master.

In reading such assertions of the Brahmin's superiority over the Kṣatriya, two qualifications must be borne in mind. First, the literature in which this superiority is being asserted is priestly. Doubtlessly, there must have been a great struggle for power between these two caste groups, but the literature is not interested in recording these challenges to Brahmanical power. Tactically, this literary "whitewash" may have been sound, but ethically it was dishonest. Second, it is questionable whether the Brahmins did, indeed, attain a clearcut supremacy over the Kṣatriyas. The ruling class did suffer a lasting setback, but two factors prevented the Brahmins from achieving any decisive superiority, namely, the development in kingly circles of an independent mode of philosophical thought that was referred to earlier and their firm grip over temporal affairs.

The priests and warriors constituted two aristocratic orders which conspired to subject the masses of the Āryan people to a position of virtual slavery. The inferior status of the Vaiśya in relation to the lordly Brahmins and Kṣatriyas is stated thus, along with some pseudo-ethical reasoning.

> And inasmuch as, in going from here, the horse goes first, therefore the Kshatriya, going first, is followed by the three other castes; and inasmuch as, in returning from there, the he-goat goes first, therefore the Brāhmaṇa, going first, is followed by the three other castes. And inasmuch as the ass does not go first, either in going from here, or in coming back from there, therefore the Brāhmaṇa and Kshatriya never go behind the Vaiśya and Sūdra; hence they walk thus in order to avoid a confusion between good and bad. And, moreover, he thus encloses these two castes (the Vaiśya and Sūdra) on both sides by the priesthood and the nobility, and makes them submissive.[153]

The submissive rank of the Vaiśya was brought about by the feudalistic tendencies in society which widened the gap between the aristocrats and the proletariat, on the one hand, and on the other hand, by the fraternizing tendencies which marked the relationship between Vaiśya and Śūdra as a result of common employment and intermarriage.

The aristocrats began to look contemptuously upon manual labour once there were enough slaves to do such jobs. Members of the Āryan community employed in farming, commerce, and the industrial arts were despised for being engaged in such degrading professions, and also because of their association with the Śūdras who came to occupy similar positions. Certain branches in the Vaiśya community were even looked upon as impure. Unlike the merchant and the farmer, the Vaiśya carpenter was considered impure. A passage in the Śatapatha Brāhmaṇa explicitly states that defilement is incurred by the touch of "a carpenter or some other impure person."[154] In the subsequent period, other such Vaiśya occupations fell in disrepute.

In addition to the contempt incurred by the manual nature of their professions, the Vaiśyas were also downgraded by the aristocracy because of their intermarriage with the Śūdras. Marriage with the Śūdras was inevitable because of the closeness of working conditions and because the Vaiśyas were shut off from the rest of the Āryan community. But once they were tainted with black blood, the Vaiśyas were all the more excluded from the priestly ruling classes who considered purity of blood more excellent than virtue.

The Śūdras constituted the fourth step within the caste system. The ethics whereby he was excluded from intercourse with the Āryan community is explained in these lines:

> Now the gods do not commune with everyone, but only with a Brāhman, or a Rājanya, or a Vaiśya; for these are able to sacrifice. Should there be occasion for him to converse with a Śūdra, let him say to one of those, 'Tell this one so and so! tell this one so and so!' This is the rule of conduct for the consecrated in such a case.[155]

This religious rationalization of ethnic prejudice gave the Āryans a clean conscience in their treatment of the Śūdras—"the Śūdra has no god and no sacrifice."[156] In the Gangetic plains the Śūdra had greater political freedom than in the Ṛgvedic period; but though elevated from a slave to a domestic servant, the Śūdra could never achieve the freedoms of an Āryan. Even so, some of the freedoms of the Śūdra during this period are overlooked by scholars.

Attention should be called to the fact that the same two steps by which the Vaiśya came down the social ladder, the Śūdra went up. Through common tasks and ties of blood the Śūdra established ethnic and cultural affinities with the Āryan community. In this process of acculturation the Śūdra was granted limited functions and privileges in the sacred rites. The Śatapatha Brāhmaṇa, for instance, specifies the form of speech which must be used in addressing various participants in a sacrifice, and one form is prescribed for the Śūdra.[157]

Though the Śūdras were the lowest within the caste system, they considered themselves superior to the savage races of pre-Dravidian stock which occupied some inaccessible areas of the country. These people had a very low culture expressed through rather loathsome behaviour, and were, therefore, treated with contempt by Āryans and Dravidians alike. Socially, they were placed in a new order, the fifth *varṇa;* and their very touch was considered defiling. It is to the discredit of the religion of these times that human worth was based on such externalities as racial stock, colour, and material standards of living. For these reasons, no efforts were made to uplift these savage tribes; instead, they were treated as pariahs and were made to pursue the dirtiest tasks.

Our investigation of the ethical thought of the Brāhmaṇas has shown that two factors were mainly responsible for the retardation of ethical and moral development: magic and caste. The magical interpretation of sacrifice deethicised good and evil. Caste robbed the Śūdra of "god and sacrifice" and elevated the Brahmins to the position of divinities of earth!

IV. Ethical Thought in the Upaniṣads

In the Ṛg Veda the *summun bonum* was harmony with the will of the gods who maintained the order of *Ṛta.* In the Brāhmaṇas the *summum bonum* was sacrificial rectitude. In the Upaniṣads the highest ideal for man's ethical endeavours is self-knowledge. Vedic ceremonialism and caste duties give way to a new spiritual quest which turns inward for the purpose of understanding Ultimate Reality. This quest is eloquently expressed in this well-known prayer:

> From the unreal *(asat)* lead me to the real *(sat)!*
> From darkness lead me to light!
> From death lead me to immortality![158]

The motivation behind this introspective search is the fundamental idea running through the early Upaniṣads that "underlying the exterior world of change there is an unchangeable reality which is identical with that which underlies the essence of man."[159] Stated in the words of the Bṛhadāraṇyaka Upaniṣad:

> Verily, he is the great, unborn Soul, who is this [person] consisting of knowledge among the senses. In the space within the heart lies the ruler of all, the

> lord of all, the king of all. He does not become greater by good action nor inferior by bad action.[160]

The formulation of this ideal was a long time in the making. Summarily stated, the Upaniṣadic sages synthesised two notions which originally had totally different connotations, namely, *'Brahman'* or the ultimate source of the external world, and *'Ātman'* or the inner self of man. These sages teach that the *Brahman* of the macrocosm is none other than the *Ātman* of the microcosm—"That self is, indeed, Brahman."[161] By equating *Brahman* with *Ātman,* each term came to signify the eternal ground of the universe, including the ground of man's being and the being of nature. Thus, in the course of his speculation, the Indian sage "at last reached the goal of his long quest after unity—a goal which left all mythology far behind and was truly philosophical."[162]

The Chāndogya Upaniṣad records a famous passage illustrating this *Brahman-Ātman* doctrine. Śvetaketu, son of Uddālaka Āruṇi, having completed his Vedic studies, "returned at the age of twenty-four, conceited, thinking himself to be learned, proud."[163] His father said to him:

> Śvetaketu, my dear, since now you are conceited, think yourself learned, and are proud, did you also ask for that teaching whereby what has not been heard of becomes heard of, what has not been thought of becomes thought of, what has not been understood becomes understood?[164]

Finding his son to be ignorant of the knowledge of *Brahman,* the father proceeds to impart divine knowledge to him. He posits an ultimate source called *Sat* or Being. Its essence lies in consciousness. *Sat* thought to itself: "Would that I were many! Let me procreate myself!"[165]

Through its act of procreation, *Sat* brought the whole of the universe into being, including human existence. The unitary World-Soul is thus the immanental reality of nature and of man. Āruṇi explains to Śvetaketu: "That which is the finest essence—this whole world has that as its soul. That is Reality. That is Ātman (Soul). That art thou, Śvetaketu."[166]

This story, along with cognate passages, has five lessons of ethical import. First, the Upaniṣads postulate that the ethical ideal of realizing one's unity with *Brahman* is the highest goal for which man can strive. Herein lies man's ultimate value, his greatest bliss, his truest freedom, his deepest peace. By uniting with the *Brahman,* the *Ātman* transcends all such vicissitudes of mortal existence as hunger and thirst, sorrow and confusion, old age and death. "As the sun, the eye of the Universe, remains far off and unaffected by all sickness that meets the eye, so also the One, the Ātman, who dwells in all creatures, dwells afar and untouched by the sorrows of the world."[167] Thus, no state can excel the state of realizing one's identity with *Brahman.*

Second, the Upaniṣads teach that though this state of perfect knowledge is so exalted, it is possible to achieve the ideal in one's present life. True, there is the view that *Brahma*-realization is only reached after death; but there is also the view known as *jīvanmukti* which states that *mokṣa* (liberation) can be reached here and now. The Kaṭha Upaniṣad affirms: "when all the desires the heart harbours are gone, man becomes immortal and reaches Brahman here."[168] The shift in the doctrine of *mokṣa* from the eschatological realm to the empirical realm is ethically significant. In place of the speculative basis contingent on faith, *mokṣa* is given a philosophical basis contingent on reason and will. The goal is still in the distant future, and few there are who attain thereto, but it is no longer a hypothetical future. The end is assured from the beginning as moral progress is made through various stages of life. The saint who reaches this goal expresses his cosmic identity in the phrase *"Ahaṃ Brahmāsmi"* (I am Brahman).

The third lesson is that liberation is not a new acquisition. It is the knowledge of *Brahman,* not the *product* of that knowledge. Causation is inapplicable to Brahman because Brahman is *being,* not *becoming.* If *mokṣa* were the product of the knowledge of *Brahman,* then, having had a beginning, it would also have an ending. "Arising from non-existence, it would again dissolve into nothingness."[169]

Fourth, since *mokṣa* is not acquired from without but realized from within, the *mokṣa* doctrine becomes the basis for moral optimism in that the capacity of the present life to achieve perfection is fully recognized.

Fifth, the story of Śvetaketu shows there is a correlation between self-knowledge and morality. The former is the foundation of the latter. The presence of pride and self-conceit in Śvetaketu was a sure sign to his father that the boy lacked knowledge of *Brahman.* It was self-contradictory for an enlightened person to entertain such vanity in his heart, because only the pure in heart see *Brahman.* Enlightenment presupposes the radical elimination of all manifestations of egocentricity.

Though *mokṣa* is the present perception of eternal Reality, ignorance prevents men from reaching it.

> So, just as those who do not know the spot might go over a hid treasure of gold again and again, but not find it, even so all creatures here go day by day to that Brahma-world *(brahma-loka)* [in deep sleep], but do not find it; for truly they are carried astray by what is false.[170]

Untruth lies in the empirical view which accepts diversity as the sole truth about the world instead of probing deep until the unity of *Brahman* is reached.

Metaphysical error translates into evil on the moral level. Whereas in the Ṛg Veda, evil lay in the contradiction of the will of the gods, and while in the Brāhmaṇas it was mostly deviation from sacrificial rectitude, in the Upaniṣads evil arises out of the mistaken notion that Reality is finite. Finiteness breeds desire. Ignorantly imagining that he is separate from others, man sees others as rivals in the fight for individual survival. All of the evils which alienate man from man, and man from nature are due to the false consciousness of individuality. Such men are prisoners of suffering, sickness, and death because they ignorantly desire what is sensuous and finite.

How does one overcome such ego-desires or *ahaṁkāra?* It is at this point that the Upaniṣads insist on the indispensability of the ethical life. Identity with the Supreme is impossible for one who has not become "calm, subdued, quiet, patiently enduring and collected."[171] Only through purification and concentration is *ahaṁkāra* overcome. However, because *ahaṁkāra* is deeply embedded in man's ego, it cannot be eradicated suddenly or automatically. Hence the need for an ascetically progressive period of moral discipline covering one's entire life.

The prescribed discipline prerequisite for *mokṣa* is known as *brahmacarya.* " *'Brahmacarya'* here takes a new meaning signifying moral conduct conducive to the contemplation of Brahman, the highest truth."[172] This meaning is borne out by the tale of Indra and Virocana who, for thirty-two years, lived together "the disciplined life of a student of sacred knowledge."[173] The Muṇḍaka Upaniṣad emphasises the oft-repeated theme:

> This Soul (Ātman) is obtainable by truth, by austerity *(tapas),*
> By proper knowledge *(jñāna),* by the student's life of chastity *(brahmacarya)* constantly [practised].[174]

First, the student must find a spiritual teacher.[175] No amount of individual thinking can take the place of a guru "who is learned in the scriptures and established in Brahman."[176]

Brahmavidyā begins as the young man approaches the teacher with sacrificial "fuel in hand."[177] The fuel symbolises the light of reason to be imparted by the teacher to the student,[178] and also the resolution of the student to follow the superior wisdom of his guru. Reason and resolution are the basic components distinguishing man, the ethical animal, from all other creatures whose lives are dictated by instinct and impulse. These human capacities which are the psychological bases for the ethical life are clearly delineated in the *Ratharūpaka* or *The Parable of the Chariot.* It reads:

> Know thou the soul (*ātman,* self) as riding in a chariot,
> The body as a chariot.

Know thou the intellect *(buddhi)* as the chariot-driver,
And the mind *(manas)* as the reins.

The senses *(indriya),* they say, are the horses;
The objects of sense, what they range over.
The self combined with senses and mind
Wise men call 'the enjoyer' *(bhoktṛ).*

He who has not understanding *(a-vijñāna),*
Whose mind is not constantly held firm—
His senses are uncontrolled,
Like the vicious horses of a chariot-driver.

He, however, who has understanding,
Whose mind is constantly held firm—
His senses are under control,
Like the good horses of a chariot-driver.

He, however, who has not understanding,
Who is unmindful and ever impure,
Reaches not the goal,
But goes on to reincarnation *(saṃsāra).*

He, however, who has understanding,
Who is mindful and ever pure,
Reaches the goal
From which he is born no more.

He, however, who has the understanding of a chariot-driver,
A man who reins in his mind—
He reaches the end of his journey,
The highest place of Vishṇu.

Higher than the senses are the objects of sense.
Higher than the objects of sense is the mind *(manas);*
And higher than the mind is the intellect *(buddhi).*
Higher than the intellect is the Great Self *(Ātman).*

Higher than the Great Self is the Unmanifest *(avyakta).*
Higher than the Unmanifest is the Person.
Higher than the person there is nothing at all.
That is the goal. That is the highest course.

An intelligent man should suppress his speech and his mind.
The latter he should suppress in the Understanding-Self *(jñāna ātman).*
The understanding he should suppress in the Great Self [=*buddhi,* intellect].
That he should suppress in the Tranquil Self *(śānta ātman).*[179]

Thus, to know the *Ātman,* the *brahmacārin* must first develop his rational faculties to control his animal impulses, especially the sex impulses. This is why chastity becomes a special connotation of *'brahmacarya'*.

The struggle between reason and passion is vividly described in the Kaṭha Upaniṣad as the struggle between *śreyas* (here, and in the Gītā = morally excellent), and *preyas* (what to most is dearer than the good).

> The better *(śreyas)* is one thing, and the pleasanter *(preyas)* quite another.
> Both these, of different aim, bind a person.
> Of these two, well is it for him who takes the better;
> He fails of his aim who chooses the pleasanter.
>
> Both the better and the pleasanter come to a man.
> Going all around the two, the wise man discriminates.
> The wise man chooses the better, indeed, rather than the pleasanter.
> The stupid man, from getting-and-keeping *(yoga-kṣema),* chooses the pleasanter.
>
> Thou indeed, upon the pleasant and pleasantly appearing desires.
> Meditating, hast let them go, O Naciketas.
> Thou art not one who has taken that garland of wealth
> In which many men sink down.
>
> Widely opposite and asunder are these two:
> Ignorance *(avidyā)* and what is known as 'knowledge' *(vidyā).*
> I think Naciketas desirous of obtaining knowledge!
> Many desires rend thee not.
>
> Those abiding in the midst of ignorance,
> Self-wise, thinking themselves learned,
> Running hither and thither, go around deluded,
> Like blind men led by one who is himself blind.[180]

Judging by this passage, the wise man is one who is guided by his reason rather than his sensations. He refuses to allow anything unedifying, no matter how pleasant, to pollute his psycho-physical constitution. Only what is spiritually uplifting is allowed to enter the doors of his five senses. And so he prays:

> Aum. May we, may we, O gods, hear what is auspicious with our ears. Oh ye, who are worthy of worship, may we see with our eyes what is auspicious. May we enjoy the life alloted to us by the gods, offering praise, with our bodies strong of limb.[181]

By purifying the intake of his senses through the proper use of reason, the *brahmacārin* purifies his whole personality. Being pure in mind and body, he is able to conserve his strength and build up his capacity for the uninterrupted flow of spiritual consciousness which ultimately leads to revelation.[182]

Together with reason, virtue constitutes the second means for attaining strength *(vīrya, bala).* Virtue thus plays a pivotal role toward liberation for "this self *(Ātman)* cannot be attained by one without strength."[183] The primary virtue in the life of the *brahmacārin* is *satya* or truth. This ancient virtue, going back to Ṛgvedic times, is integral to the Upaniṣads. Asked to identify "the mystic doctrine" *(upaniṣad),* the sage replies, "Truth is its abode."[184] Truth helps the disciple build up soul-force by bringing his speech and mental states under the guidance of reason. The first practical precept mentioned by a teacher in his farewell address to his students reads: "Speak the truth."[185] One should guard himself against speaking falsehood "as a sword-walker guards himself from falling into a pit."[186]

Truth starts with reason but does not stop with it. The deepest knowledge can only be seen through the eyes of faith. The disciple must, therefore, have faith in the guru's teaching. This is clearly brought out in the discourse between Śvetaketu and his father. Explaining the subtle essence which cannot be perceived but which is nevertheless real, the father says, "Believe me, my dear."[187]

The second exhortation of the teacher to his departing students is: "Practice virtue *(dharma).*"[188] Dharma is related to truth as action is related to knowledge. There are three active modes of *dharma: yajña, adhyayana,* and *dāna* (sacrifice, study, and dedication).[189]

Yajña or sacrifice is qualified as *tapas.* The meaning of *tapas* is soul-force. It refers to the spiritual energy which is generated by bringing one's physical nature under the control of his rational will. Austerities produce a certain spiritual combustion which frees the soul of narrow, selfish accretions of *preyas,* and expands it in the direction of *śreyas.*

The second mode of *dharma* is *adhyayana* or study. Revelatory knowledge is stored in *śruti* literature; therefore, it is considered a virtue to make a careful study of the Vedas. Since virtue is relative to personal needs, study is the determinative virtue of the student because it fulfils the specific purpose of his stage of life, namely, the acquisition of knowledge. Failure to gather knowledge would be the undoing of all other virtues the student may otherwise have acquired. Goodness is only good when it is good for something, and in the student's case it is the gathering of knowledge.

Related to the study of scriptures is the exposition of the scriptures or *pravacana. Pravacana* has two values. First, through teaching, one is himself taught. Second, by teaching others, one pays his debt to his preceptor and thereby keeps alive the Vedic tradition, the source of all religion and morality. Together, *adhyayana* and *pravacana* provide the common framework for the other virtues such as *ṛta* (the right), *satya* (the truc), *tapas* (austerity), *dama* (self-control), *sama* (tranquility), *mānuṣa* (humanity).[190]

The third mode of *dharma* is *dāna.* The Chāndogya Upaniṣad describes it as "absolutely controlling his body in the house of the teacher." This form of commitment of the pupil to the guru, carrying him beyond the normal period of the *Brahmacarya* stage, is called *dāna* because the pupil is offering himself as a gift.

Dāna in the Upaniṣads is also the ideal of charity that must govern all human relations. Being a social animal, it is man's *dharma* to relate to his fellows in a supportive and helpful manner even though this may sometimes entail personal sacrifices. The story of Naciketa offering himself as a gift is an inspiring model of this ideal. However, "the gift without the giver is bare." Therefore, it is not only important that charity be practised but that it be practised in a moral manner. The Taittirīya Upaniṣad speaks to this requirement.

> One should give with faith *(śraddhā).*
> One should not give without faith.
> One should give with plenty *(śri).*
> One should give with modesty.
> One should give with fear.
> One should give with sympathy *(sam-vid).*[191]

Commenting on these three modes of *dharma,* Professor G. Mukhopadhyaya summarises the interrelatedness and ethical intentionality of the ideas expressed above:

> By *yajña* or sacrifice one is linked with the world of the gods, through study or *adhyayana* one is joined with the supreme sphere of Śabda-Brahman, and lastly through *dāna,* self-giving or gift of things one gets connected with the human world. Dharma thus covers all the spheres of life and is not an isolated state of thing.[192]

There are two other lists of virtues worth noting. The Chāndogya Upaniṣad provides an allegorical interpretation of life as a great soma festival.[193] We have here "a miniature ethical system" built around the notion of sacrifice to be performed in spirit, without recourse to physical rites. The *dikṣā* or initiatory rite is allegorized as privation. Gifts to the priests are in the form of "austerity, almsgiving, uprightness, nonviolence, truthfulness."[194] It should be pointed out that here is the sole reference to *ahiṁsā* in the Upaniṣads. Nonviolence was only elevated as a supreme virtue in subsequent Buddhist tradition.

A second list of virtues is found in a myth where Prajāpati, the great moral lawgiver, speaks through the roll of thunder—*'da'! 'da'! 'da'!* The myth begins:

> The threefold offspring of Prajāpati, gods, men and demons, lived with their father Prajāpati as students of sacred knowledge. Having completed their studentship the gods said, 'Please tell (instruct) us, sir.' To them, then, he uttered the syllable *da* (and asked) "Have you understood?" They (said) 'We have understood', you said to us *"damyata"*, "control yourselves." He said, 'Yes, you have understood.'[195]

In this first instance, *'da'* is associated with *'damyata'* or self-control. The gods are requested to cultivate this virtue inasmuch as they are naturally disposed to being unruly. The 'gods' are those men who are graced with benevolent qualities, but lack self-restraint.

Next, the men ask Prajāpati for instruction and to them he utters the same syllable, *'da'*. They associate it with *'datta'* or give. Since men naturally tend to be penurious, they are asked instead to be liberal with their wealth.

In similar fashion, the demons ask for instruction. When they hear the syllable, *'da'*, they associate it with *'dayadhvam'*, meaning 'be compassionate'. Demons represent beings whose *guṇas* tend to cruelty; therefore, they are asked to share the milk of human kindness with all people.

The two social institutions meriting our attention are the family and caste. For all their emphasis on renunciation, the Upaniṣads never minimize the importance of the family. The departing student is instructed by his teacher: "cut not off the line of progeny."[196] A man is incomplete and unfulfilled without a wife, children, and earthly possessions.[197] All aspects of the householder's life are ethically regulated. He must especially be hospitable to guests, otherwise, "hope and expectation, intercourse and pleasantness, sacrifices and meritorious deeds, sons and cattle"—all of these will be snatched away from him for the niggard shows himself to be a "man of little understanding."[198] Before he can understand *Brahman* the householder must propitiate the gods and gratify his father.[199] In order to share, the householder must first possess; he therefore prays for all the good things in this life: wealth, cattle, clothes, food, drink, prosperity, and longevity. A typical prayer: "May I become glorious among men! May I be better than the very rich! Hail!"[200] The speaker, here, is a teacher. All the teachers of major Upaniṣads, like Yājñavalkya, were *gṛhasthas*.

As far as the woman's status within the family, "the Brihadaranyaka records one of the best periods of Indian history, when women were admitted into these philosophical groups and were allowed to discuss the highest spiritual truths of life."[201] The Aitareya Upaniṣad suggests that it was possible for elderly married women to be admitted to Vedāntic discourses.[202] There are several references in the Upaniṣads to women functioning as teachers, though it is not certain if they were married.

Maitreyī, wife of Yājñavalkya, is known as a *Brahmavādinī* (desirous of the knowledge of *Brahman*). Her conversation with Yājñavalkya on the Absolute Self shows that "the later subjection of women and their exclusion from Vedic studies does not have the support of the Upaniṣads."

Another *Brahmavādinī* was Gārgī. So great was her desire to know the nature of *Brahman* that she could not cease questioning Yājñavalkya, despite his threat: "Gārgī, do not question too much lest your head fall off."[203] Gārgī was undeterred. She kept probing the sage's mind until she had extracted from him one of the profoundest definitions of *Brahman*.

The value placed on the intellectual achievement among women becomes apparent in ritual prayers that are prescribed for the birth of a daughter who, it is hoped, will achieve the status of *paṇḍitā* or learned woman.[204] Women's education was not limited to household affairs; they also had the right to study the Vedas. Śaṅkara's denial of the latter privilege finds no support from the Upaniṣadic text and from other related beliefs and practices.

Feminine sexuality is lauded as the creation of the divine, and, therefore, is good. Spirit and flesh are blended in this descriptive analogy meant both for excitement and reverence.

> Her lap is a sacrificial altar; her hairs the sacrificial grass; her skin, the soma-press. The two labia of the vulva are the fire in the middle. Verily, indeed, as great as is the world of him who sacrifices with the Vajapeya ('Strength-libation') sacrifice, so great is the world of him who practices sexual intercourse, knowing this; he turns the good deeds of women to himself. But he who practices sexual intercourse without knowing this—women turn his good deeds unto themselves.[205]

Sexual intercourse performed with spiritual knowledge is a thing of joy because of the "loveliness among women."[206] When a woman yields her favours to her lover, exultingly he says: " 'With power, with glory I give you glory!' Thus they two become glorious."[207]

We now turn our attention to a second important social institution, namely, caste. The impact of Upaniṣadic thought on the caste system had the effect of somewhat relaxing its rigidity. The story of Satyakāma illustrates the fact that often ethical considerations prevailed over caste considerations in the selection of students to discipleship. When Gautama asked him of his family background, the boy made this candid confession:

> I do not know this, sir, of what family I am. I asked my mother. She answered me, "In my youth, when I went about a great deal as a maid-servant, I got you. So I do not know of what family you are. I am Jabālā by name and you are Satykāma by name." So I am Satyakāma Jabālā, Sir.[208]

Given such a truthful reply, the teacher responded: "None but a Brahmana could thus explain. Bring the fuel, my dear, I will receive you as a pupil. Thou hast not departed from the truth."[209]

Another illustration of the softening of caste attitudes is seen in the admission of women into philosophical circles, as our observations on the status of women have already shown. Women like Gārgī and Maitreyī were able to participate in philosophical discussions because the exclusive rights of Brahmins as the purveyors and dispensers of religious truth had been radically questioned and curtailed.

The Brahmins began losing their religious prerogatives with the onslaught of Upaniṣadic thought upon the value of ritualism. It is plain from our study that the metaphysics and ethics of the Upaniṣads are quite contrary to the system of ideas on which the sacrificial notions of the Brāhmaṇas are based. The Upaniṣadic hostility toward sacrificial ceremonialism is most clearly expressed in the Muṇḍaka Upaniṣad. Deriding the effectiveness of sacrificial forms against rebirth, the Upaniṣad says:

> Unsafe boats, however, are these sacrificial forms,
> The eighteen, in which is expressed the lower work.
> The fools who approve that as the better,
> Go again to old age and death.[210]

The belittling of the ritualistic system also involved the undermining of the priests who presided over the system. As with their work, they were deemed inferior and devoid of knowledge.

This turn of events in religious authority made it possible for Kṣatriya religious philosophers to rise to positions of intellectual and spiritual leadership. The Upaniṣads mention several royal philosophers such as Ajātaśatru, Aśvapati, Sanatkumāra, Janaka, and Pravāhana Jaivali. Sometimes these sages even demonstrated superior wisdom over their priestly counterparts as evidenced by the words of Pravāhana Jaivali to Śvetaketu Āruṇeya who came to him for enlightenment about the course of the soul after death. The young man assured the king that his father had instructed him, but, upon being questioned, it became apparent that the lad was indeed ignorant. Distressed, the boy returned to his father and said: "Verily, indeed, without having instructed me, you, sir, said: 'I have instructed you.' Five questions a fellow of the princely class *(rajanyabandhu)* has asked me. I was not able to explain even one of them."[211]

The father responded: "As you have told them to me here, I do not know even one of them. If I had known them, how would I not have told them to you?"[212]

With that, Gautama Āruṇi went to the king's place and said to him, "The word which you said in the presence of the young man, even that do you speak to me." This made the king perplexed. He then commanded him to stay for some time, and said, "As to what you have told me, O Gautama, this knowledge has never yet come to Brahmans before you; and therefore in all the worlds has the rule belonged to the Kṣatriya only."[213]

On the basis of this evidence it seems correct to conclude that by the time of the early Upaniṣads the Brahmans' superiority in religious knowledge began to be questioned, Kṣatriyas came to acquire an upper hand, or at least equality, in matters of religion and philosophy. Women also were freely allowed to participate in learned public discussions. In short, there was a slackening of the rigour and rigidity of caste and sex.

The purpose of the personal and social ethics we have just described was to build up soul force by which alone the *Ātman* is realized. The Bṛhadāraṇyaka Upaniṣad says: "having become calm, subdued, quiet, patiently enduring and collected, one should see the self in the self."[214] It is not our intention to explicate the further stages of religious development; suffice it to say that on the highest stage of contemplation one attains an immediate certainty of *Brahman.*[215]

When the supreme knowledge of the *Ātman* is realized, the individual is transported beyond the ethical plane to the religious plane. This is the level of *mokṣa* or supreme liberation. On this level one is not only beyond evil, but beyond the good, for the one presupposes the other. The Bṛhadāraṇyaka Upaniṣad paradoxically describes this state of freedom: "In the highest state a thief is not a thief, a murderer is not a murderer. He is not followed by good nor followed by evil, for he then overcomes all sorrows of the heart."[216]

The secret of this state is that the enlightened one is devoid of fear and is therefore untroubled about the past. "Him does not afflict the thought, why have I not done what is good, why have I committed sin."[217] The reason he is fearless is because, whereas on the moral level the individual is the doer, on the religious level he is no longer a doer. The individual is now identified with the *Ātman* who is essentially a nondoer, and hence, for the *Ātman* the issue of good and evil simply does not arise. The Absolute is above all moral distinctions. Thus, the categorical imperative that one ought to do what is good is significant only on the moral level because here the battle between the *devas* and the *asuras* is very real; but on the religious level, because the *Ātman* knows no struggle, the battle ceases; therefore, the command to do what one ought to loses its former meaning.

Regrettably, this supraethical teaching of the Upaniṣads is taken for the antithesis to morality. Robert Hume voices the surprise of several Western scholars who are shocked by this "unethical character" of Hindu religion. He says:

> There is a wide difference . . . between the Upanishadic theory and the theory of the Greek sages that the man who has knowledge should thereby become virtuous in character, or the result of the teaching should be a virtuous life. Here the possession of metaphysical knowledge actually cancels all past sins and even permits the knower unblushingly to continue in 'what seems to be much evil,' with perfect impunity, although such acts are heinous crimes and are disastrous in their effects for others who lack that kind of knowledge.[218]

Hume overlooks the fact that morality is the *sine qua non* of *jñāna* or saving knowledge. The Kaṭha Upaniṣad clearly states: "Truly, that which is steadfast is not obtained by those who are unsteadfast."[219] The same warning is sounded in a score of other texts.[220] All of these passages reinforce the central Upaniṣadic teaching that spiritual perception is only possible to one whose nature has first been transformed by virtuous living.

Though the religious level seems to be discontinuous with the moral level of existence, since the one is the preparation of the other, there is really a continuity between the two. The law of the moral life is fulfilled in the love of the spiritual life. The deliberate, conscious struggle of the moral life is joyfully transcended by the natural, spontaneous expressions of the spirit. "The soul delights in that supreme blessedness, perceives the unity of all, and loves the world as we love our separate selves."[221]

The Upaniṣads are realistic enough to recognize that there are few who attain to this sublime level of existence. The Kaṭha Upaniṣad observes:

> He who by many is not obtainable even to hear of,
> He whom many, even when hearing, know not—
> Wonderful is the declarer, proficient the obtainer of Him!
> Wonderful the knower, proficiently taught![222]

Until the higher self is realized through intuitive perception, the individual is ruled by the lower self. Though it is the higher self which is the basic reality of the lower self, it is the latter, the phenomenal self, which undergoes birth and death. The wheel of births and deaths around which most lives revolve is known as *saṁsāra* (transmigration). The Chāndogya Upaniṣad describes the doctrine of *saṁsāra* as follows:

> Those who are pleasant conduct here—the prospect is, indeed, that they will enter a pleasant womb, either the womb of a Brahman, or the womb of a Kshatriya, or the womb of a Vaisya. But those who are of stinking conduct

> here—the prospect is, indeed, that they will enter a stinking womb, either the womb of a dog, or the womb of a swine, or the womb of an outcast *(caṇḍāla).*[223]

While the roots of this doctrine of transmigration go back to earlier sources, its branches spread across the entire history of Indian thought, reaching out to the present. The significant element in this doctrine from the ethical point of view is its moral optimism. There is strong motivation for moral activity in the hope that there is always some form of existence through which the individual may strive toward freedom. "As every existent thing has the form of the Divine, it has also the promise of the good."

Connected with the doctrine of *saṁsāra* is the correlative doctrine of the law of *karman. Karman* is the link between rebirth and desire for "whatever a man desires he wills, and whatever he wills, he acts."[224] As the moral principle in the universe, the law of *karman* regulates the rebirth of the *jīvas* (individual embodied souls) according to their acts. No birth is an accident. It is all within a chain of moral causality. Responsibility is placed squarely where it belongs—on human freewill. The present is linked to the past. This does not mean that man is a prisoner of his past. Rather, the past, present, and the future are all equally grounded in freedom, and, therefore, there is always hope and incentive to moral living. The evil that has been done can be undone, and the good that has been left undone can be done.

The final significance of these two doctrines of *saṁsāra* and *karman* does not lie in their eschatological speculations, but in the ethical principle underlying their eschatology. This principle is one that seeks a rational explanation for the sufferings and inequities of life. The primary concern is for what happens here on earth. The present is determinative for the future. Heaven and hell belong to this world of time and space.

Looking back over our study, the Upaniṣads provide no grist for the mill of those Western scholars who charge Indian philosophy with being unethical, or not giving morality its due status. The Upaniṣads presuppose a rigorous ethical discipline prior to the student's introduction to his study. However, it must be admitted that though the Upaniṣads assume ethical excellence in the *brahmacārin,* they do not systematically develop any set of ethical principles. Even so, the Upaniṣads contain sufficient moral teaching that is grounded in philosophical reflection. The sum of its philosophical ethics is in three short words: *damyata, datta, dayadhvam.* The cultivation of self-control, generosity, and compassion suggest that the Upaniṣads are not only conconcerned with personal ethics, but also with social ethics.

It is quite true that ethics is not an end in itself, but only a means toward reaching the experience of Brahman which transcends the moral conflicts of the relative world. But this should not suggest that the enlightened person can act unethically. The actual moral influence of the Upaniṣads on the society of its times is reflected in these words of King Aśvapati:

> 'Within my realm there is no thief,
> No miser, nor drinking man,
> None altarless, none ignorant,
> No man unchaste, no wife unchaste.[225]

CHAPTER 2

The Ethics of the Sūtra and Epic Period

I. Ethical Thought in the Dharma Sūtras, Dharma Śāstras, Epics

Up to this point we have studied the ethics of the Vedic period based on an examination of Hinduism's *śruti* literature. Our present task is to study the development of Hindu ethical thought in *smṛti* literature covering the period 500 B.C. to 300 A.D.

Smṛti means "that which is remembered." It incorporates all authoritative texts outside the Vedas. For the purpose of ethics, the most important works in this collection are the Dharma Sūtras, Dharma Śāstras, and the two epics.

The Dharma Sūtras are aphoristic codes (*sūtras* = threads), succinctly designed to teach students the general principles of *dharma* or moral law. The sanctions for ethical behaviour were religious and not judicial. There is nothing systematic about these textbooks, nor are their treatments of law very thorough. In the area of civil and criminal law their teachings are negligible. Among these early lawbooks the most significant for our purpose are the Dharma Sūtras of Gautama, Baudhāyana, Vasiṣṭha, and Āpastamba. They date from approximately the sixth to second centuries B.C.

The Dharma Śāstras date later than the Dharma Sūtras and are more precise and complete. Like the early lawbooks, the Dharma Śāstras are not too keen about legal distinctions and technical definitions as they are concerned with moral duties. The most authoritative text on the subject of *dharma,* professing divine origin, is The Laws of Manu. It is claimed: "What Manu says is medicine." The date of its composition is sometime between the first century B.C. and the second century A.D. Next in rank to the code of Manu is the Yājñavalkyasmṛti. It is later than Manu, probably belonging to the early Gupta period when there was a renaissance of Brahmanical culture.

The Mahābhārata and Rāmāyaṇa are the two most cherished works of popular Hinduism. "There is hardly a Hindu who has not heard the stories and teachings of these epics from childhood, imbibing them as it were with his mother's milk."[1] The epics are splendid illustrations of the evolutionary character of Hindu thought, having undergone successive accretions and transformations over a period of four to five centuries.

The Mahābhārata or "Great War of the Bhāratas" is a history of the conflicts between two royal houses, the Pāṇḍavas and Kauravas. Its present form was substantially completed by the second century B.C. It reflects an era when Hinduism was being challenged by such heterodox movements as Jainism and Buddhism, and attempting to come to terms with the new liberal spirit that was in the air. Its voluminous verses contain teachings pertaining to statecraft, religion, and morals. In its later portions its heroes are much taken up with the performance of religious duties. The comprehensiveness of its religious and ethical teaching is enunciated in its final section: "Whatever is worthy to be known in matters relating to the welfare of man is here; and what is not here is nowhere else to be found."

The heart of the Mahābhārata is the Bhagavadgītā; indeed, the Gītā is the heart of Hinduism itself. "The song of the Lord" was developed out of the philosophical matrix of the Upaniṣads, but unlike the metaphysical preoccupation of the Upaniṣads, the spirit of the Gītā is practical. It emphasises *bhakti* (religious devotion) and *dharma* (moral law). As the incarnation of Viṣṇu, Kṛṣṇa the charioteer engages in a charming dialogue with Arjuna the warrior-prince who is up against a prodigious moral dilemma. In the course of arguments and counterarguments, important issues of moral duty are raised, and the ethical validity of disinterested action is clearly explained. Because of its unparalleled influence in shaping Hindu ethics through the ages, a special section has been devoted to the ethical thought in the Gītā.

The second epic, the Rāmāyaṇa, is more secular and smaller than the Mahābhārata (recensions vary from 50,000–90,000 lines against the Mahābhārata's more than 200,000 lines). It imparts the kinds of ideals that most characterise the personal, domestic, social, and public life of the Hindus. Like the Mahābhārata, the Rāmāyaṇa gradually developed into a textbook of *dharma*. Vālmīki, the author, probably gave poetic form to the Rāma legends he had collected in approximately the third century B.C. However, extant versions of the poem date from about 200

A.D. The story is about Rāma who is an incarnation of Viṣṇu. As the embodiment of *dharma,* he defeats Rāvaṇa the king of the demons. Sītā, Rāma's wife, is the epitome of womanly virtues because of her faithfulness and unwavering devotion to her husband. The ethical influence of the Rāmāyaṇa has been popularised through devotional movements in which Rāma and Sītā are worshipped as divinities. Mahatma Gandhi was inspired by the epic's ideal of *Rāmarājya* in his nonviolent struggle for India's independence. Judged by its impact both on India's leaders and the masses of her illiterate people, the prophecy in this poem seems to be correct, that as long as mountains stand and rivers flow on the face of this planet, so long shall the fame of the Rāmāyaṇa story and its author be perpetuated.

With this thumbnail sketch of the literature, we turn to its contents. The *smṛtis* continue to maintain the Upaniṣadic ideal of enlightenment as the *summum bonum.* Their institutionalization of the third and fourth *āśramas* emphasizing the ideals of contemplation and renunciation as the means to liberation, attest to the *smṛti's* acceptance of this philosophical ideal. At the same time, the *smṛti* literature continues the tradition of the Brāhmaṇas with a view to evolving a definite order of Brahmanical society. Thus, by espousing the ideals of the Upaniṣads and the Brāhmaṇas, the *smṛti* writers unite "the realm of desires with the perspective of the eternal."[2] However, of these two goals, the practical goal receives greater attention than the transcendental one. This is evidenced by the formulation of the *puruṣārthas* (human values) constituting the 'aims of man'. The three aims *(trivarga)* emphasised are: *dharma, artha,* and *kāma.* The *puruṣārthas* provide the psycho-moral basis for the *āśrama* scheme.

The key to understanding Brahmanical society is found in the first *puruṣārtha,* namely, *dharma.* Indeed, *dharma* is the key to understanding the whole of Hindu culture, past and present. The Sanskrit root-meaning of this protean word is *dhṛ,* 'to hold together'. It is a development of the earlier Ṛgvedic idea of *Ṛta* which, as we have seen, represented cosmic law operating in all phenomena—natural, religious, and moral. It provided the Vedic seers with the ethical norm by which men could relate to nature, to one another, and to the gods. In the *smṛti* period this law permeating the whole universe was called *dharma.* Within the social order, *dharma* was explicitly defined in terms of certain duties and obligations which were codified in the great lawbooks. These codes of social behaviour are divided into three main classes: *Varṇadharma*—duties pertaining to the four castes; *Āśramadharma*—duties pertaining to the four stages of life; and *Sādhāraṇadharma*—common duties binding on all persons, regardless of caste or station in life.

The preceding ideal social structure provided the framework within which all questions of social and moral behaviour were answered. *Dharma,* expressed through specific duties and obligations, served as the criterion for ethical conduct. Ethical decisions were to be resolved, not on the basis of the private conscience, but social conscience. The authority of the social conscience lay in the Vedas, the *smṛtis,* and in the practices of good men. Only as a last resort could the individual determine moral behaviour through his own conscience and the satisfaction of his heart.[3] Thus, there is no gainsaying the fact that the ethics of the *smṛtis* is authoritarian, being rooted in revelation. Even when the individual makes his own decision in some unusual situation, it must entail the rational application of Vedic authority.

We will start with the special duties known as *Varṇadharma.* The basic social ideal is the division of society into four castes: Brahmins, Kṣatriyas, Vaiśyas, and Śūdras. These divisions are of divine origin. The Brahmin was created from the mouth of Brahmā; the Kṣatriya from his arms; the Vaiśya from his thighs; and the Śūdra from the Lord's feet.[4] The ethical implication of the divine origin of caste is that it is an integral part of a divine pattern "for the sake of the prosperity of the worlds,"[5] and, therefore, it is morally incumbent that one obediently accepts his role in compliance with "sacred law."[6]

To the Brahmin is assigned the roles of "teaching and studying (the Veda), sacrificing for their own benefit and for others, giving and accepting (of alms)."[7]

By virtue of his birth from Brahmā's mouth, being firstborn, and possessing the Veda, the Brahmin is considered "the lord of this whole creation."[8] No created being can surpass him "through whose mouth the gods continually consume the sacrificial viands and the manes the offerings of the dead."[9] A Brahmin who dutifully performs his *dharma* is the most excellent of created beings.[10] "The very birth of a Brāhmaṇa is an eternal incarnation of the sacred law; for he is born to (fulfil) the sacred law, and becomes one with Brahman."[11]

Of course, the Brahmin was expected to live up to his lordly status. As the educator of youth, the minister of religious and spiritual needs of the family, and as the protector of *dharma,* the Brahmin had to lead an exemplary life. He was to be a man of *tapas,* persistently striving for enlightenment.[12] He had to be humble—"a Brāhmaṇa shall not name his family and (Vedic) gotra in order to obtain a meal; for he who boasts of them for the sake of a meal, is called by the wise a foul feeder."[13] The Brahmin had to "fear homage as if it were poison; and constantly desire to (suffer) scorn as (he would long for) nectar."[14] He had to be courteous —"a Brāhmaṇa who does not know the form of returning a salutation, must not be saluted by a learned man, as a Śūdra, even so is he."[15] A

Brahmin teacher was to be a man of "sweet and gentle speech," whose "thoughts are pure and ever perfectly guarded."[16] He must place wisdom above wealth, and should be more ready to give than to receive.[17]

The preceding description of the Brahmin's character is based on Manu Smṛti, but other sources would equally support the underlying moral logic that the higher the caste, the greater the ethical expectation. By virtue of the same ethic, the sins of the Brahmin were most grievous. Gautama says: "If a learned man offends, the punishment should be very much increased."[18] Similarly, the Mahābhārata adds, the higher the status, the greater the punishment.[19]

Regrettably, due to four evil influences of the caste system, the ethical norm we have just looked at did not always prevail. First, the caste system had the effect of attributing greater moral depravity to the non-Brahmin. A Brahmin violating a Śūdra's wife was considered less guilty than a Śūdra ravishing the wife of a Brahmin.[20]

Second, the criterion for being a good Brahmin was often more biological than ethical. The law stated it was better to give alms to a Brahmin, unworthy though he be, than to a non-Brahmin possessed of merit.[21] In the same vein, when making offerings to the gods, one must "not enquire into the qualities or descent of a Brāhmaṇa whom he means to invite."[22] Apparently, his being a Brahmin by birth was a sufficient qualification of merit.

Third, notwithstanding the ideal calling for humility in respect of birth, there was the arrogant claim: "A Brāhmaṇa, though ten years old, and a member of the kingly caste, though a hundred years old, must be considered as a father and son," and of these two, the Brahmin was the father.[23] With equal arrogance it is stated that should a Brahmin and Kṣatriya cross paths, the Brahmin assumes the right-of-way.[24] The real height of contempt and exorbitant self-importance is reached in the law which ordinarily forbids a Brahmin to give leftover food to non-Brahmins, but this law is waived, provided the Brahmin "shall clean his teeth and give the food after having placed in it the dirt from his teeth."[25]

Fourth, despite the ideal that privilege entails responsibility, a great deal of the caste legislation was aimed at securing all kinds of preferential treatment for the Brahmins. These privileges included preferential treatment in respect to sacrifice,[26] marriage, means of livelihood,[27] offerings,[28] property,[29] and judicial treatment.[30] The last mentioned privilege became the breeding ground for flagrant injustices.[31] All of these discriminatory laws were enforced by invoking rewards and punishments.

The evil influences of caste should not detract from the fact that the lawmakers did try to uphold ethical standards. A good Brahmin is still one who supports "the moral order in the world," is "deeply versed in the Vedas," and "looks to these (alone), and lives according to these."[32] When these spiritual and ethical concerns of life are neglected, "(noble) families even are degraded."[33]

Next, let us examine the legislations pertaining to Kṣatriyas for their ethical and moral content. The Kṣatriyas constituted the warrior caste, but all warriors were not Kṣatriyas.[34] Even so, it was possible for non-Kṣatriyas "who live by the use of arms" to move upward into Kṣatriya ranks as a result of devoting themselves to the duties of the warrior. From an ethical point of view, the most significant feature of this caste revolves around the king. The law-books abound with details connected to the ethics of royalty, an area we must now explore.

Government as an extension of the king was invested with the responsibility of upholding *dharma,* the eternal divine order of society.[35] Prof. Basham reminds us that in ancient and classical India, government, no matter what its shape, was not an end in itself. "The Hegelian concept of the state as an organism of supernatural size and power, transcending all other entities upon earth and mystically linking man with the Absolute, is completely foreign to anything ever thought of in India."[36] The state as protector of *dharma* comes closer to the Thomistic doctrine of government as the means for promoting salvation.

The protection of *dharma* by government was deemed necessary because it was believed that mankind was living in an age of cosmic decline. "Kingship came into existence, in order to preserve as much as was possible of the age of gold in a period of universal degeneration."[37] According to one legend of the Mahābhārata, the king was divinely appointed, upon the request of mankind, to prevent life from becoming "mean, brutish and short."[38] A second legend has it that kingship is a purely divine imposition upon mankind, designed to help people live by the laws of *dharma.*[39]

The means by which the king ruled his subjects was *daṇḍa* (punishment).[40] The use of force was morally legitimised because of the anarchical tendencies in man. Justifying the use of *daṇḍa,* Manu argues:

> If the king did not, without tiring, inflict punishment on those worthy to be punished, the stronger would roast the weaker, like fish on a spit.
>
> The crow would eat the sacrificial cake and the dog would lick the sacrificial viands, and ownership would not remain with any one, the lower ones would (usurp the place of) the higher ones.
>
> The whole world is kept in order by punishment, for a guiltless man is hard to find; through fear of punishment the whole world yields the enjoyments (which it owes).[41]

In addition to protecting *dharma,* the duty of the king was to fulfil other social needs represented by *artha* and *kāma.*[42] Thus, the duty of the king encompassed the total welfare of the people. By upholding *dharma,* he protected social order and brought peace and justice to the land. By promoting *artha,* he provided people with material prosperity and political stability. And by cultivating *kāma,* he helped bring pleasure into the life of his subjects. All of this is significant evidence that the *Puruṣārthas* had a strong hold upon the life of the people in ancient and classical India.

Proof that these values were not merely held as ideals but were actively cultivated by royalty is supplied by the testimony of early travellers. Chinese and Arab travellers have substantiated the reports of Megasthenes on the administration of Chandragupta Maurya. Like the ideal king envisaged by such jurists as Manu,[43] Chandragupta was a benevolent autocrat concerned with the freedom and prosperity of his people.[44]

Motivation for such benevolent autocracy was twofold. Negatively, the ruler was afraid of rebellion if he acted otherwise. Positively, he was motivated out of a concern for *dharma,* and a desire to abide by the general will.[45]

A striking illustration of the preceding is the story of King Rāma. The Rāmāyaṇa tells of how the king, though convinced of his wife's conjugal purity, was nevertheless prepared to banish her out of deference to his subjects. The people were suspicious that Sītā had illicit connections while in the court of Rāvaṇa, and the guilt of her deed could bring ruin to the realm. Rāma had no such doubts, but was willing to bow to the will of the people. This shows that even within an autocratic form of government without any formal checks and balances on the ruler's power, the king could not act unrighteously or in unashamed arbitrariness.

Turning from the ethics of domestic affairs to that of foreign affairs, we find that the chief ethical principle of royalty was expediency. The Arthaśāstra reflects a situation in which several "mini" kingdoms existed in a precarious state of coexistence. It was a case of the survival of the fittest, with the big fish always ready to swallow up the little fish.[46] In such a situation the fundamental value, requiring no higher justification, was survival itself. Any course of action making for survival was deemed politically sound and morally justifiable.

Kauṭilya's principle of expediency becomes clear by examining the sixfold policy one state can adopt toward another. The six principal policy-relations are: "armistice, war, neutrality, invasion, alliance and peace."[47] Interpreting other ancient thinkers, Kauṭilya recommends:

> Any power inferior to another should sue for peace; any power superior in might to another should launch into war; any power which fears no external attack and which has no strength to wage war should remain neutral; any

power with high war-potential should indulge in invasion; any debilitated power should seek new alliances; any power which tries to play for time in mounting an offensive should indulge in bilateral policy of making war with one and suing peace with the other.[48]

Faced with the threat of battle, the king and other members of the military caste must consider it their *dharma* to be willing to sacrifice their lives for the state. "A soldier must not die in a house."[49]

Though the jurists consider the protection of the state by war as "righteous killing," ordinarily, such warfare was governed by codes of chivalry. Laws for conduct proper to war are described by Āpastamba,[50] Gautama,[51] and Baudhāyana.[52] Manu sums up these duties for honourable warriors:

> When he fights with his foes in battle, let him not strike with weapons concealed (in wood), nor with (such as are) barbed, poisoned, or the points of which are blazing with fire.
>
> Let him not strike one who (in flight) has climbed on an eminence, nor a eunuch, nor one who joins the palms of his hands (in supplication), nor one who (flees) with flying hair, nor one who sits down, nor one who says 'I am thine'.
>
> Nor one who sleeps, nor one who has lost his coat of mail, nor one who is naked, nor one who is disarmed, nor one who looks on without taking part in the fight, nor one who is fighting with another (foe);
>
> Nor one whose weapons are broken, nor one afflicted (with sorrow), nor one who has been grievously wounded, nor one who is in fear, nor one who has turned to flight; (but in all these cases let him) remember the duty (of honourable warriors).[53]

The ethics of war were particularly framed to protect the dignity of royalty, a fact that should remind us that the ethics we are dealing with is the ethics of royalty. The Institutes of Viṣṇu declare:

> A king having conquered the capital of his foe, should invest there a prince of the royal race of that country with the royal dignity.
>
> Let him not extirpate the royal race; unless the royal race be of ignoble descent.[54]

While codes of chivalry were generally adhered to in usual circumstances, "in case of need," duties of morality yielded to demands of necessity in which the only thing considered sacred was the preservation of the state. Thus the ethics of political theory was completely situational.

Next, we examine the *dharma* of the Vaiśyas. By the time of the Sūtras, the Vaiśya caste was shorn of some of its earlier nobility. Distinctions between Vaiśyas and Śūdras were becoming progressively diffuse. The chief cause for this ignominious descent was not even remotely connected with moral considerations but with externalities of professionalism. The Brahmins had developed a postive antipathy toward some Vaiśya occupations such as trade, agriculture, and cattle breeding. So despised were these professions that under no circumstance could a Brahmin personally engage in them. Baudhāyana states the penalty for any infraction of the law:

> Let him treat Brāmaṇas who tend cattle, those who live by trade, (and) those who are artisans, actors (and bards), servants or usurers, like Śūdras.[55]

Evidence of the Vaiśya's humiliation was apparent in several discriminatory ways.[56] For instance, a Vaiśya guest was to be treated on par with a Śūdra in respect to all items of hospitality.[57]

Though the Vaiśya was reduced to a despicable object because of the menial nature of his profession and because of his occupational and marital contacts with the Śūdra caste, nevertheless, by virtue of being an Āryan, he still retained certain religious and status privileges.

On the other hand, Śūdras who had assimilated the habits and manners of their masters while serving as domestics, were granted certain religious, civic, and professional rights and privileges, as we shall see.

The Āryanised Śūdra was treated as possessing a moral character and was expected to behave in accordance with "truthfulness, meekness, and purity."[58] He was not considered permanently defiled, but could cleanse himself through such purificatory ceremonies as "sipping water," and the washing of the "hands and feet."[59] He could also take part in minor religious ceremonies, such as offering the *Pākayajñas.*[60] Professionally the Śūdra was encouraged to "serve the higher castes"[61] as a way of gaining merit, but he could also "live by (practising) mechanical arts."[62] The Śūdra serving an Āryan had the right to full support, even when disabled.[63] Materially, some of these Āryanised Śūdras were well off, possessing hoards of wealth.[64]

Despite these and other allowances made to certain select Śūdras, the majority was still a despised lot, especially the ones who were nonacculturated. Another passage from Gautama starkly brings out the arbitrary and unjust way in which the activities of this caste were rigidly defined.

> A Śūdra who intentionally reviles twice-born men by criminal abuse, or criminally assaults them with blows, shall be deprived of the limb with which he offends.
>
> If he has criminal intercourse with an Āryan woman, his organ shall be cut off, and all his property be confiscated.
>
> If (the woman had) a protector, he shall be executed after (having undergone the punishments prescribed above).

> Now if he listens intentionally to (a recitation of) the Veda, his ears shall be filled with (molten) tin or lac.
> If he recites (Vedic texts), his tongue shall be cut out.
> If he remembers them, his body shall be split in twain.
> If he assumes a position equal (to that of the twice-born men) sitting, in lying down, in conversation or on the road, he shall undergo (corporal) punishment.[65]

When all of the castes within the hierarchical system follow their own appointed *dharma* in the manner prescribed, harmonious results ensue, both in this life and the next.[66] Harmony is the proof of the divine origin and character of the social structure. This explains the severity with which violations of *dharma* were handled. The scriptures warn of the dire repercussions attendant upon a failure to preserve the system. The Bhagavadgītā, through its own "domino theory" of social degeneration, describes the consequences of caste violations.

> In the ruin of a family, its immemorial laws perish; and when the laws perish, the whole family is overcome by lawlessness.
> And when lawlessness prevails, O Krishna the women of the family are corrupted, O Vārshneya, a mixture of caste arises.
> And this confusion brings the family itself to hell and those who have destroyed it; for their ancestors fall, deprived of their offerings of rice and water.
> By the sins of those who destroy a family and create a mixture of caste, the eternal laws of the caste and the family are destroyed.
> The men of the families whose laws are destroyed, O Janārdana, assuredly will dwell in hell; so we have heard.[67]

The moral principle regulating rebirth in accordance with the *varṇa* system is the law of *karman.* A good life merits birth in a high caste; but the deserts of an evil life are rebirth in a low caste. Thus, one's present caste is determined by the past, and has a moral basis. A man should, therefore, make atonement for past misdeeds by adhering to the *dharma* of his own *varṇa,* and by practising a life of virtue. In this way he acquires great glory and ascends to a higher birth in the next life.

This moral explanation of caste as the social consequent of an individual's past *karman* seems to answer the question about how the system was allowed to prevail without any serious protests against it on the part of the downtrodden. The despised Śūdra, ridden roughshod over by members of the higher castes, could not think of cursing his overlords; after all, both he and they were only reaping what they had sown. In such an ethos it was impossible for some Indian Karl Marx to raise the cry: "Śūdras of Hindustan arise, you have nothing to lose but your caste," and get a following—on moral grounds!

The second major aspect of *dharma,* having examined the ethics of *Varṇadharma,* is the scheme of *Āśramadharma.* In the earlier period the stages of life were less definite than is the case in the lawbooks. Now, for Manu and the other lawmakers, the *āśramas* are clearly four in number. These writers devote a great part of their material to a treatment of the *dharma* belonging to each stage, especially the second one.

The *Brahmacarya* stage is entered upon through the *upanayana saṁskāra.* This initiation ceremony takes place for a Brahmin at age eight; for a Kṣatriya at age eleven; and for a Vaiśya at age twelve.[68] Before the ceremony, the boy is a virtual Śūdra; after the ceremony he is a *dvija* or twice-born. He is now born into the world of the Ārya, and all its privileges and responsibilities will be taught to him during his years of Vedic studentship.

The Āśvalāyana Gṛhya Sūtra gives detailed descriptions of the elaborate rites of initiation, the intention of which was to create a sense of dignity, duty, and responsibility within the student.[69] The rituals were not important as ends in themselves, but were means for generating ethical values. Regrettably, some of the earlier *dharma* writers, such as Āpastamba, attribute magical properties to the *upanayana* ceremony which detracts from its moral aspects.[70] Yājñavalkya is silent about these superstitions, such as the promise of longevity, manly vigour, and so on, which suggests that they were not believed in during his time.

The type of teacher-student relationship envisioned by the educational system is dramatised in one part of the *upanayana* ceremony. The Āśvalāyana Gṛhya Sūtra stipulates:

> On the region of the student's heart the teacher should place his hand with the fingers stretched upwards and say: 'Into my vow I put thy heart; after my mind may thy mind follow; with single-aimed vow do thou rejoice in my speech; may God Brihaspati join thee to me.[71]

The joining of student to *guru* involved the student living in the residence of the teacher. The importance of this step for mental and moral development of the student was profound. It provided him with an optimum environment for personal growth under the tutelage of a man who by training and character was best qualified for the nurture of his emotional and intellectual capacities. The epics cite several teachers remembered both for their erudition and quality of life; men like Viśvāmitra, Vasiṣṭha, Sāndīpani, and Droṇācārya, only to mention a few.

Because the guru was responsible for bringing to birth the mental and spiritual potential of the pupil, he was honoured as the pupil's father. Āpastamba says:

> He from whom (the pupil) gathers *(ākinoti)* (the knowledge of) his religious duties *(dharmān)* (is called) the Ācārya (teacher). Him he should never offend.
>
> For he causes him (the pupil) to be born (a second time) by (imparting to him) sacred learning. The (second) birth is the best. The father and mother produce the body only.[72]

Honour to the teacher was shown in several concrete ways.[73] The relationship was to be reciprocal:

> Loving him like his own son, and full of attention, he shall teach him the sacred science, without hiding anything in the whole law. And he shall not use him for his own purposes to the detriment of his studies, except in times of distress.
>
> The pupil who, attending to two (teachers), accuses his (principal and first) teacher of ignorance, remains no (longer) a pupil.
>
> A teacher also, who neglects the instruction (of his pupil), does no (longer) remain a teacher.[74]

The purport of education was the moral and intellectual growth of the students. These two elements were never separated. Indeed, the latter was contingent upon the former. According to the Sacred Law, only the person who is pure may be instructed in the Veda.

> Neither (the study of) the Vedas, nor liberality, nor sacrificies, nor any (self-imposed) restraint, nor austerities, ever procure the attainment (of rewards) to a man whose heart is contaminated (by sensuality).[75]

Moral culture not only preceded intellectual culture, but was the weightier of the two:

> A Brāhmaṇa who completely governs himself, though he knows the Sāvitrī only, is better than he who knows the three Vedas, (but) does not control himself.[76]

The secret of self-control was not so much a matter of restraint and repression as "a constant (pursuit of true) knowledge."[77] In pursuance of virtue the student of *dharma* was expected to be "grateful, non-hating, intelligent, pure, healthy, non-envious, honest, energetic."[78] Sexual purity was highest in the list of virtues. A *Brahmacārin* was forbidden "to gaze at and to touch women, if there is danger of breach of chastity."[79] He may "talk to women only for what is absolutely necessary." Should a breach of sexual morality occur, the student must sacrifice an ass at a crossroad to the goddess Nirṛti; don the skin of a donkey; and for a period of one year, proclaim his asinine deed.

The presence of virtuous fruit in the student's life indicated that true knowledge had taken root. Says the Mahābhārata: "Knowledge of the śāstras is said to bear fruit when it produces modesty and virtuous conduct."[80]

Thus, the cultivation of the moral life through simplicity, austerity, chastity, and obedience, leads to the pure, undistracted development of the intellect. Manu limits the intellectual curriculum to a study of the three Vedas,[81] but, by the time of Yājñavalkya, the *Brahmacārin's* studies were expanded to include the Purāṇas, Nārāśaṃsīs, the Gāthikās, the Itihāsas, and the Vidyās.[82] The Vidyās included professional training in such subjects as medicine, astrology, military arts, music, and so forth. All of these branches of knowledge were integrated with the sacred knowledge of the Vedas, thus linking expertise with ethics, and the acquisition of information with the development of character.

Two negative effects of *Brahmacarya* discipline need to be mentioned in passing. First, since the transition from one stage of life to the other was to be smooth and natural, it was inevitable that the ascetical outlook moulded in the student stage should be carried over into that of the householder stage. Some students continued the life of celibacy by becoming *Sannyāsins* directly, which gives some indication of the impact of the ascetical training to which they were rigorously subjected.

The second negative effect of student life was the inculcation of what N. K. Dutt describes as the "pride of scholasticism" among the professed scholars.[83] Compounded with racial and sacerdotal pride, the pride of scholasticism elevated barriers between Brahmins and non-Brahmins. In this way "the good effect of the strictness of *Brahmacarya* in specialising learning and in enforcing high moral discipline was neutralised by the increased rigidness and hauteur of caste, which is one of the many factors making India a land of contrasts."[84]

The second *āśrama* is that of the householder. The *Gārhasthya* stage of life was considered of supreme importance for several reasons. First, as Gautama points out, the *Gārhasthyāśrama* is the source of the other *āśramas* "because the others do not produce offspring."[85] Second, Yājñavalkya correctly observes that this was the only stage in which all of the *puruṣārthas* were jointly realised.[86] Third, it is the opinion of all the writers that the family was basic to the caste system. It provided the regulatory machinery for the strict enforcement of caste, informing its members of their duties, and imbuing them with the caste spirit. These are some of the reasons why the householder stage was given a central place and why the ethical codes governing it were invested unequivocally with divine authority.

The rules of *dharma* regulating the *Gārhasthyāśrama* are voluminous in scope, intricate in detail, and often variant in prescription.

We start with the list of ethical duties prescribed for the householder by Yājñavalkya. It consists mainly of ritual, procreational, and conjugal functions of the family.

> A householder should perform every day a Smṛiti rite [that is, a domestic rite prescribed by the Sacred Law, Smṛiti] on the nuptial fire or on the fire brought in at the time of the partition of ancestral property. He should perform a Vedic rite on the sacred fires.
>
> Having attended to the bodily calls, having performed the purificatory rites, and after having first washed the teeth, a twice-born (Aryan) man should offer the morning prayer.
>
> Having offered oblations to the sacred fires, becoming spiritually composed, he should murmur the sacred verses addressed to the sun god. He should also learn the meaning of the Veda and various sciences. . . .
>
> He should then go to his lord for securing the means of maintenance and progress. Thereafter having bathed he should worship the gods and also offer libations of water to the manes.
>
> He should study according to his capacity the three Vedas, the Atharva Veda, the Purānas, together with the Itihāsas (legendary histories), as also the law relating to the knowledge of the Self, with a view to accomplishing successfully the sacrifice of muttering prayers [*japa-yajña*].
>
> Offering of the food oblation [*bali*], offering with the proper utterance [*svadhā*], performance of Vedic sacrifices, study of the sacred texts, and honouring of guests—these constitute the five great daily sacrifices dedicated respectively to the spirits, the manes, the gods, the Brahman and men.
>
> He should offer the food oblations to the spirits [by throwing it in the air] out of the remnant of the food offered to the gods. He should also cast food on the ground for dogs, untouchables, and crows.
>
> Food, as also water, should be offered by the householder to the manes and men day after day. He should continuously carry on his study. He should never cook for himself only.
>
> Children, married daughters living in the father's house, pregnant women, sick persons, girls, as also guests and servants—only after having fed these should the householder and his wife eat the food that has remained. . . .
>
> Having risen before dawn the householder should ponder over what is good for the Self. He should not, as far as possible, neglect his duties in respect of the three ends of man, namely, virtue, material gain, and pleasure, at their proper times.
>
> Learning, religious performances, age, family relations and wealth—on account of these and in the order mentioned are men honoured in society. By means of these, if possessed in profusion, even a shūdra deserves respect in old age.[87]

This passage is self-explanatory, but a few comments are in order. Mention of the *five* daily sacrifices points to a broadening of ethical awareness as compared with the earlier notion of the three debts to the ancestors, gods, and sages.

The concept of daily sacrifices also shows the sense of obligation and interdependence the *gṛhastha* felt toward his total environment—seen and unseen, animate and inanimate. This awareness motivated him to engage in ethical actions out of feelings of gratitude and belonging.

Gratitude easily spilled over into liberality—"the *gṛhastha* should never cook for himself!"

What is cooked for himself must first be shared with guests and members of the household, including servants who were *Śūdras.* It was an iron law of the householder: service before self.

To ensure that the householder had time to "ponder over what is good for the Self," he had to rise before dawn! The good is defined in terms of three cardinal values: *dharma, artha,* and *kāma.* By including *kāma,* Yājñavalkya emphasised a value dimension of personality that is not given equal recognition by other writers. For instance, Manu[88] and the Mahābhārata[89] sometimes overlook *kāma,* emphasising only the acquisition of *dharma* and *artha.*

The concluding verse classifies the things for which the householder was honoured by society. Learning (knowledge having both intellectual and ethical aspects) stands first. Then follow: religious performance, age, family relations, and last of all, wealth. Money was not devalued, but dharmic concerns always held it in a state of relativity to spiritual values. Even a poor Śūdra possessing spiritual and moral qualities was to be treated with the highest honour.

Special attention should be given to Yājñavalkya's description of the duties of the householder to his wife. He must be solely devoted to her, having become one through sacramental bonds; he must satisfy her sensuous yearnings, only refraining from sexual intercourse on inauspicious days. Care of the wife is essential because through her the householder begets sons whereby the family is continued, both in time and in eternity.[90]

This brings us to our second ethical concern: attitude toward women. This subject is a tangled web, laced with many contradictions and inconsistencies. Sometimes woman is worshipped as a goddess; at other times she is shunned as a temptress. She is praised as the personification of virtue, and is branded as the incarnation of vice. Though honoured as a queen, she is a prisoner in her own castle.

In several instances these contradictory judgments are real. But when the literature is taken as a whole, most of the contradictions can be explained. The clue to resolving the discrepancies lies in the threefold recognition that the literature is not monolithic in thought; that points of view changed with the passage of time; and that women were at the same time judged from different perspectives.

Regarding the first proviso, it is clear that there is a whole spectrum of opinion ranging from the conservative views of Āpastamba to the more liberal views of Yājñavalkya. Therefore, instead of pitting contradictory judgments against each other, it is more accurate to identify these opinions by their authors. Similarly, the disparities must be assessed historically, for images of women changed with time and place. These two points of literary and historical criticism are straightforward. The third point requires substantial explanation.

Women were simultaneously judged from different perspectives; hence, differences of judgment. From the point of view of female nature, women were regarded morally inferior to men. Some early Dharma Sūtra writers equate women with Śūdras in terms of their capacity for moral achievement. That explains why the penalty for killing a Brahmin woman was no more than that for killing a Śūdra.[91] Similar views are recorded in the Dharma Śāstras. For instance, according to Manu, women are naturally wicked:

> (When creating them) Manu allotted to women (a love of their) bed, (of their) seat and (of) ornament, impure desires, wrath, dishonesty, malice and bad conduct.
>
> For women no (sacramental) rite (is performed) with sacred texts, thus the law is settled; women (who are) destitute of strength and destitute of (the knowledge of) Vedic texts, (are as impure as) falsehood (itself), that is a fixed rule.[92]

The Mahābhārata also considers women to be of weak and undesirable character. "Bed, seat, ornament, food, drink, meanness, harshness of speech and love—these Prajāpati gave to women."[93] In another passage, Bhīṣma, enlightening Yudhiṣṭhira about female nature, says that women are seducers, lacking strength to resist temptations.[94]

Such depreciative assessments of female nature provided the moral justification for depriving women of social freedom, and keeping them totally dependent upon the strong male. Vasiṣṭha[95] and Baudhāyana[96] concur with Manu:

> Her father protects (her) in childhood, her husband protects (her) in youth, and her sons protect (her) in old age; a woman is never fit for independence.[97]

This curtailment of female freedom was probably reinforced by the fear of the Āryans for the purity of their race and culture against the intrusions of the surrounding black population eager to mingle with their womenfolk.

For a totally opposite view of female nature to the one just outlined, we turn to Yājñavalkya. In praise of women, this jurist says: "Soma gave them purification; the Gandharva, sweet speech, Agni, perfect purity; therefore verily women are always pure."[98] The same high opinion of the fair sex can be culled from Vātsyāyana's Kāma Sūtra.

However, though Yājñavalkya and Vātsyāyana are positive in their assessment of female character, they share the consensus of the other jurists that women must always be guarded by men. From this it follows that the primary virtue of women is obedience to the male sex. Only by obeying the lordly male could women ascend to the joys of heaven.

Thus, aside from the minority opinion represented by Yājñavalkya and Vātsyāyana, the Dharma Sūtras, the Dharma Śāstras, and the Mahābhārata adopt an uncomplimentary view of female nature. This not only deprived women of freedom, as we have seen, but also of their responsibility. Since it was assumed that women were inherently of weak character, guilt could not be justifiably imputed to them.[99] Thus, "by committing an act of adultery, only the man becomes sullied with sin." This sounds morally fair for guilt is relative to responsibility, but it is also dehumanising, reducing women to a species that is below the capacity for answerability.

Turning from the cynical attitudes toward women, we come to another set of attitudes based on the biological and maternal aspects of womanhood. Here, there is an unmistakable attribution of honour, respect, and dignity to women. A profusion of adulations provide us with an accurate picture of the status of women in the family as wives and as mothers.

The dirge of Manu dies as he suddenly changes his tune and begins to sing in praise of women. Woman is no more *woeman,* as the following sentiments attest:

> Women must be honoured and adorned by their fathers, brothers, husbands, and brothers-in-law, who desire (their own) welfare.
>
> Where women are honoured, there the gods are pleased; but where they are not honoured, no sacred rite yields rewards.
>
> Where the female relations live in grief, the family soon wholly perishes; but that family where they are not unhappy ever prospers.
>
> The houses on which female relations, not being duly honoured, pronounce a curse, perish completely, as if destroyed by magic.
>
> Hence men who seek (their own) welfare, should always honour women on holidays and festivals with (gifts of) ornaments, clothes, and (dainty) food.
>
> In that family where the husband is pleased with his wife and the wife with the husband, happiness will assuredly be lasting.
>
> For if the wife is not radiant with beauty, she will not attract her husband; but if she has no attraction for him, no children will be born.

> If the wife is radiant with beauty, the whole house is bright; but if she is destitute of beauty, all will appear dismal.[100]

The Mahābhārata echoes the same chorus of compliments.[101] It is true, as N. K. Dutt observes, that "even in such passages women are honoured as potential mothers and obedient wives," but even so, a higher note is struck than the generally low tones of the Dharma Śāstras.[102]

In addition to her biological role, woman is accorded highest respect for her maternal role. It is quite possible that these sentiments were fostered by the sociological influence of the Dravidian matriarchal system upon the Āryan culture. Be that as it may, Āpastamba gives expression to this appreciation for motherhood thus:

> A mother does very many acts for her son, therefore he must constantly serve her, though she be fallen.[103]

Vishṇu is more positive than Āpastamba:

> A man has three *Atigurus* (or specially venerable superiors):
> His father, his mother, and his spiritual teacher.[104]

Gautama goes still further:

> The teacher is chief among all Gurus. Some (say) that the mother (holds that place).[105]

Vasiṣṭha sheds the tentativeness of Gautama and boldly quotes the opinion which elevates motherhood to the highest:

> The teacher (ācārya) is ten times more venerable than a sub-teacher (upādhyāya), the father a hundred times more than the teacher, and the mother a thousand times more than the father.[106]

This positive emphasis on womanhood helped nurture certain ideals. The story of Sītā in the Rāmāyaṇa is one illustration of this process of idealisation. Her husband, Rāma, had been exiled by his father, king Daśaratha, to the forest for fourteen years. Rāma breaks the news to Sītā and admonishes her respectfully to continue in the home and to keep her mind "steady and calm." When Sītā heard it all, her love turned a violent outcry at the suggestion that she should enjoy the luxuries of the palace while her beloved wanders homeless in a pathless jungle. She says to Rāma:

> A fine speech you have made, O Knower of *dharma*. It is to me a strange doctrine that a wife is diverse from her husband and that his duty is not hers, and that she has no right to share in it. I can never accept it. I hold that your fortunes are mine, and if Rama has to go to the forest, the command includes Seeta also, who is part of him. I shall walk in front of you in the forest ways and tread the thorns and the hard ground to make them smooth for

your feet. Do not think me obstinate. My father and mother have instructed me in *dharma.* What you tell me is totally opposed to what they have taught me. To go with you wherever you go—that is my only course. If you must go to the forest today, then today I go with you. There is no room here for any discussion. Do not think that I cannot bear forest life. With you by my side it will be a joyous holiday. I shall not be a source of trouble to you. I shall eat fruit and roots like you and I shall not lag behind as we walk.

I have long wished to go to the woods with you and to rejoice in the sight of great mountains and rivers.

I shall spend the time most happily among the birds and flowers, bathing in the rivers and doing the daily rites. Away from you I do not care for Heaven itself. I shall surely die if you leave me behind. I implore you to take me with you. Do not forsake me now.[107]

In addition to Sītā, other ideal women who still exercise an inspiring influence upon the Hindu mind are: Ahalyā, Draupadī, Tārā, and Mandōdarī. The recollection of such personalities is said to cleanse the soul of its great sins *(mahāpātaka).*

In describing the ethical aspects of the *Gārhasthyāśrama,* it remains for us to say something about marriage. This subject is important because, as a primary social institution, it is charged with governing sex relations, and fixing the ties of a child to his society.

First, regarding standards for the spouse, the Āśvalāyana Gṛhya Sūtra prescribes:

One should first examine the family (of the intended bride or bridegroom), those on the mother's side and on the father's side. . . . One should give his daughter in marriage to a young man endowed with intelligence, beauty, and good character, and who is free from disease. . . .[108]

Next, regarding the forms of marriages, there are eight different types. Following Manu, these eight forms are:

The gift of a daughter, after decking her (with costly garments) and honouring (her by presents of jewels), to a man learned in the Veda and of good conduct, whom (the father) himself invites, is called a Brhāma rite.

The gift of a daughter who has been decked with ornaments, to a priest who duly officiates at the sacrifice, during the course of its performance, they call the Daiva rite.

When (the father) gives away his daughter according to the rule, after receiving from the bridegroom, (the fulfilment of) the sacred law, a cow and a bull or two pairs, that is named the Ārsha rite.

The gift of a daughter (by her father) after he has addressed (the couple) with the text, 'May both of you perform together your duties,' and has shown honour (to the bridegroom), is called in the Smriti the Prajāpatya rite.

When (the bridegroom) receives a maiden, after having given as much

> wealth as he can afford, to the kinsmen and to the bride herself, according to his own will, that is called the Āsura rite.
>
> The voluntary union of a maiden and her lover one must know (to be) the Gāndharva rite, which springs from desire and has sexual intercourse for its purpose.
>
> The forcible abduction of a maiden from her home, while she cries out and weeps, after (her kinsmen) have been slain or wounded and (their houses) broken open, is called the Rākshasa rite.
>
> When (a man) by stealth seduces a girl who is sleeping, intoxicated, or disordered in intellect, that is the eighth, the most base and sinful rite of the Paiśācas.[109]

With the exception of Āpastamba who lists six forms of marriage,[110] all of the other writers, such as Gautama, Baudhāyana, Yājñavalkya, and Kauṭilya, have lists similar to that of Manu with only slight variations. The first four categories of marriage are morally approved; the remaining are generally disapproved on the grounds that they are based on physical force, and do not have the consent of the father or guardian.

An important rule of marriage was that the girl should not be an agnate.[111] Monogamy was the marital norm, though polygamy was permitted, especially if the wife were barren. Rules of divorce varied among the Arthaśāstra and Dharmaśāstra writers. The latter were against divorce on the grounds that marriage was a sacrament and therefore inviolable; the former accepted divorce, regarding marriage as a contract. At any rate, both schools of thought continue to uphold the Vedic ideal of marriage as the means by which the householder is enabled to realize the *puruṣārthas,* to offer sacrifice to the gods, and to beget many sons.

We come now to the *Vānaprasthyāśrama.* The law reads:

> When a householder sees his (skin) wrinkled, and (his hair) white, and the sons of his sons, then he may resort to the forest.
>
> Abandoning all food raised by cultivation, and all his belongings, he may depart into the forest, either, committing his wife to his sons, or accompanied by her.
>
> Taking with him the sacred fire and the implements required for domestic (sacrifices), he may go forth from the village into the forest and reside there, duly controlling his senses.
>
> Let him offer those five great sacrifices according to the rule, with various kinds of pure food fit for ascetics, or with herbs, roots, and fruit.
>
> Let him wear a skin or a tattered garment; let him bathe in the evening or in the morning; and let him always wear (his hair in) braids, the hair on his body, his beard, and his nails (being unclipped).
>
> Let him perform the Bali-offering with such food as he eats, and give alms according to his ability; let him honour those who come to his hermitage with alms consisting of water, roots, and fruit.

> Let him always be industrious in privately reciting the Veda; let him be patient of hardships, friendly (toward all), of collected mind, ever liberal and never a receiver of gifts, and compassionate towards all living creatures.[112]

On the basis of the preceding description of the *Vānaprasthya āśrama,* certain points of ethical interest stand out.

First, the ideal of life at this stage is *mokṣa,* and, therefore, it is in the light of this spiritual value that the ascetical discipline should be understood and evaluated. The same is true of the following stage of *Saṁnyāsa.* Asceticism was not an end in itself, but only a means toward achieving self-control and spiritual power—the prerequisites of *mokṣa.* In ascetic practice, the body is not treated as an enemy of the spirit; and hence, there is no correlation between asceticism and mortification of the flesh.

Second, the life of a hermit was not one of ethereal passivity but ethical activity—"let him be always industrious." Like the householder, he continued to offer the five great sacrifices. But whereas the activity of the householder was prompted by *artha* and *kāma,* the activity of the hermit was devoid of any motives of personal gain and pleasure. Inspired by the Vedas, he fulfilled his *dharma* by exercising friendship, liberality, wisdom, and compassion "toward all living creatures."

Though he lived "without a fire, without a house," the silent sage patiently endured all manner of hardships, and thus gained power through austerity.

The fourth and final stage is that of the *Sannyāsin.* The law reads:

> Having thus passed the third part of (a man's natural term of) life in the forest, he may live as an ascetic during the fourth part of his existence, after abandoning all attachment to wordly objects.[113]

The goal is final liberation, and to attain it he must "always wander alone, without a companion." He should be "indifferent to everything, firm of purpose, meditating (and) concentrating his mind on Brahman." He should be free of all desire, whether to live or to die, and must wait for his appointed time "as a servant (waits) for the payment of his wages."

Though he is beyond ethical striving, his conduct is ethical, in keeping with his goal of *mokṣa.*

> Let him put down his foot purified by his sight, let him drink water purified by (straining with) a cloth, let him utter speech purified by truth, let him keep his heart pure.
>
> Let him patiently bear hard words, let him not insult anybody, and let him not become anybody's enemy for the sake of this (perishable) body.

> Against an angry man let him not in return show anger, let him bless when he is cursed, and let him not utter speech, devoid of truth, scattered at the seven gates.[114]

Thus, by restraining his senses, by destroying love and hatred, and by abstaining from injury to all creatures, the *sannyāsin* becomes fitted for immortality. As the text states it:

> A twice-born man who becomes an ascetic after the successive performance of the above-mentioned acts, shakes off sin here below and reaches the highest Brahman.[115]

Questions might be raised about the ethical and social significance of the *Saṁnyāsa* stage. In the earlier stage, through a life of duty and discipline he contributed his share to the welfare of the community, but the *Sannyāsin's* life is completely individual and fiercely spiritual. Alone, he strives to unite with the Alone.

The answer to these questions is that while the *Sannyāsin's* quest is indeed highly individual, it does have a social impact. Without knowing it, he continues to uplift the group to a degree which was not possible heretofore. In terms of wealth, time, and services the *Sannyāsin's* contribution is nil, but to those who are struggling toward purity and self-knowledge, his life serves as "an example of fulfilment and a promise of the future of all."[116]

Our study of the specific duties in the *Varṅāśrama* scheme brings us now to a consideration of common duties under the rubric of *Sādhāraṇa dharma.* In addition to the moral rules pertaining to the four castes and four orders, the law-books include ethical standards for all men, regardless of caste and order. Āpastamba enumerates the "faults" and "good qualities" which either destroy or save mankind. These are:

> Anger, exultation, grumbling, covetousness, perplexity, doing injury (to anybody), hypocrisy, lying, gluttony, calumny, envy, lust, secret hatred, neglect to keep the senses in subjection, neglect to concentrate the mind. The eradication of these (faults) takes place through the means of (salvation called) Yoga.
>
> Freedom from anger, from exultation, grumbling, from covetousness, from hyprocrisy (and) hurtfulness; truthfulness, moderation in eating, silencing slander, freedom from envy, self-denying liberality, avoiding to accept gifts, uprightness, affability, extinction of the passions, subjection of the senses, peace with all created beings, concentration (of the mind on the contemplation of the Ātman), regulation of one's conduct according to that of the Āryas, peacefulness and contentedness;—these (good qualities) have been settled by the agreement (of the wise) for all (the four) orders; he who, according to the precepts of the sacred law, practises these, enters the universal soul.[117]

Similar standards are enunciated by Gautama,[118] Vasiṣṭha,[119] Manu,[120] and Yājñavalkya.[121]

These virtues constituting the moral preparation necessary for entrance into the "universal soul" help place in perspective the relative value of ceremonialism and legal rectitude *vis à vis* ethical excellence.

Like the Brāhmaṇas, the Kalpa Sūtras are replete with commands for the performance of sacrificial rites. In addition, there are the myriads of traditional duties supposedly based on the Vedas. A perusal of these rites and duties is apt to convey the impression that the morality of this literature is exclusively authoritarian, external, ceremonial, and formal: and that ethical and moral values receive short shrift.[122] Such conclusions fail to take into consideration the fundamental place given to ethical excellence, over against the purely ceremonial and formal observance of the law.

Āpastamba's list of common virtues should make it quite explicit that the lawbooks not only talk about overt acts of ceremonial behaviour, but of virtues of the spirit, as well. They probe beyond the deed and the word to the underlying thought. As a matter of fact, all three components of a moral situation—thought, word, and deed—are integrally connected so that only he who is ethically pure can enter the path of karman and be qualified to perform the sacred rites and duties. Vasiṣṭha says:

> Neither austerities, nor (the study of) the Veda, nor (the performance of) the Agnihotra, nor lavish liberality can ever save him whose conduct is vile and who has strayed from this (path of duty).
>
> The Vedas do not purify him who is deficient in good conduct, though he may have learnt them altogether with the six Angas; the sacred texts depart from such a man at death, even as birds, when full-fledged, leave their nest.
>
> As the beauty of a wife causes no joy to a blind man, even so all the four Vedas together with the six Angas and sacrifices give no happiness to him who is deficient in good conduct.[123]

With similar emphasis on the spirit, after describing the forty sacred ritual observances which a good man should practise, Gautama proceeds to explain the "eight good qualities of the soul." They are: "compassion on all creatures, forbearance, freedom from anger, purity, quietism, auspiciousness, freedom from avarice, and freedom from covetousness."[124] The jurist then warns:

> He who is sanctified by these forty sacraments, but whose soul is destitute of the eight excellent qualities, will not be united with Brahman, nor does he reach his heaven.
>
> But he, forsooth, who is sanctified by a few only with the eight excellent qualities, will be united with Brahman, and will dwell in his heaven.[125]

The significance of this passage lies in its double-barreled fire both upon the ritualists and the mystics. "It proclaims very definitely that salvation is a matter of spiritual excellence as exhibited by the ethical, not by ritualistic, observances, and it eliminates the mystic intuition of God in favour of compassion, contentment, purity, and a generous, earnest disposition."[126]

The motivation behind all of these codes of conduct and prescriptions of virtues is eschatological—to be "united with Brahman" and to "dwell in his heaven." One's future state was morally continuous with one's present state; as Baudhāyana says: to deserve heaven, one must avoid meanness, hardheartedness and crookedness." Eschatology thus becomes the determinant for ethics. Since the soul survives death, it would be shortsighted to settle for ethical standards that take only this life into view. Hence the admonition of Vasiṣṭha: "Practice righteousness, not unrighteousness; seek truth, not untruth; look far, not near; look toward the Highest, not toward that which is not the Highest."[127] Vasiṣṭha is not advocating the elimination of desire, because heaven is as much an object of desire as is earth. His ethical stance may, therefore, be described as "self-seeking beyond the grave."[128] The things of the earth must not be sought as ends in themselves; but this calls not for renunciation—only restraint.

II. Ethical Thought in the Bhagavadgītā

The teaching of the Bhagavadgītā has for its starting point the misery of mundane existence.[129] The soul is viewed as trapped in the cycle of rebirths because impeded empirical consciousness deludes it into imagining that it is dependent on the body and that it undergoes all the sufferings of finite existence. Essentially, the soul is quite independent of the body; but as long as it is ignorant of its true nature, it remains a prisoner in "this perishable, unhappy world."[130]

In the light of the human predicament, 'good' and 'evil' are defined in relation to the soul's release from or resignation to the weary round of rebirths. Release leads to the attainment of *Nirvāṇa,* poetically described in these words of Kṛṣṇa:

> When the embodied soul transcends these three *guṇas,* whose origin is in the body, it is freed from birth, death, old age and pain, and attains immortality.[131]

The *summum bonum* is approached from metaphysical and theological points of view. Metaphysically, it is the identity of the *ātman* with *Brahman.* "He who is happy within, whose joy is within and whose light is within; that yogin becomes Brahman and attains to the bliss of

Brahman."[132] Theologically, the goal of life is union with Īśvara: "He who is disciplined by the yoga of practice and meditates on the supreme Person, his mind not straining after some other object, he reaches, O Pārtha, that supreme divine Spirit."[133]

Neither identity with Brahman nor union with Īśvara is possible without the aid of practical morality. Morality provides the "foundation on which the superstructure of the holy life culminating in Nirvāṇa is built."[134]

What is the nature of the Gītā's ethics? We find a clue as its drama begins to unfold. The opening scene pictures Arjuna standing in his chariot between the armies of the Kauravas and Pāṇḍavas. Seeing all his kinsmen standing arrayed, Arjuna is overcome with grief and utters these words of distress to his charioteer:

> My limbs collapse, my mouth dries up, there is trembling in my body and my hair stands on end;
>
> (The bow) Gāndīva slips from my hand and my skin also is burning; I am not able to stand still, my mind is whirling.
>
> And I see evil portents, O Keshava (Krishna), and I foresee not good in slaying my own kinsmen in the fight.
>
> I do not desire victory, O Krishna, nor kingdom, nor pleasure. Of what use is kingdom to us, O Govinda (Krishna), of what use pleasure or life?
>
> Those for whose sake we desire kingdom, pleasures and happiness, they are arrayed here in battle, having renounced their lives and riches.
>
> Teachers, fathers, sons, and also grandfathers; uncles, fathers-in-law, grandsons, brothers-in-law and (other) kinsmen:
>
> These I do not wish to kill, though they kill me, O Madhusūdana (Krishna); even for the kingdom of the three worlds; how (much less) then for the sake of the earth![135]

Arjuna's depression is a form of self-indulgent pity which prevents him from doing his duty because it will harm his kith and kin. Such sentimentality incurs the rebuke of Kṛṣṇa who exhorts him to act bravely. The charioteer asks:

> Whence hath this despair come to thee in this (time of) crisis? It is unbecoming to an *āryan,* it does not lead to heaven, it is disgraceful, O Arjuna.
>
> Yield not to this impotence, O Pārtha (Arjuna), for it is not proper of thee. Abandon this petty weakness of heart and arise, O oppressor of the foe.[136]

These words of Kṛṣṇa are a clarion call to action, and therein lies the main thrust of the Gītā's ethical teachings. Through several (and sometimes contradictory) arguments, it attempts to show the kind of action that must be undertaken in the world.

The Gītā's formula for ethical activism is a synthesis of two conflicting modes of discipline, both of which were considered orthodox paths to salvation.

The first form of discipline was known as *pravṛtti* or 'active life'. Those who embraced this ideal engaged in Vedic rituals and all of the duties prescribed in the Kalpa Sūtras. The motive for their actions was reward in heaven. The object of desire did not mitigate the basic selfishness of these religious rites. Their selfishness lay in being devoted to the fruit of action, and it made little moral difference as to where the fruit were reaped—on earth or in heaven.

The second form of discipline was known as *nivṛtti* or 'quietism'. Those who espoused this ideal abandoned all religious and social obligations, relying solely on *jñāna* or knowledge as the pathway to salvation. It was their reasoning that since all actions—good and bad—must have their consequence in reincarnations, the most direct way to escape the evil of rebirth was by minimizing all 'works', good ones included.

The Gītā counters the preceding argument that *karman* is evil and should be abandoned because it leads to rebirth by making a shrewd analysis of human behaviour. It does not stop with *karman,* but goes beyond *karman* to *kāma.* Behind the deed lies the desire. Aversions and attachments determine a man's behaviour, therefore, a man's real enemies are not actions but passions.[137] Actions are only the motor manifestations of the impulse to love or to hate.

The implications of this analysis are that the power to bind one to continued existence resides not in *karman* but in *kāma.* Accordingly, *karman* without *kāma* has no consequence for rebirth. Once desire is removed from the deed, the deed loses its fateful sting. He who knows this is wise. He can work and yet does nothing. As the Gītā expresses it:

> Having no desires, with his mind and self controlled, abandoning all possessions, performing actions with the body alone, he commits no sin.
>
> He who is content with what comes by chance, who has passed beyond the pairs (of opposites), who is free from jealousy and is indifferent to success and failure, even when he is acting he is not bound.[138]

The same applies to the performance of Vedic *yajña.* Devoid of any hope for reward, the performer of *yajña* works, but his actions have no future effect.

> The offering is Brahman, Brahman is the oblation; it is poured by Brahman in the (ritual) fire of Brahman. Brahman is to be attained by him who concentrates his actions upon Brahman.[139]

The foregoing analysis of action as the extension of desire, along with the inference that detached actions per se have no binding power, brings one to the conclusion that what is ethically required is not "renunciation *of* action" but "renunciation *in* action."[140]

The Gītā's expression for detached activism is *karmayoga. Karmayoga* treats the act as an end in itself and not as a means to another end. The classic formulation of *karmayoga* is contained in these words:

> In action only hast thou a right and never in its fruits. Let not thy motive be the fruits of action; nor let thy attachment be to inaction.[141]

Thus, in the principle of *karmayoga* the Gītā synthesises the positive elements of *pravṛtti* and *nivṛtti.* "While it does not abandon activity, it preserves the spirit of renunciation. It commends the strenuous life, and yet gives no room for the play of selfish impulses. Thus it discards neither ideal, but by combining them refines and ennobles both."[142]

Explained in this way, *karmayoga* sounds ethically desirable. It is said to impart inner poise, self-mastery, and to free one from passion and pride.[143] But granting *yoga* is desirable; is it possible?

Examine the Gītā's description of the *Sannyāsin.* "He who does the action that should be done without concern for its fruits, he is a *Sannyāsin,* he is a yogin, not he who does not light the sacred fires and performs no rites."[144] *Saṁnyāsa* or renunciation is described here as an inward attitude—not something connected with outward works. Psychologically, this detached attitude seems impossible. All voluntaristic activity presupposes decision, and there can be no decision without desire. Human behaviour, unlike the instinctive behaviour of animals, is always motivated; hence its moral character. How then are we to understand the Gītā's description of the *Sannyāsin* as one who performs his prescribed duty "without concern for its fruit"?

Upon closer examination it becomes clear that the detachment which the Gītā inculcates is only in respect to worldly aspirations, such as the desire of Arjuna for the recapture of his ancestral kingdom. Preoccupation with mundane interests prevents the mind from attending to the needs of the inner life and must, therefore, be eliminated. But while *karmayoga* enjoins the renunciation of all temporal ends, its concept of the self does provide motivation for seeking ends in consonance with its higher nature. When the self's destiny is conceived of as achieving oneness with *Brahman, yogins* are told to "perform actions only with the body, the mind, the intellect or the senses, without attachment, for self-purification."[145] The concluding words, "for self-purification," illustrate the sole purpose for which the Gītā legitimates motivated action. In serving society the *yogin* is perfectly disinterested, performing works "only with the body," and so on, but this detached action is not without motive. Its motive is cleansing of the heart whereby the goal of self-realization is achieved. In the case of those *yogins* whose hearts have already been cleansed, they are encouraged to work for the welfare of the world, and also to set ideals for others.[146]

Similarly, when the self's destiny is conceived within a theological framework, the devotee is told, "Whatever thou doest, whatever thou eatest, whatever thou offerest, whatever thou givest, whatever austerities thou performest, do that, O son of Kuntī, as an offering to Me."[147] The concluding words, again, illustrate the ultimate objective of all the service that is performed as God's work. The devotee disinterestedly performs divine service to place himself in the hands of God—eternally secure. Arjuna is assured, "know thou that My devotee never perishes."[148]

Up to this point we have explored the ethical meaning of *karmayoga* which teaches that a man must perform his duties as a member of society without any thought of personal gain. Our next task is to fix a more precise definition of duty.

Sometimes by duty is meant the performance of religious rites. Contrary to the view that "action should be given up as an evil," the Gītā affirms, "acts of sacrifice, gift and austerity ought not to be abandoned, rather they should be performed; for sacrifice, gift and austerity are purifiers of the wise."[149] Religious duties are, therefore, enjoined because of their purificatory effects.

At other times duty refers to the commandments of God without any specific mention of what they are definitely. For example, Arjuna is told: "They who constantly follow My doctrine, who are filled with faith and are uncomplaining, they too are freed from (the bondage of) actions. But those who carp at my teaching and do not follow it know these mindless ones, deluded in all knowledge, to be lost."[150]

The most common connotation of duty in the Gītā is that of social obligations. *Karmayoga* concretely understood is the disinterested performance of customary and traditional duties. Arjuna is commanded: "perform action as the ancients did long ago."[151] Just as men of old in quest of liberation carried out their customary work, so also must Arjuna rise to his duty as a Kṣatriya.

The fact that Arjuna was born a Kṣatriya meant that he was endowed with the full nature of a warrior. A person is born into a particular caste because God had considered his natural endowments appropriate for that caste. Kṛṣṇa explains:

> The actions of Brahmins, Kṣhatriyas and Vaishyas, and of Shūdras, O conqueror of the foe, are distinguished according to the *guṇas* that arise from their innate nature.
>
> Calmness, self-control, austerity, purity, patience, uprightness, wisdom, knowledge and religious belief are the actions of the Brahmin, born of his nature.

> Heroism, majesty, firmness, skill and not fleeing in battle, generosity and lordship, are the actions of the Kshatriya, born of his nature.
>
> Agriculture, cattle-tending and trade are the actions of a Vaishya, born of his nature; action whose character is service is likewise that of the Shūdra, born of his nature.[152]

By birth, and therefore it is assumed by nature also, Arjuna's own *dharma (svadharma)* dictated his taking up arms in the cause of righteousness. He is reminded, "having regard for thine own *dharma,* thou shouldst not tremble. There exists no greater good for a Kshatriya than a battle required by duty."[153] Good Kṣatriyas welcome such holy war as an "open door to heaven."[154] On the contrary, failure to combat evil is to "incur sin."

It is plain that the Gītā is committed to the maintenance of caste. In addition to the above religious and biological endorsements, caste is approved on sociological grounds. Arjuna says:

> In the ruin of a family, its immemorial laws perish; and when the laws perish, the whole family is overcome by lawlessness.
>
> And when lawlessness prevails, O Krishna, the women of the family are corrupted, and when women are corrupted, O Vārshneya, a mixture of caste arises.
>
> And this confusion brings the family itself to hell and those who have destroyed it; for their ancestors fall, deprived of their offerings of rice and water.[155]

Thus, on religious, biological and sociological grounds, the ideal of caste enshrined in immemorial customs and traditions is upheld by the Bhagavadgītā.

However, it is necessary to show that the Gītā does differ from the orthodox view of caste in two critical areas. First, as Professor K. N. Upadhyaya traces, under the influence of Jainism and Buddhism, the Gītā universalises its concept of salvation to make it accessible to all men, regardless of race, sex, or caste.[156] With open arms, Kṛṣṇa says:

> They who take refuge in Me, O Pārtha, even though they be born of sinful wombs, women, Vaishyās and even Shudrās, they also reach the highest goal.[157]

Second, because the Gītā lays so much store by the internal value of an act, it refuses to categorise meritorious actions according to hierarchical standards. To the contrary, irrespective of one's place in the caste structure, a man obtains perfection by being devoted to "his own proper action."[158]

The discussion of the caste duties of the Kṣatriya gives rise to a related problem: the ethics of war. Can war ever be compatible with morality? Harking back to the poem, we find Arjuna utterly bewildered about his duty. His problem is not one of metaphysics but ethics. He pleads, "tell me decisively which is better."[159] "As a man of action he asks for the law of action, for his dharma, for what he has to do in this difficulty."[160]

Arjuna's own conclusion is that killing one's own kinsmen, even for a righteous cause, is morally untenable, to say nothing of killing out of greed for a "kingdom on earth" or for the "sovereignty of the gods."[161] "It would be better for me if the sons of Dhritarāshṭra, with weapons in hand, should slay me, unresisting and unarmed, in the battle."[162]

Having spoken these words in agony and in love, "Arjuna cast away his bow and arrow and sank down on the seat of his chariot, his spirit overcome by grief."[163] The situation is clear: Arjuna has laid down his bow, not out of cowardice but conscientiousness. He is afraid not of dying but killing.

Kṛṣṇa sympathetically smiles over the moral quandary in which Arjuna finds himself and proceeds to explain the grounds on which war can be morally justified when waged against evildoers. Repeatedly the moral aspect of the problem is emphasised.[164]

Kṛṣṇa starts by telling Arjuna that his nonviolent protest indicates a lack of intelligence. "Thou grievest for those thou shouldst not grieve for, and yet thou speakest words that sound like wisdom. Wise men do not mourn for the dead or for the living."[165] The wise are not perplexed because they know that man is the combination of two distinct modes of being—body and self.

The body is mortal.[166] It is perpetually subject to change and is constantly rotating within the world of becoming. "Death is certain for one that has been born, and birth is certain for one that has died."[167] These unavoidable facts of our mortal nature should give one poise and a sense of proportion.

By contrast with the body, the Self is "never Born, nor does it die, nor having once been, will it again cease to be. It is unborn, eternal and everlasting."[168] Changes in the body do not affect the self.[169] "Just as a man casts off worn-out clothes and takes on others that are new, so the embodied soul casts off worn-out bodies and takes on others that are new."[170] Being immutable and indestructible, the self does not slay, nor is it slain.[171] "Weapons do not cut it, nor does fire burn it; waters do not make it wet, nor does wind make it dry."[172]

Insights into these facts concerning the body and the soul should deliver Arjuna from grieving over any creature.[173] Instead of sorrow, because the physical embodiment of the eternal soul must inevitably come to an end, Arjuna should take up his sword and join the battle!

These arguments legitimising warfare on the basis of metaphysical concepts of the body/soul relation raise some ethical issues. True, human existence is short, but does the brevity of life and the inevitability of death justify a premature end, albeit for a righteous cause?

Furthermore, physical embodiments in the world do have their bearing on the soul's destiny, hence, are they not to be treated significantly? Does not the Gītā itself admit the meaningfulness of worldly existence by emphasising activism; and does it not also accept the belief that several embodiments are necessary for the ascent of the soul before liberation? Is it then ethically permissible to destroy the body without greater regard for the body's service to the soul than these metaphysical considerations seem to allow?

The real danger of arguments based on the metaphysical knowledge of the imperishable soul lies in its positing a purely speculative basis as the ground for practical morality. By making ethics dependent on strictly intellectual theories that have not been nurtured in the crucible of moral experience, the purport of ethics is subverted. Starting with the metaphysical assertion of the inviolability of the soul, it is possible logically to justify righteous killing, for, on such presuppositions, no one is really killed, and, therefore, there is no killer, no guilt, no blame! The argument may be logical, but it is not legitimate. K. N. Upadhyaya, addressing himself to this problem, clearly describes the kind of reciprocal relation that must exist between metaphysics and ethics if the former is to serve as the legitimate basis for the latter. He explains:

> The transcendental truth of the supramundane unity where the multiplicity of the world melts away, has to be realised in one's own direct experience by means of gradual development of the natural faculties through proper ethical conduct. Ethics is, thus, only the means to the transcendental or metaphysical plane. . . . It is only on that higher plane that ethics loses its significance, for it can have meaning only in the midst of multiplicity or society of individuals. But if one, instead of going from ethics to metaphysics reverses the process and proceeds from some *a priori* metaphysical assumptions to ethics, one will inevitably be caught in contradictions.[174]

Further objections are not necessary because Kṛṣṇa himself seems dissatisfied with the purely metaphysical approach. That is why he follows up the metaphysical argument by appealing to Arjuna's sense of duty. He states: "Further, having regard for thine own *dharma,* thou shouldst not tremble. There exists no greater good for a Kṣatriya than a battle required by duty."[175]

A Kṣatriya's *svadharma* was preparedness to combat the enemies of society. As a Kṣatriya, Arjuna must, therefore, be true to his law of action and take up arms rather than assume the posture of an ascetic by "shaving off the hair." Fighting a just war is a noble duty which should be happily accepted because it is "an open door to heaven."[176] On the other hand, should Arjuna fail to engage in lawful battle, he will be violating his sacred duty and shall "incur sin."[177] The warning is clear:

> Men will forever speak of thy dishonor, and for one who has been honored, dishonor is worse than death.
> The great warriors will think that thou hast abstained from battle because of fear and they who highly esteemed thee will think lightly of thee.
> Many words which ought not to be spoken will be spoken by thy enemies, scorning thy strength. What is more painful than that?[178]

It may be noted in passing that this anxiety expressed over such mundane concerns as fame, earthly reward and heavenly gain, is in embarrassing contrast to Kṛṣṇa's later teaching, about to be examined, enjoining on Arjuna a transcendental attitude toward such ephemeral considerations.

Having explained the propriety of duty, Kṛṣṇa believes the path of action is clear. If Arjuna performs his duty in the correct spirit, he is bound to come through victoriously, one way or the other. "If thou art slain, thou wilt obtain heaven, or if thou conquer, thou wilt enjoy the earth. Therefore arise, O son of Kuntī, resolved to fight."[179]

It is ethically important that the battle be fought in the right spirit. This means that Arjuna must adopt the transcendental attitude of equal-mindedness. Treating alike pleasure and pain, gain and loss, victory and defeat, Arjuna will be able to fight without incurring sin. This teaching asking Arjuna to rise above praise and blame is on a higher level than the earlier teaching urging their consideration.

To enable Arjuna to achieve the proper spirit, Kṛṣṇa tells him to consider himself an instrument in the hands of God—he then cannot fight for selfish ends. God has already sealed the fate of his enemies because of their unrighteous past. Even without Arjuna's intervention, all the warriors standing arrayed in the opposing army shall soon cease to be. Arjuna must therefore consider himself a mere sword being wielded by the hand of God.[180]

Should Arjuna at this point lose his nerve and decide, "I will not fight," it will be impossible for him to sustain such self-conceited sentimentality. By nature Arjuna was a Kṣatriya, and sooner or later his martial nature would surely assert itself. Arjuna, therefore, is warned not to allow egotism *(ahaṃkāra)* to hoodwink him into imagining that he is someone other than a man who was born to fight. "That which thou wishest not to do, through delusion, O son of Kuntī, that thou shalt do helplessly, bound by thine own action born of thy nature."[181]

Delay is detrimental. If driven to fight by the inner momentum of his Kṣatriya nature, the egotism that now prevents him from following his *dharma* will then propel him to fight with vengeance! Caught up in the heat of emotions, it will be impossible for him to conduct his actions as the wise warrior Kṛṣṇa would have him be. So the real issue is not whether to fight, but whether to fight out of desire and incur sin, or out of duty and act righteously.

The difficulty with the arguments stated earlier is that they seem to undercut man's self-determination. The importance of this for ethics is vital. The grand premise of ethics is that man is able to surpass himself. This capacity presupposes freedom. But if it is true that human activity is only the enactment of a ready-made scenario conceived in the mind of God; or if the present is only a projection of the past, then could it be that the Gītā in which these ideas are enunciated has been inappropriately called an ethical treatise on the active life?

The key to an understanding of the Gītā's psychology of conduct lies in its view of life as embracing both *prakṛti* and *puruṣa. Prakṛti* is the psychical apparatus with which a man is endowed at birth, being a carry-over from his mental development in a previous existence. Its process is clearly delineated:

> Having attained the world of the doers of right, and having dwelt there for many years, he who has fallen from yoga is born in the house of the pure and prosperous;
>
> Or he may be born in the family of wise yogins; for such a birth as this is hard to attain in the world.
>
> There he acquires the mental characteristics associated with his previous existence, and he strives from that point on to perfection.[182]

Since all beings are involved in the process of following the inner workings of their nature, repression is of no avail.[183] "The excited senses of even a wise man who strives (for perfection) . . . violently carry away his mind."[184] Such passages make it clear that to control the effects of one's past *karmans* is difficult indeed.

However, though sense-control is difficult, it is not impossible. By virtue of his higher nature, it is possible for man to achieve transcendence over *prakṛti.* The discipline involved here is one that brings the lower faculties under the control of the higher faculties, until the governance of *puruṣa* is attained. The hierarchical aspect of the discipline is stated thus:

> The senses, they say, are great; greater than the senses is the mind *(manas);* greater than the mind is the reason *(buddhi);* and greater than the reason is He.[185]

The rationale behind this discipline is that freedom is correlative to consciousness—the greater the consciousness the greater the freedom.

The outward life of sense is least free, because consciousness is constricted by the sway of senses. Freedom emerges when the senses are made dependent on the mind. Freedom is enhanced when the mind is yoked with intelligence. Greatest freedom is achieved when intelligence is informed by the consciousness of the Self. Thus, starting from the bondage of the outward life of sensations, the *yogin* moves inward and upward until he discovers the central and greatest reality of his own being. This is the highest level of consciousness, and with it, the maximization of freedom.

The psychological significance of the Gītā's analysis of freedom is that it does not fall into the customary traps of modern Behaviourists or Existentialists who argue either for freedom or determinism.[186] Instead of taking a polaristic position, the Gītā tries to do justice to all ranges of human experience. On the lowest range, it concurs with Behaviouristic thought that nature is determined. But, unlike the Behaviourists, the Gītā does not stop there. In existentialistic fashion it proceeds to qualify the determinism of nature by man's mental and spiritual capacities to control nature. The lower self is progressively brought under the control of the higher Self, but in so doing, the lower is not abrogated by the higher. Instead, the interests and activities of the empirical self are sublimated, so that all aspects of personality are made to function helpfully and harmoniously.

Finally, what is the character of the free man? What is his style of life? How does he transcend nature? The Gītā responds with this portrait of the free man:

> He does not abhor illumination, activity or delusion when they arise, O Pāndava, nor desire them when they cease.
>
> He who is seated like one indifferent and undisturbed by the *gunas,* who thinks "the *gunas* alone act," who stands apart and remains firm,
>
> To whom pleasure and pain are alike, who abides in the self, to whom a lump of clay, a rock, and gold are the same, to whom the pleasant and unpleasant are equal, who is firm, to whom blame and praise of himself are the same;
>
> To whom honor and dishonor are the same, to whom the parties of friends and enemies are the same, who has abandoned all undertakings—he is called the man who transcends the *gunas.*[187]

Such a free man, having transcended the *guṇas,* and serving the Lord with unswerving *bhaktiyoga,* is "fit to become Brahman."[188]

CHAPTER 3

The Ethics of the Darśana Period

I. Introduction

The evolution of Hindu thought continued from the Epic period into the age of the Systems. Simultaneous with the popularisation of Hinduism along the pattern of the Purāṇas and the Tantras (A.D. 300–750) was a movement among the intelligentia which led to the systematisation of Hinduism into the philosophical sūtras of the six orthodox schools. This development was the rational legacy of the attack of Buddhism and Jainism upon the dogmatic foundations of traditional Hinduism.

> Critics forced their opponents to employ the natural methods relevant to life and experience, and not some supernatural revelation, in defence of their speculative schemes . . . The force of thought which springs straight from life and experience as we have it in the Upaniṣads, or the epic greatness of soul which sees and chants the God-vision as in the *Bhagavad-gītā* give place to more strict philosophising . . . the spirit of the times required that every system of thought based on reason should be recognised as a *darśana.*[1]

The word *darśana* means 'point of view' (from the root *dṛś,* meaning "to see"). Hence, the six classic systems are regarded as six points of view from which the single orthodox tradition may be considered. Despite the contradictions among them, these independent systems are taken to be "complementary projections of the one truth on various planes of consciousness, valid intuitions from differing points of view—like the experiences of the seven blind men feeling the elephant, in the popular Buddhist fable."[2]

The adoption of a critical and analytical point of view explains the systematic focus placed by all of these schools on *pramāṇas. Pramāṇa* means "the essential means of arriving at valid knowledge or *pramā.*"[3] Generally stated, there are three *pramāṇas:* (1) perception *(pratyakṣa),* (2) inference *(anumāna),* and (3) verbal testimony *(śabda).*

The systems start with Noetics, but having answered the question, "How do we know?" press on to their ultimate aim, namely, *mokṣa.* All of the systems concur that "the *summum bonum* of life is attained when all impurities are removed and the pure nature of the self is thoroughly and permanently apprehended and all other extraneous connections with it are absolutely dissociated."[4] Liberation is not just an eschatological possibility but is attainable in this life as *jīvanmukti.*

Ethically speaking, the systems recognize all three levels of moral development. On the Objective level, emphases vary as to the need for adherence to the *Varṇāśrama* scheme of life. On the Subjective level, purity of heart *(cittaśuddhi)* is insisted upon. With cleansed heart one must work disinterestedly and unselfishly. Finally, there is the Transcendental level upon which the good is no longer an object of labour but a realized reality. The liberated man transcends the plane of moralistic individualism while bound to the orbit of *saṁsāra,* and now becomes like a lovely lotus unblemished by the muck and mire whence it grows.

The common ethical concepts enunciated earlier—*avidyā, karman, dharma, saṁsāra, jīvanmukti*—provide the basis for the orthodox character of these systems. These ideas are taken from the Vedas, and by virtue of accepting the validity of the Vedas, these systems are called *āstika,* to be distinguished from the *nāstika* systems (Buddhism, Jainism, and Cārvākas) which deny Vedic authority. However, it must be pointed out that orthodoxy is very liberal in its handling of Vedic testimony, relying mainly on the *jñānakāṇḍa* (the Upaniṣads) side of the *śruti* literature. The manner in which Vedic texts are interpreted is considerably coloured by the peculiar predilections of the exegete.

The Brahmanical *darśanas* we are now ready to study are: Gautama's Nyāya, Kaṇāda's Vaiśeṣika, Kapila's Sāṁkhya, Patañjali's Yoga, Jaimini's Pūrva Mīmāṁsā, and Bādarāyaṇa's Uttara Mīmāṁsā, or the Vedānta. Apart from their names, we know nothing of these actual or purported founders. We shall be justified in treating them as schools and not individuals. Of these systems, the one of greatest contemporary significance is the Vedānta. For this reason the author has devoted special attention to two Vedāntic schools: Śaṅkara's, representing the philosophic rendering of the Vedānta, and Rāmānuja's, representing its theistic interpretation.

Since this is a work in ethics, we shall not concentrate on all the philosophical details of each system, but only on those which are relevant to ethical theory and practice. Unlike Western philosophic systems, the ethical ramifications of these *darśanas* have not been worked out, but every philosophical system has a reciprocally related structure of values, and this makes it incumbent upon us to identify those values which have been explicitly or implicitly determined by the profound philosophical ideas of these systems.

Their theoretical conclusions aside, we are inspired in this quest by the ethical attitude of these philosophers toward the truth they investigate. Reverence for truth, and an indomitable will that it shall prevail, mark these men not only as scholars to respect but to admire. With intellectual bravery they work out their principles and candidly admit the consequences of their theories.

> If they are idealists, even to the verge of nihilism, they say so, and if they hold that the objective world requires a real, though not necessarily a visible or tangible substratum, they are never afraid to speak out. They are *bona fide* idealists or materialists, monists or dualists, theists or atheists, because their reverence for truth is stronger than their reverence for anything else.[5]

Furthermore, their vision of the great world rhythm—endless successions of creation, maintenance, and dissolution—make these philosophers believers in progress. Rise and fall do not imply new beginnings, and absolute cosmic annihilation. "The new universe forms the next stage of the history of the cosmos, where the unexhausted potencies of good and evil are provided with the opportunities of fulfilment. It means that the race of man enters upon and retravels its ascending path of realisation."[6] Thus, their belief in the possibility of discovering truth provides them with the necessary impetus to incarnate its essence in progressively greater degrees.

II. Ethical Thought in Nyāya-Vaiśeṣika

Though not as well known to the West as the Sāṁkhya-Yoga and Vedānta philosophies, the Nyāya and Vaiśeṣika systems of logic and realism are "able and earnest efforts to solve the problems of knowledge and being on the basis of reasoned argument."[7] Scriptural authority is recognized, which is why they are included within the orthodox systems, but they rely chiefly on rational endeavour to illuminate Reality.

We propose to treat both of these philosophic schools as one system. There is historical precedence for this syncretic approach going back to the time of Vātsyāyana (400 A.D.). The two systems have been traditionally synthesised because of their single world view and because of their common approach to ethics.

Of the two works, the Vaiśeṣika is the older. Its earliest exposition, composed in ten books of aphorisms, has come down to us in the name of Kaṇāda. Kaṇāda means 'atom (of grain) eater', a nickname obviously connected to his theory. The earliest exposition of the Nyāya school contained in five books of aphorisms has been passed on under the name of Akṣapāda Gautama. Akṣapāda was also probably a nickname, denoting 'one whose eyes are directed at his feet'.

By themselves, the aphorisms of both schools are difficult to decode. Stylistically, this was intentional to maintain the veil of secrecy. Futhermore, "it must be assumed that they represent the summing up in definite form of doctrines long discussed in the schools, and that they were meant to do no more than serve as mnemonics, on which to string a full exposition given in the oral method traditional in India."[8] However with the aid of commentaries these works become readily comprehensible. The earliest commentary on Kaṇāda is Praśastapāda's Vaiśeṣika Sūtra Bhāṣya, and that on Gautama is Vātsyāyana's Nyāya Sūtra Bhāṣya.

The word *'vaiśeṣika'* signifies 'difference' and points to the fundamental diversity in the universe. The word *'Nyāya'* means argumentation and stands for the intellectual and analytical method that has made the system both distinctive and formative. Taken together, 'Nyāya-Vaiśeṣika' represents a cosmological theory that is realistic and pluralistic, and which is arrived at through the method of logic.

Like the other darśanas, the *summum bonum* of the Nyāya and Vaiśeṣika systems is the attainment of salvation. *Mokṣa* is brought about by a knowledge of the sixteen great topics of Gautama's philosophy or the six or seven categories advanced by Kaṇāda.[9] The *summum bonum* consists in the "final cessation of pain." The cause of possible pain, namely, *adṛṣṭaṁ* (the resultant energy persisting in the self as a consequence of its prior activities) and *saṁskāra* (potential tendencies), are neutralised, and thereby pain permanently ceases. The cessation of pain cannot be described as a state of bliss, because pleasure and pain are inextricably mixed.[10] Rather, salvation is a state of absolute unconsciousness, devoid of thought, feeling, and will. The self transcends all of its specific qualities, such as pain and pleasure, for none of these belong to its essential nature. Rid of these qualities, the self enters a condition of timeless freedom, untouched by the weary cycle of birth and death.

The pain from which deliverance is sought is the last link of a chain of suffering that begins with false knowledge *(mithyājñāna)*. As the sūtra states it, "pain, birth, activity, faults (defects) and misapprehension (wrong notion)—on the successive annihilation of these in the reverse order, there follows release."[11] Diagramatically, the chain of bondage can be illustrated thus:

(False knowledge)—(Defects)—(Activity)—(Birth)—(Pain)

We shall now examine each of these links to discover their ethical import.

First, 'False knowledge'. False knowledge refers to various objects of cognition, and is of several forms. In respect to the soul, 'False knowledge' is in the form, 'there is no such thing as Soul.' Similarly, Not-Soul is regarded as Soul; pain as pleasure; the noneternal as eternal; nonsafety as safety; the fearful as free from fear; what is fit to be rejected as worthy of being kept; activity as, 'there is no such thing as karman, nor any result of karman'; defects as, 'metempsychosis is not due to defects'; rebirth as, 'the birth of living beings is without cause'; the Highest Good as, 'it is something terrible, involving as it does the cessation of activity', 'in the Highest Good which consists in dissociation from all things, we lose much that is desirable,' 'how can any sane person have any longing for such Good, in which there is neither pleasure nor pain, nor any consciousness at all?'[12]

Second, 'Defects'. From 'False Knowledge' proceeds attachment to the pleasant and aversion for the unpleasant; and under the influence of this attachment and aversion, 'Defects' appear. The sūtra states, "There are three Groups of Defects;—[all being included under] Desire, Hatred and Illusion, which are distinct from one another."[13]

Vātsyāyana enlarges upon this sūtra, developing each of the three types.

(1) Desire—under which are included Love (for the other sex), Selfishness, Longing for acquiring, in a lawful manner, what belongs to another, Hankering (for Rebirth) and Greed (desire for obtaining, in an unlawful manner, what belongs to another).
(2) Hatred—under which are included Anger, Jealousy, Envy, Malice and Resentment.
(3) Illusion—under which are included Error, Suspicion, Pride, and Negligence.[14]

Third, 'Activity'. Urged by the preceding 'Defects', when a man acts he commits evil in connection with the body, speech, and mind. Misdeeds pertaining to the body are: "killing, stealing, illicit intercourse." Misdeeds pertaining to speech are: "lying, rude talking and incoherent babbling." Misdeeds pertaining to the mind are: "malice, desire for things belonging to others, and materialism." These evil acts constitute sin and tend to *adharma* (vice, demerit).

On the other hand, there are good acts consisting of the following: pertaining to the body: "charity, protecting and service"; pertaining to speech: "telling the truth, saying what is wholesome and agreeable, studying the Veda"; pertaining to the mind: "compassion, entertaining no desire for the belongings of other people, and faith." All such activities are good and tend to *dharma* (virtue, merit).[15]

Vātsyāyana further explains that the meaning of 'activity' *(pravṛtti)* in the preceding sūtra is the result of activity, "in the form of Merit and Demerit; just as life being the result of food, we speak of the life or living beings as 'food'."[16]

Fourth, 'Birth'. *Pravṛtti* in the form of merit brings about high birth, and in the form of demerit causes low birth. "Birth consists in the collective appearance (in one congregated group) of the Body, the Sense-Organs and the Consciousness."[17]

Fifth, 'Pain'. From the moment of birth there is pain. It is experienced as *'bādhanā'* (harrassment), *'pīḍā'* (suffering), and *'tāpa'* (affliction). Everything is intermingled with pain. Life itself is "nothing but pain." 'Pain' is symptomatic of the soul's uneasiness with itself.[18]

Thus empirical existence is a chain which holds the individual in bondage from one cycle of existence to the next. On the basis of this analysis of the human condition, it seems correct to conclude that the Nyāya-Vaiśeṣika philosophy is pessimistic.

However, while the Nyāya-Vaiśeṣika system is pessimistic regarding the *way things are,* it is optimistic about the *way things can become.* Ethically, this optimism lies in its affirmation of man's voluntary capacities to initiate, select and choose *dharma* against *adharma.* Kaṇāda's sūtras open on an ethical note: "Now, therefore, we shall explain Dharma."[19] The pain in the world is connected directly or indirectly to man's selfishness on an individual or social scale, but the moral training prescribed by this system is confident about man's power to overcome selfish desires and impulses.

The system is also intellectually optimistic. It insists: knowledge of the truth does absolutely abolish pain. "Dharma (is) that from which (results) the accomplishment of Exaltation and of the Supreme Good."[20] Since the Nyāya and Vaiśeṣika philosophies teach the doctrine of release from the coil of mortality, they are properly referred to as *Mokṣa-śāstras.* We shall now enquire into the details of this optimistic doctrine of emancipation from pain.

Release comes through right knowledge. True knowledge destroys the ignorance *(moha)* which falsely imparts the notion of 'I' (egoism, *ahaṃkāra).* In the light of this saving knowledge, one can no longer mistake the purely adventitious features connected with the self (pain, pleasure, knowledge, desire, volition, and so on) for its essential characteristics. No doubt, the body and *manas* are closely related to the self, but this relationship is not at all necessary.

When *moha* is destroyed, *dveṣa* (hatred) and *rāga* (narrow love) fail to arise. With the passing of aversion and attachment, there is no reason for activity, and, therefore, no cause for *saṁsāra.* No more birth means no more pain, and thereby one attains the highest good.[21]

The final question is: How does one acquire this true knowledge that brings about the *summum bonum?*

The discipline leading to the *summum bonum* is twofold: ethical and intellectual. The intellectual discipline consists of study, reflection, and meditation. The sūtra recommends:

> [There should also be] repetition of the study of the Science, as also friendly discussion with persons learned in the Science.[22]

The "Science" referred to is the "Science of the Soul." It is to be read, retained, and continuously reflected upon. By "friendly discussion with persons learned in the Science" is meant the consolidation of the knowledge acquired. It consists in:

> (1) the removing of doubts
> (2) the knowing of things not already known
> (3) the confirmation (by the opinions of the learned) of the conclusions already arrived at (by one's self).[23]

In addition to the Science of the Soul, the Science of Yoga is enjoined. Through it, "methods of internal discipline" are learned.[24] These consist of "Penance, Controlling of the Breath, Abstraction of the Mind, Contemplation and Concentration of mind; and the practice of the renouncing of objects of sense."[25] Yogic meditation leads to a direct experience of Ultimate Truth.

This brief description of the intellectual discipline impresses us with the necessity of an uncommon degree of seriousness which is indispensable for its undertaking. To help the *yogin* achieve this intense, undivided level of mental poise and power, the ethical discipline is prescribed. The ethical discipline is only preparatory to the intellectual discipline, but without it the second step is impossible to take.

A clear and concise description of the ethical path toward *mokṣa* is found in the Padārthadharmasaṁgraha of Praśastapāda (400 A.D.). We shall focus on two key categories of ethics; *dharma* (merit or virtue), and *adharma* (lack of merit, demerit).

Dharma is described as the property of man.

> It brings about to the agent happiness, means of happiness and final deliverance; it is supersensuous; it is destructible by the experiencing of the last item of happiness; it is produced by the contact of the man with the internal organ, by means of pure thoughts and determinations; and with regard to the different castes and conditions of men there are distinct means of accomplishing it.[26]

The means of *dharma* are found in the Veda and the lawbooks. They comprise the traditional *varṇas* and *āśramas,* along with the duties common to all men. The latter consists of the following: "faith in *dharma,* harmlessness, benevolence, truthfulness, freedom from desire for undue possession, freedom from lust, purity of intentions, absence of anger, bathing, use of purifying substances, devotion to deity, fasting, and non-neglect (of duties).[27]

Adharma is also described as a quality of the self. It makes for sin and has dire consequences. It is imperceptible and is removed by the cognition of the last item of pain which results from it. The causes of *adharma* are:

(1) the doing of actions which are prohibited in the scriptures and which are contrary to the causes of dharma, for example, harmfulness, untruthfulness, undue possession
(2) the nonperformance of actions enjoined in the scriptures, and
(3) neglect (of duties).[28]

These causes, along with impure motives, contaminate the mind, bringing about *adharma.*

When a man who is not yet enlightened, performs the ceremonial acts of *dharma* for the sake of achieving worldly gain, his virtuous deeds lead him to "contact with desirable bodies and sense-organs and consequent experience of pleasures etc., in accordance with the impressions (left by his previous actions)—in such regions as those of Brahmā, of Indra, of Prajāpati, of *pitṛs* (ancestors), or of men."[29]

By the operation of the same moral law of *karman,* when a man performs acts which are predominantly of the nature of *adharma,* these acts bring about his "contact with bodies and sense-organs and consequent experience of pains etc., in such regions as those of ghosts and of the lower animals. And thus by the performance of such virtuous deeds as are in the form of outgoing activity (of the self), accompanied by sin, the man passes through the various divine, human and animal regions, again and again; and this is what constitutes his 'wheel of bondage'."[30]

On the other hand, rising to an ethically higher plane, when a man performs *dharma,* motivated by spiritual insight, with no thought for worldly prosperity but only the desire for spiritual good, the result of such *dharma* for this soul is birth in a pure family. He has a longing to escape "the wheel of bondage," and with the help of a qualified teacher, he studies the six categories of Kaṇāda which banish from his mind all the spectres of illusion. With ignorance removed, he acquires the dispassion that frees him from all attachments and aversions. When such feelings are eliminated, the production of *dharma* and *adharma* ceases. Then, when the *dharma* and *adharma* of his past lives are depleted, and all his affections have ceased, his future actions are characterised by pure *dharma* which tends toward "peace." These actions of pure *dharma* create in him a sense of happy contentment and a disregard for his physical existence. This *dharma* also ceases. "Thus there being a complete cessation, the self becomes "seedless," and the present body falling off, it takes no other bodies, and this cessation of equipment with bodies and organs, being like the extinguishing of fire on all its fuel being burnt up, constitutes what is called "mokṣa" ("final deliverance")."[31]

III. Ethical Thought in Sāṁkhya-Yoga

The authorship of the Sāṁkhya system has been attributed to the nigh legendary figure known as Kapila (*circa* 7 B.C.). The Sāṁkhya-Sūtra which bears his name, though incorporating some ancient material, is a later work belonging to the fourteenth century A.D. The earliest text on hand dealing with Sāṁkhya philosophy is the Sāṁkhya kārikā of Īśvara-kṛṣṇa. Its date is the third century A.D. This "pearl of the whole scholastic literature of India" has been the subject of several famous commentaries, including Sāṁkhya-tattva-Kaumudī by Vācaspati Miśra, 850 A.D.

Though originally opposed to the religion of the Brahmins, the Sāṁkhya system was accepted as 'orthodox' because of its acknowledgment of the infallibility of the Vedas. Its own influence upon the sacred literature has been profound and far-reaching, moulding some of the ideas in the Mahābhārata, the Laws of Manu, and the Purāṇas. As one source strongly states it, the whole of Indian literature "has been saturated with the doctrines of the Sāṁkhya."[32]

The sister system to the Sāṁkhya is the Yoga. It is also ranked as one of the orthodox systems of Brahmanic philosophy. Its founder, Patañjali (5 A.D.), is author of the classical text called the Yoga-sūtra, probably composed after A.D. 450. If this date put forth by Jacobi is correct, then the author is not to be identified with the grammarian, Patañjali, who lived in the second century B.C. Important commentators on the Yoga-sūtras include Vyāsa (A.D. 500) and Bhoja (A.D. 1000).

Both of these systems are treated together because the Yoga system concurs with the Sāṁkhya on all major points pertaining to physiology, psychology, and metaphysics. The only difference is in respect to the question of God. Whereas Sāṁkhya is atheistic, Yoga is theistic. However, even here, the notion of God is not integral to Yoga, being inserted to placate the theists, and to make available the means of grace for human deliverance. In respect to ethics, the difference between these two schools lies in the fact that while Sāṁkhya is theoretical, Yoga is practical.

The *summum bonum* of all ethical endeavours is the realisation of the perfection of *Puruṣa*. This is brought about by the highest knowledge or *vivekajñāna.* Intuitively, the *jīva* learns to discriminate between the *Puruṣa* and *Prakṛti*, and thereby returns to its true self.

> Every jīva has in it the higher puruṣa, and to realise its true nature has no need to go out of itself, but only to become conscious of its real nature. The ethical process is not the development of something new, but a re-discovery of what we have forgotten.[33]

This brief description of the *summum bonum* shows that the ethics of this system is founded upon its metaphysics. Therefore, ere we get into the latter we must explicate its metaphysical basis.

The Sāṁkhya-Yoga system is ontologically dualistic. It postulates two uncreated, independent, and eternal principles known as *Puruṣa* and *Prakṛti. Puruṣa,* the spiritual principle, and *prakṛti,* the material principle, are the transcendental essences of our conscious and unconscious experiences. All experiences arise from this duality between *Puruṣa,* the knower, and *Prakṛti,* the known. Together they form the matrix from which the phenomenal universe evolves.

Prakṛti, the changing object, is the *causa materialis* of the whole world of becoming. Kapila's affirmation of the reality of matter is in direct opposition to those doctrines that would treat it as illusory appearance.[34]

The theory of causality explaining this evolution is known as *pariṇāmavāda.* It holds that the effect is only a modification of the cause. The effect resides in the cause in a potential form prior to manifestation. When we say, for instance, that curd is produced from milk, we mean that milk containing the potency of the curd has brought it out into actuality. Several proofs are offered in support of this theory.[35]

The existence of *Prakṛti* is proved through inferential reasoning, and not by recourse to revelation.[36] This shows the consistently rationalistic posture of the Sāṁkhya system.

By the aid of reason, the nature of *Prakṛti* is also explained. Since the effect is only a modification of the cause, the nature of the cause can be deduced from the nature of the effect. Upon analysis, the physical universe is seen to possess three basic properties called *guṇas*: therefore, the Unmanifest cause must also be characterised by similar constituents.[37]

It should be noted that while *guṇas* are translated as "attributes" and "qualities," these attributes are properties nondistinguishable from substance. The *sattva, rajas,* and *tamas guṇas* are described as of the nature of "pleasure, pain, and delusion; they serve the purpose of illumination, action, and restraint; and they are mutually subjugative and supporting, and productive and cooperative. The Sattva attribute is held to be buoyant and illuminating; the rajas attribute exciting and mobile; and the tamas attribute sluggish and enveloping. Their functioning is for a single purpose, like that of a lamp."[38] Expanding on the figure of the lamp, the commentator Vācaspati explains:

> We have all observed how the wick and the oil—each, by itself, opposed to the action of the fire—co-operate, when in contact with fire, for the single purpose of giving light; . . . the three attributes, though possessed of mutually contradictory properties, co-operate towards a single end;—"for the single purpose" of the emancipation of the spirit.[39]

When the *guṇas* are in a state of equilibrium, there is no evolution. The *guṇas* maintain their dynamic character, but do not interact with one another.

Change within unconscious *Prakṛti* from the state of dissolution *(pralaya)* to that of evolution *(sarga)* is attributed to the proximity of conscious *Puruṣa (saṁnidhimātra).* Acting like a magnet, the presence of *Puruṣa* draws the *guṇas* into a state of excitation, and starts them off on their evolutionary cycle. By combining in various proportions, the *guṇas* give rise to the manifold variety in the physical world.

The union between conscious though inactive *Puruṣa* with active though unconscious *Prakṛti* is compared to the union that exists between a blind man carrying a lame man on his shoulders. "From this union proceeds evolution."[40]

The order of evolution is clearly drawn.[41] The first product of evolving *prakṛti* is *mahat* ("the great one"). It is the basis of the individual's intelligence *(buddhi).* Looked at in its cosmic aspect as that which holds in it potentialities for further development, it is called *mahat.* Seen from the point of view of forming the physical basis for psychical activity in each individual, it is called *buddhi.* Though physical, *buddhi* functions psychically, because of its proximity to, and temporary association with, *Puruṣa.*

Ahaṁkāra (egoism) is derived from *buddhi.* It is the principle of individuation. According to the Sāṁkhya-kārikā, there are three types of *ahaṁkāra* corresponding to the three *guṇas.*[42] The five sensory organs and the five motor organs are derived from the *sattva* aspect of *ahaṁkāra manas* (mind). The five subtle elements are produced from the *tamas* aspect of *ahaṁkāra*, and from these, the five gross elements are derived. *Rajas guṇa* provides the energy for these productions of *ahaṁkāra.*

Some comments need to be made on how these twenty-five principles of *Prakṛti* are related to the ethical process.

Unlike some other systems where the principle of matter is equated with the principle of evil, the Sāṁkhya system suggests no such moral dualism. To the contrary, both the design and function of *Prakṛti* are aimed at liberation of *Puruṣa.* The kārikā says: "As the insentient milk flows out for the growth of the calf, so does Nature act towards the emancipation of spirit."[43] Hiriyanna comments,

> The noteworthy point here is the physical accompaniment of man as well as his environment is neither hostile or indifferent to his attaining the ideal of freedom. Through them rather, Prakṛti is ever educating him into a fuller knowledge of himself with a view to securing that result. Nature therefore cannot, in the end, be said to enslave spirit. In fact, it behaves towards man as a "veritable fairy godmother."[44]

The doctrine of the *guṇas* also has "great ethical significance."[45] The *guṇas* provide the foundation for three types of ethical activities.[46] *Sattva guṇa* gives rise to virtuous conduct *(dharma)* expressed as kindness, sense control, absence of hate, reflection. *Rajas guṇa* gives rise to indifferent conduct shown by anger, avarice, passion, discontent, rudeness, and violence. *Tamas guṇa* gives rise to bad conduct through apathy, sloth, laziness, enslavement to women, intoxication, and impurity. The fact that all of these ethical activities are superseded when enlightenment breaks, should not detract from the preparatory significance of ethics. Through *sattva guṇa,* the *buddhi* arrives at its original condition of purity, and only then is in a position to experience intuitive knowledge. Goodness does not touch the *Puruṣa* inasmuch as the ethical life is limited to the empirical sphere, but without goodness the *Puruṣa* cannot be distinguished from *Prakṛti.*

The principle next to *buddhi,* namely, *ahaṁkāra,* is also understood in ethical terms. Unselfish actions, arising from this principle of individualisation, are an indirect means of *mokṣa.*[47]

Other elements conceived ethically are those which comprise the subtle body or *liṅgaśarīra.* In addition to the *buddhi* and *ahaṁkāra,* these are the eleven organs of sense and the five *tanmātras.* The subtle body is attached to the self. It is the empirical storehouse of all past *karman.* Unlike the gross body, it is unaffected by birth and death.[48] The ethical significance of the *liṅgaśarīra* resides in the prerequisite that before saving knowledge can dawn, the storehouse, especially in the area of *buddhi,* must be morally cleansed. Then, when right knowledge comes, the *liṅgaśarīra* leaves the self.

We had stopped to point out some ethical aspects of *Prakṛti.* We must now move on to a consideration of the second ultimate principle in this dualistic philosophy, and that is *Puruṣa.*

Like *Prakṛti, Puruṣa* is without beginning and without end. In all other respects, *Puruṣa* is essentially different from *Prakṛti.* Positively stated, all that can really be said of *Puruṣa* is that it is 'pure spirit'.[49] Negatively, *Puruṣa* is unbound, inactive, impassive, motionless, and attributeless.

Five proofs are offered for the existence of *Puruṣa.*[50] Reasoned arguments are also presented for the "multiplicity of selves."[51] Individual souls are of an infinite plurality and are not to be mistaken for emanations from a World Soul.

The relation between the soul and the inner organ *(buddhi, ahaṁkāra,* and *manas*) is somewhat difficult to grasp. Though completely passive and independent, 'by virtue of its nearness', the soul excites the incessant processes of the inner organ into a state of consciousness. This influence of *Puruṣa* is metaphorically described as illumination, or is illustrated by comparing the soul to a mirror in which the inner organ is reflected.

The experience of consciousness which the soul brings about in the internal organ is characterised by suffering. Even pleasure 'is accounted pain by the wise'. The soul, being "by nature, eternal, and eternally pure, enlightened, and unconfined,"[52] does not suffer; but because, as in a looking glass, it reflects the inner organ which is the seat of all suffering, it seems that the soul itself is bound by pain.[53]

The cause of bondage is ignorance of the true nature of *Puruṣa.* Through 'want of discrimination' *(aviveka),* the essential distinction of the soul from the inner organ and senses is not recognized. This ignorance goes back to the disposition inherited from previous births.

Release from bondage comes through the highest knowledge *(vivekajñāna).* It is intuitive and consists in the clear recognition that all activity and suffering takes place in *Prakṛti,* and that *Puruṣa* stands above all the change and sorrow connected with the weary round of rebirth and death. When this enlightenment dawns, the activity of *Prakṛti* ceases. "As a dancer desists from dancing, having exhibited herself to the audience, so does Primal Nature desist, having exhibited herself to the spirit."[54] Enlightenment does not bring life to an immediate end. As the following verse explains, life persists for some time.

> Virtue and the rest having ceased as causes, because of the attainment of perfect wisdom, the spirit remains invested with the body, because of the force of past impressions, like the whirl of the potter's wheel, which persists for a while of the momentum imparted by a prior impulse.[55]

How does one attain *vivekajñāna?* The most important path is through the practice of *yoga.* The Sāṁkhya Sūtra gives prominence to the discipline of *dhyāna* (meditation) as the means for restoring *buddhi* to its original *sāttvika* condition. With controlled senses and tranquil mind, purified *buddhi* is able to reflect the effulgence of *Puruṣa.*[56]

On account of the ascetic element engendered by *yoga*, it would be unfair to say that asceticism stifles the spring from which the moral life flows. Sāṁkhya does not discourage virtuous conduct. It only says that good deeds must be performed in a spirit of detachment if they are to lead to liberation.[57] Good deeds done with the hope of happiness receive their reward in a temporary heaven. But such morality is shortsighted. It only postpones the conquest of evil. It is not the final answer to terminating the "threefold misery."[58]

Good deeds performed in the spirit of detachment are free of hopes and fears, rewards and punishments. Their chief characteristic is kindness for all forms of life—not only human, but animal and vegetable also. The Sāṁkhya-kārikā boldly labels the host or religious rites laid down in the Veda as the means of terminating misery, categorically inefficient and impure. Vācaspati comments:

> The impurity lies in the fact of the Soma and other sacrifices being accompanied by the killing of animals and the destruction of grains and seeds.[59]

As part of its tirade against Vedic morality, the Sāṁkhya forbids gifts to priests in the expectation of collecting merit. This is not to say it devalues the ancient honour ascribed to the teacher of spiritual wisdom. A good teacher is one who is himself free; and it is not important whether he is a Brahmin or not. Finding such a *guru* is contingent on virtuous conduct in the past. And as another strike against caste, Śūdras are not barred from receiving instruction in the highest knowledge.

Thus, while granting ethical conduct its correct place in the economy of life, Sāṁkhya radically reinterprets ethics in the light of its metaphysics. As J. Ghosh puts it:

> It is based on a revision of values, in fact, on a new conviction that our joys and sorrows form a chequered procession of empty pageantry with which the soul can have no real concern. And it involves renunciation of prizes and pleasures within our grasp as well as abstinence from active service of the human race, so that if it does not furnish the motives for a resolute application of our energy to what are generally regarded as important tasks, neither does it check and defeat our manhood, for in asking us to give up good things, it asks us to be strong against the strength of our rebellious passions and to curb the madness of our wills. . . . It holds that the man of the world does not see life steadily or see it whole, and it rejects in consequence the remedies that he suggests for the evils that beset life, while it seeks in thought alone a way out of them because they are found to arise out of a persistent obliquity of vision.[60]

For a fuller treatment of the means toward the acquisition of saving knowledge, we must turn to the Yoga system of Patañjali. Its emphasis is twofold: ascetic preparation and yogic training.

In keeping with the metaphysical presuppositions which are almost identical with Sāṁkhya, the Yoga system holds the mental state of desirelessness *(vairāgya)* as its ethical ideal. The Yoga Sūtra defines desirelessness as the "consciousness of supremacy in him who is free from thirst for perceptible and scriptural enjoyments."[61] The *bhāṣya* on this verse explains:

> A mind free from attachment to perceptible enjoyments, such as women, foods, drinks, and power, and having no thirst for scriptural enjoyables, such as heaven and the attainment of the states of *videha* (disembodied) and the *prakṛtilaya* (absorbed in Nature), has, when it comes into contact with such divine and worldly objects, a consciousness of its supremacy due to an understanding of the defects of the objects, brought about by virtue of intellectual illumination. This consciousness of power is the same as the consciousness of indifference to their enjoyment, and is devoid of all desirable and undesirable objects as such. This mental state is desirelessness *(vairāgya)*.[62]

Vairāgya is of a lesser and higher quality, the latter being consequent upon the knowledge of *Puruṣa*.[63]

Turning from the ethical norm to the practical method of its achievement, we come to the Eightfold Means *(aṣṭāṅga)* of Yoga.[64] These eight accessories are: "Restraint, observance, posture, regulation of breath, abstraction (of the senses), concentration, meditation and trance."[65] Of these, the first two, restraint *(yama)* and observance *(niyama)*, are of direct ethical significance.

The moral ingredients of *yama* are: "abstinence from injury, veracity, abstinence from theft, continence, and abstinence from avariciousness."[66] The first ingredient, noninjury or *ahiṁsā*, provides the ethical framework for all the other virtues. *Ahiṁsā* is more than nonviolence; it is nonhatred *(vairatyagah)*.[67] Its scope is universal. It is "not limited by life-state, space, time and circumstance."[68] That is to say, *ahiṁsā* cannot be relativised by a series of "if's", "and's", and "but's." The *bhāṣya* on this verse exposes some of the rationalisations that would constrict the universal character of *ahiṁsā*.

> Abstinence from injury is limited to life-state, as for example, the injury inflicted by a fisherman is limited to fish alone, and to none else. The same is limited to space, as, for example, in the case of a man who says to himself, "I shall not injure at a sacred place." The same is limited to time, as for example, in the case of the man who says to himself, "I shall not cause injury on the sacred day of the *caturdaśī* (the fourteenth) of the lunar fortnight."
>
> The same in the case of the man who has given up the three injuries is limited by circumstance, as, for example, when a man says to himself, "I shall cause injury only for the sake of gods and *brahmins* and not in any other

way." Or, as for example, injury is caused by soldiers in battle alone and nowhere else. . . . Universal is that which pervades all conditions of life, everywhere, always, and is nowhere out of place. They are called the great vow.[69]

The second ethical value of the Eightfold Means is observance or *niyama*. The ingredients of *niyama* are: "cleanliness, contentment, purificatory action, study and the making of the Lord in the motive of all action."[70] The ideas are amplified in the following passage:

> By cleanliness is meant disgust with one's body, and cessation of contact with others.
>
> And upon the essence (of mind) becoming pure, come high-mindedness, one-pointedness, control of the senses, and fitness for the knowledge of the self.
>
> By contentment, the acquisition of extreme happiness. By purificatory actions, the removal of impurity and the attainments of the physical body and the senses.
>
> By study come communion with the desired deity. The attainment of trance, by making Īśvara the motive of all actions.[71]

Just as *ahiṁsā* is normative for goodness, it is also normative for evil. "Sins are the causing of injury to others and all the rest." The moral ramifications of an evil deed are analysed with respect to agent, cause, scope, and consequence. . . .

> [Sins] are done, caused to be done, and permitted to be done; they are preceded by desire, anger, and ignorance; they are slight, middling, and intense; their result is an infinity of pain and unwisdom.[72]

The method for avoiding the contemplation of an evil deed is by saturating the mind with thoughts of its disgusting effects. "The habituation to the contrary tendencies becomes the cause of removing sins. . . ."[73]

Thus, by cultivating *yama* and *niyama*, "the Ten Commandments of Yoga," and by avoiding sin, the yogin develops a serene detachment from the pleasures of this world, and from blessings in the world to come.[74]

Once the individual is ethically prepared, he embarks upon a rigorous course of yogic training aimed at disciplining the body and mind, both of which are seen as closely connected.

> The principle underlying the whole discipline is that man's faculties are by long habit adjusted to the preservation of the empirical self and that they must be readjusted so as to secure the totally opposite aim of restoring the purusa-element in it to its true condition.[75]

The stages in the yogic training are: posture *(āsana)*, breath control *(prāṇāyāma)*, withdrawal of senses from their objects *(pratyāhāra)*, attention *(dhāraṇā),* contemplation *(dhyāna),* and meditative absorption *(samādhi).*

Step by step, the psychophysical discipline of yoga elevates the seeker from the gross levels of existence to its subtle heights, until the pinnacle of concentration is achieved. This is the state of *asamprajñāta samādhi.*[76] It is 'superconscious' *samādhi,* leading directly to *kaivalya* which is complete isolation. In this state the originally pure nature of *Puruṣa* is experienced, and all mortal sufferings—psychological *(ādhyātmika),* environmental *(ādhibhautika),* and supernatural *(ādhidaivika)*—are totally transcended.

IV. Ethical Thought in the Pūrva Mīmāṁsā

The *summum bonum* in the early Mīmāṁsā was the attainment of heaven through the due performance of rituals. Jaimini explains in his Mīmāṁsā Sūtra that the purpose of sacrifice was to merit the reward of heaven in another world: "Let one desirous of heaven perform a sacrifice."[77] In conjunction with this goal, *dharma, artha,* and *kāma (trivarga)* were adopted as the values for which men must aspire. The absence of *mokṣa* from this threefold scheme of values differentiated the Mīmāṁsā from other systems of Hindu philosophy.

Later developments in the Mīmāṁsā doctrine entailed the acceptance of the prevailing ideal of *mokṣa* as the ultimate aim of life. In place of *svarga,* the highest good is now defined as *apavarga* or escape from *saṁsāra.* When the cycle of rebirths is stopped, the soul enters the state of *mokṣa* where it abides in its own essential nature.

What is the nature of the soul? While the Mīmāṁsaka writers deny the existence of a Creator God, they entertain no doubts about the existence of the soul.[78] Both Prabhākara and Kumārila extrapolate the arguments for the soul's existence contained in Śabara's Bhāṣya.[79] Since the fruits of sacrifice are to be reaped in another world, there must be a permanent spiritual entity which survives the death of the body and which reaps what it has sown. If this were not the case it would mean that the Vedas which advocate the rewards of sacrifice in heaven would be of doubtful validity.

A moral objection to the argument claiming it is necessary to posit an eternal entity which sows seed and reaps their result, is that the reaper has no knowledge of what he has sown in his previous existence. This missing link between the deed and the consciousness of the deed undercuts the value of assuming the need for a permanent moral agent. Besides, it is natural to expect that the agent could engage in forbidden acts, and yet take comfort in the realisation that when the day of reckoning dawns, he shall be blissfully ignorant of the sins he has sown on earth.

Lack of terrestrial memories is irrelevant, replies Kumārila. Who is worthy of sacrificing? Only those who are morally and spiritually fit: and men of such character fully realise that what they do is governed by the moral law of the universe even though they cannot establish all the links within the causal nexus.

The nature of the soul as "I" is perceived through mental intuition *(mānasa-pratyakṣa)*. In common with Nyāya-Vaiśeṣika schools, the conception of the soul is realistic and pluralistic. There are many souls, different in each body, all of which are eternal, universal, and permanent substances.[80] Though eternal, the soul undergoes modifications. On this point of modal change in the soul, the Bhaṭṭa school parts ways with the view of the Prabhākaras. The Bhaṭṭas find no contradiction between permanence and change. Everyday experience demonstrates that things can change constantly without becoming different. The movement of the waves does not change the identity of the ocean, nor does the uncoiling of the snake change its essence. It is, therefore, quite consistent to believe in the eternality of the soul and at the same time to affirm that it undergoes change of form.

The soul as eternal, permanent substance is completely different to the body, the senses, and the understanding. Through the instrumentality of its psychophysical organism the soul experiences pleasure and pain, and is able to relate within the world. The soul survives the death of its body, and in the next world assumes another body whose character is fixed by the moral quality of the soul in its previous existence.

This shackling of the soul to the world by virtue of the body, the sense, the motor organs, and the mind, constitutes the bondage of the soul. Bondage continues through an unending cycle of lives, each of which has been morally determined by *karman*. Since *karman* is the cause of bondage, emancipation is brought about by the removal of *karman*.

One path leading to emancipation is the way of *dharma*. The purpose of the Mīmāṁsā Sūtra, as stated by Jaimini, is "the enquiry into dharma (duty)."[81] He defines the subject as follows: "Dharma is that which is indicated by means of the Veda as conducive to be the highest good."[82] Central to this scheme of the good life was sacrificial action. There were three kinds of actions: (1) *Kāmyakarmas* or optional deeds which gather merit; (2) *Pratiṣiddhakarmas* or forbidden deeds which incur demerit; and (3) *Nityakarmas* or unconditional duties, such as the regular offering of twilight prayers *(sandhyā)*.

The Veda is "the means of arriving at the right notion of 'dharma' ", says the Ślokavārttika.[83] The Mīmāṁsakas generally apply the word 'Veda' to the ritualistic texts of the second stage of Vedic literature and less frequently to the Ṛgvedic hymns. If the question of the authority of these ritualistic texts were raised, the Mīmāṁsā writers would respond with Jaimini that the Veda is superhuman, eternal, uncreated, and therefore not open to doubt.

The unquestioned authority of the Vedas is maintained with utmost tenacity, because, if the texts were the works of men, like other human creations, they would be limited and fallible, and, therefore, in no position to legislate duty or promise any rewards, especially the rewards of heaven. Replying to the objection that the Veda's authorship is identified with certain persons and therefore cannot be eternal, Kumārila tries to offer reasons why this is not the case and concludes with this statement:

> The Veda naturally abandons the denotation of non-eternal meanings,—inasmuch as such denotation is found to be impossible with regard to the Veda, by considering alternatives of eternality and non-eternality with regard to it. Because if the Veda be eternal its denotation cannot but be eternal; and if it be noneternal (caused), then it can have no validity (which is not possible, as we have already proved the validity of the Veda); and as for the theory that the Veda consists of assertions of intoxicated (and senseless) people, this theory has been already rejected above—(and as such the validity and hence the eternality of the Veda cannot be doubted).[84]

In their anxiety to uphold the supreme authority of the Vedas, the Mīmāṁsakas deny the existence of a creator.[85] Though they continue the Vedic cult of sacrifice to the gods, their only interest is in ceremonialism, and the gods "gradually recede and fade into mere grammatical datives."[86]

> A deity comes to be described not by its moral or intellectual qualities, but, as that which is signified, in a sacrificial injunction, by the fourth case-ending (the sign of a dative, to which something is given). In short, a deity is necessary merely as that in whose *name* an oblation is to be offered at a sacrifice. But the primary object of performing a sacrifice, says an eminent Mīmāṃsaka, is not worship: it is not to please any deity. . . . A ritual is to be performed just because the *Vedas command us* to perform them.[87]

Having no divine dispenser of rewards and punishments, how does the Mīmāṁsā explain the reaping of *dharma* and *adharma* in view of the long lapse between act and consequence? Jaimini finds the solution to this problem in the notion of *apūrva.* Literally, it refers to something without previous existence, hence something new. *Apūrva* provides the necessary link between act and consequence.[88] It may be viewed either as "the imperceptible antecedent of the fruit, or as the after-state of the act."[89] Thus, the deferred consummation of an act is attained through the unseen efficacy of *apūrva* which remains in the performer and is realized in the future life.[90] Jaimini says: "There is *apūrva* because action (is enjoined)." Through this concept the Mīmāṁsā philosophy lays down an idealistic and mystical basis for ethical action.

Thus far we have stated that *dharma* is the means to *mokṣa* and that the revelation of *dharma* is found in the Vedas. This *dharma* is based on the eternal validity of the scriptures; its standard is supernatural; and it is constituted of such duties whose spiritual potency is conserved through the efficient medium of *apūrva*.

This definition of *dharma* obviously excludes common morality. Kumārila explicitly states: "We should distinguish between what relates to dharma and moksa which is known from the Veda and what relates to artha and kāma which is learnt by worldly discourse."[91] At the same time, ordinary morality is considered an essential prerequisite of spirituality, so that though ceremonialism may be distinct from morality, it is not divorced from morality. The correlation is clear: "the Vedas cleanse not the unrighteous." The only time moral laws are suspended is on those rare occasions when the injunctions of *dharma* are granted precedence as in the case of ritualistic offerings of animals, despite the common ban on injury to living beings.

The role of *dharma* in the process leading to *mokṣa* is as follows. First, according to the Prabhākara school, there is the experience of disenchantment with mortal existence because it is pervasively fraught with pain. To be sure, life has its pleasures, but to gain them is pain and to lose them is pain. This experience of disillusionment over what the world has to offer moves the aspirant to free himself from life in the world. He has the choice to follow a twofold path—the path of *karman* and the path of knowledge.

The discipline of *karman* calls for the control of passions. By abstaining from forbidden deeds *(pratiṣiddha)* which incur demerit and consequent punishment and by eschewing optional deeds *(kāmya)* which produce merit and subsequent reward, the disciple eliminates those *karmans* which bind him to the world. The only *karmans* he is obliged to perform are *nityakarmas* (unconditional duties). The object of *nityakarmas* is not worship, nor purification, nor moral improvement, but obedience to the commands of the Vedas.[92] These commands being categorical, must be carried out in the spirit of disinterest. Failure to do so is violation of Vedic law, and this is tantamount to the conscious commital of forbidden sins. Thus, by abstention from *pratiṣiddha* and *kāmyakarmas* which give rise to demerit and merit, and by adherence to the *nityakarmas* for no other reason than that are enjoined by the Vedas, passion is controlled, and deeds binding one to *saṁsāra* are eliminated. Simultaneously, *karmans* accumulated in the past are gradually exhausted through experience.

In addition to the discipline of *karman* is the discipline of *jñāna*. Through the cultivation of meditation, one gains insight into the true nature of the self, and this self-knowledge ensues in liberation. Prabhākara argues that liberation must be the product or *jñāna* because the Vedas prescribe the cultivation of knowledge with no ulterior purpose. Many moral virtues accompany the birth of knowledge, such as equanimity, continence, and self-control.

The Kumārila school is substantially in agreement with the Prabhākaras in respect to the process of liberation. However, it emphasises that *jñāna* is only an indirect means to *mokṣa*. Positively, knowledge of the self and its distinction from the body is an aid to performing obligatory sacrifices. Negatively, it prevents the production of future *karman*. By itself, *jñāna* is incapable of cancelling the accumulation of past *karmans*. The only way the moral stock of past deeds can be dissipated is through the consuming effect of experience. *Jñāna* is therefore not a direct, but an indirect, means to *mokṣa*.

How does the Mīmāṁsā conceive of *mokṣa?* Since bondage is the attachment of the self to the world through the physical body, the organs of sense, and the *manas*, *mokṣa* is the elimination of these ties through the cessation of rebirth.[93] For Prabhākara, *mokṣa* is "the absolute cessation of the body caused by the disappearance of dharma and adharma." Kumārila defines *mokṣa* as a condition in which the self is delivered from pain. Though the enlightened self realizes that its relation to the world is not essential, there is no implication in either writer that the relationship between the individual self and the world is not real; nor is there any hint of the Vedantic notion suggesting the sublation of the world in *mokṣa*. The reality of the physical world is at all times emphasised, because, for one thing, it provides the basis for differentiating between virtue and vice.

In the state of *mokṣa* the self is unconscious. Consciousness only arises out of the relation of the self to the world by the instrumentality of its psychophysical organism. When this association of body and soul ceases, consciousness and such other mental states as *jñāna,* pleasure and pain also cease. The self is not even conscious of itself![94] It is, therefore, erroneous to assert that the state of *mokṣa*, is one of 'pure bliss'. All that can be said is that the soul abides in its intrinsic nature as absolute substance having existence, and though not conscious, as having the potentiality for consciousness. So the goodness of *mokṣa* is not based on the attainment of bliss, but on the total transcendence of pain.[95] Later Bhaṭṭas introduced the Advaitin view of *mokṣa* as the experience of *ānanda,* but this development has no foundation in Kumārila's teaching.[96]

In respect to social ethics, we shall briefly touch on the Mīmāṁsā's views of caste and the position of women. Jaimini helps perpetuate the caste cult. Replying to the contention that "all four castes [are entitled to the performance of sacrifices],—there being no distinctions," Jaimini offers the 'true view' on those eligible to perform sacrifices.

> In reality, the acts in question can be performed by the three (higher) castes only; as in connection with the "Installation of Fire" these three only have been mentioned: (the śūdra) therefore can have no connection with sacrifices; the Veda being applicable to the brāhmin (and the other two castes) only;—such is the opinion of Ātreya.[97]

The rationale for arriving at the preceding value judgment is based upon the exact meaning of the castes derived from the words used in the texts. Brahmins, Kṣatriyas, Vaiśyas, and Śūdras respectively refer to: (1) intellect, (2) *ahaṁkāra* and mind, (3) the senses and (4) the objects of senses.[98] Since Śūdra has reference to objects of senses, it seems plain to Jaimini that the fourth caste cannot perform any act connected with the intellect. This means the Śūdra lacks the capacity to perform such spiritual acts as sacrifices.

Regarding the Śūdra and material matters, Jaimini states: "The three castes can acquire wealth because it is acquired through action."[99] The acquisition of wealth is accomplished by intellect, mind and the senses —faculties which represent the three upper castes. On the other hand, the Śūdras or objects of senses cannot appropriate wealth because they themselves are wealth.[100]

Whereas a Śūdra cannot be considered an actor, a woman can. Jaimini clarifies the actor in terms of man and woman. He says:

> According to *Aitiśāyana,* an actor should be described as a man (or a word in the masculine gender), because that is the best way of doing so. We should accept his view; but, if in spite of this, we misinterpret or find fault with the text, the error would lie in our own lack of knowledge. Bādarāyana says that the reference to "man" is to the species or the human race (as opposed to an individual), and so the term is used without any special distinction of sex. For that reason even a woman should be regarded as an actor, because so far as the species is concerned, there is no distinction (between man and woman); and we cannot admit that there is any. But if the term "man" is distinctly said to refer to the male, we should take it to be in accordance with what the sacred books have said.[101]

Next, does the woman have the right to possess property? Against those who answer the question in the negative, Jaimini argues that she can, but with a certain provision of limitation.

> So far as effort to secure a certain result is concerned, there is no distinction between a man and a woman; and this is proved by the fact that the two

> are united together to secure a common end (an offspring). So far as the purchase of a woman is concerned, it is only a matter of custom; for if we can see for ourselves that women do possess wealth; and if a woman can do so, it follows that she can also act; and this can easily be proved. But even if a woman is "bought," she can still own property through someone else (or through devotion to her man). Indeed, she is closely connected with the ownership of property, because we see that both man and woman seek the fruit of action jointly; and we see that it accrues to both.
>
> It is for this reason that the union of the two is said to be like a sacrifice of both. But, as in an action we have a principle and a subordinate part, the word "second" should refer to the wife, for she is not the equal of man; but what belongs specially to her is the power to bless and to remain chaste.[102]

It is a matter of regret that the ethics of the Mīmāṁsā system has not received more careful attention of modern scholars, especially in view of the fact that Mīmāṁsā rules are fundamental for the interpretation of the laws by which Hindu society has been traditionally governed.

One merit of this system is its attempt to show that the good life is an integrated development of all four *puruṣārthas—kāma, artha, dharma,* and *mokṣa.* The spiritual aspirations of Jainism and Buddhism during these times neglected physical and social values by concentrating exclusively on spiritual values. The one-sided thrust of these heterodox religions created an ascetical ethos in which material and social values were played down. Such an ill-conceived repudiation of the world and the values of *artha* and *kāma* had to be stopped. This prompted the Mīmāṁsā sages to "reassert the faith in morality, to revive the ethico-social tendencies expressed in the Vedas and Upaniṣads, and to bring home to the common man that true renunciation consisted not in giving up ardour for and zest of life, but in subordinating enjoyment to Dharma, sensuousness to the sense of duty and attachment to spiritual realization."[103]

It is also a matter of commendation that the Mīmāṁsakas infused new conviction in the moral conduct of life by upholding the standard of duty for duty's sake. "Here the Mīmāṃsā ethics reaches, through ritualism, the highest point of its glory. . . ."[104]

The Mīmāṁsā's concept of duty is more stringent than that of the Gītā inasmuch as its understanding of disinterestedness is so pure that it excludes even such spiritual motives as *ātmaśuddhi* ('purifying the self'), and subserving the purposes of God.[105]

There is an obvious parallel between this concept of law operative in *dharma* and the Categorical Imperative of Immanuel Kant. Both state that a moral deed is to be performed because one ought to do it and not because of any attached benefits. The Mīmāṁsā also agrees with Kant that though an unconditional deed is to be done with absolute disinterest, the doer is finally rewarded because such is the constitution of the universe. However, whereas the Mīmāṁsā attributes reward to the governance of the impersonal moral law, Kant attributes it to God. The two also differ in postulating the locus of authority. The Mīmāṁsā finds the source of authority in the injunctions of the Vedas, while Kant traces it to the commands of the higher rational self.

It is further creditable that though the Mīmāṁsakas distinguish between the ideal of *dharma* with its superhuman standard and extraempirical concerns, and the lesser ideal of common morality with its utilitarian standard and empirical concerns; nevertheless, the two spheres are integrated, and common morality is thereby duly recognized. Commenting on this aspect of Mīmāṁsā ethics, Prof. I. C. Sharma remarks:

> The critics forget that when Mīmāṃsā names the obligatory acts like Yajña as Dharma, and the prohibited acts (Nisiddha Karmas) like gambling and killing as Adharma; and when the effects of both these acts are regarded as Apūrva, the invisible power of the conservation of the acts (Karmas), it is evident that social and spiritual well-being have been given equal status in the Mīmāṃsā ethics. If the Nitya Karma, or the obligatory acts of performing a Yajña (sacrifice), lead to Mokṣa, negligence towards the prohibited acts would hinder the spiritual progress of an individual. It is wrong to suppose that the fields of social morality and spiritual morality are bifurcated.[106]

The view of man on which the Mīmāṁsā system is based is, for the most part, ethically sound. Freedom is assumed as the prerequisite for responsible action. Freedom is not controverted by the law of *karman* when this impersonal moral law of the universe is correctly understood. Jaimini makes a clear distinction between natural action and deliberate action that is purposively oriented. He observes: "We see that when people have a purpose or aim in action, it is the result of deliberate intention or precise thinking."[107] In the same vein, the Prabhākaras analyse the voluntaristic basis of action. The Siddhāntamuktāvalī presents Prabhākara's analysis of volition in the following progression: the awareness of some duty to be done *(kāryatājñāna);* the wish to do it *(cikīrsā),* implying the awareness that the task can be accomplished *(kṛtisādhyatājñāna);* the resolve *(pravṛtti);* the motor reaction *(ceṣṭā);* and performing the deed *(kriyā).*[108]

The Mīmāṁsā's appeal to the judgment of men of ethical stature as guides for Vedic conduct indicates that man is viewed as a spiritual entity living in a society of similar ethical beings.

Unfortunately, by appealing to Vedic authority as the source of obligation which categorically enjoins *dharma,* the Mīmāṁsā postulates a supernatural standard of authority. Its ethics is therefore authoritarian in character, to be accepted on faith and not reason. Of course, the Tantrarahasya[109] and other writings allow for the judgment of "one's own conscience" in determining what is good, but conscience is not viewed autonomously. Far from being a free agency of moral perception, the role of conscience is limited to that of providing a conscientious appeal for the doing of duties learned from external authority. Such a conscience is good for tribalism but is bad for individuality.

V. Ethical Thought in the Vedānta

The Vedānta System of Bādarāyaṇa is based on the *jñānakāṇḍa* portion of the Vedas. The Vedānta Sūtra (variously known as Brahma Sūtra, Śārīraka Sūtra, Uttara Mīmāṁsā) deals with the final aim of the Veda. The word 'Vedānta' literally means 'the end of the Vedas'. Without the help of commentators, it is impossible to grasp the meaning of the 555 sūtras which attempt to systematise the doctrine of the Upaniṣads. Chief among these commentators are Śaṅkara (eighth century A.D.) and Rāmānuja (twelfth century A.D.) who provides us with nontheistic and theistic interpretations of the Vedānta, respectively. Śaṅkara's system is monistic, and is known as Advaita. Rāmānuja follows a qualified monism called Viśiṣṭādvaita.

A. Advaita

The purpose of Śaṅkara's philosophy is stated in his introduction to the Vedānta Sūtra. He declares:

> With a view to freeing one's self from that wrong notion which is the cause of all evil and attaining thereby the knowledge of the absolute unity of the Self the study of the Vedānta-texts is begun.[110]

In keeping with the aim of this study, the *summum bonum* is the intuitive realisation that there is one and only one Reality which is the negation of all plurality and difference. This rigorous monism is the key to Śaṅkara's system. It is capsulized in the well-known phrase: "Brahman is real; the world is unreal; the individual self is only the Supreme self and no other."[111]

As sole Reality, *Brahman* is *nirguṇa* or indeterminate. This is not to say that *Brahman* is blank. It means that the Absolute cannot be objectively categorized by empirical thought because it is incapable of objectification. At best it can be indirectly described as not unreal, not unconscious, and not of the nature of pain. But though the Absolute is indefinable and unknowable in terms of discursive thought, it can be directly grasped through experience. One can know *Brahman* by being *Brahman*.

If this be true that *Brahman* is alone Real, what is the explanation for the world of variety and multiplicity which is part of everyman's ordinary experience?

Śaṅkara answers this question by introducing the principle of nescience. This principle of cosmic illusion which is somehow connected with *Brahman* is neither *sat* nor *asat*. Not being the product of fantasy, it is *sat*; but inasmuch as it is phenomenal it is *asat*. This eternal power is the source of phantasmal appearances. Though *Brahman* is pure intelligence, without form, qualities, or the limitations of time, space, and causality, it appears to possess a phenomenal character because this is erroneously superimposed upon it.

Śaṅkara illustrates the process of superimposition springing from nescience by the following example. He says:

> It is a matter not requiring any proof that the object and the subject whose respective spheres are the notion of the 'Thou' (the Non-Ego) and the 'Ego', and which are opposed to each other as much as darkness and light are, cannot be identified. All the less can their respective attributes be identified. Hence it follows that it is wrong to superimpose upon the Subject—whose Self is intelligence, and has for its sphere the notion of the Non-Ego, and the attributes of the object, and vice-versa and to superimpose the subject and the attributes of the subject on the object. In spite of this it is on the part of man a natural procedure—which has its cause in wrong knowledge—not to distinguish the two entities (object and subject) and their respective attributes, although they are absolutely distinct, but to superimpose on each the characteristic nature and the attributes of the other, and thus coupling the Real and the Unreal, to make use of expressions such as "That am I", "That is mine."[112]

Regarding the definition of 'superimposition', Śaṅkara describes it as "the apparent presentation of the attributes of one thing in another." This definition is illustrated by such expressions as: 'mother-of-pearl appears like silver', 'The moon although one only appears as if she were double'.[113]

Superimposition defined in this way is called nescience *(avidyā)* by the wise, whereas knowledge *(vidyā)* is the correct determination of the being-in-itself of things. The source of *avidyā* is the knowing subject, but the intelligent Self is unaffected thereby.

Avidyā is the basis of all human knowledge as well as knowledge found in the sacred scriptures. The reason both empirical and scriptural modes of thought spring from ignorance is because "the means of right knowledge cannot operate unless there be a knowing personality, and because the existence of the latter depends on the erroneous notion that the body, the senses and so on, are identical with, or belong to, the Self of the knowing person."[114] Thus the common delusion of sacred and secular thought lies in the superimposition of the 'I' on the body.

A further proof that human cognitional activity has for its presupposition the preceding kind of superimposition follows from the similarity in that respect between men and animals. Both animal and human knowledge have egoistic aims. Śaṅkara builds up his case in a most interesting way.

> A cow, for instance, when she sees a man approaching with a raised stick in his hand, thinks that he wants to beat her, and therefore moves away; while she walks up to a man who advances with some fresh grass in his hand. Thus men also—who possess a higher intelligence—run away when they see strong fierce-looking fellows drawing near with shouts and brandishing swords; while they confidently approach persons of contrary appearance and behaviour. We thus see that men and animals follow the same course of procedure with reference to the means and objects of knowledge. Now it is well known that the procedure of animals bases on the non-distinction (of Self and Non-Self); we therefore conclude that as they present the same appearances, men also—although distinguished by superior intelligence proceed with regard to perception and so on, in the same way as animals do; as long, that is to say, as the mutual superimposition of Self and Non-Self lasts.[115]

In sharp contrast to the egoistic aims of Vedic and worldly knowledge which keep man bound to *saṁsāra,* Vedāntic knowledge conceives "the true nature of the self as free from all wants, raised above the distinctions of the *Brāhmaṇa* and Kshatriya classes and so on, transcending transmigratory existence."[116]

The ultimate purpose of Vedāntic knowledge is to bring to an end this endless process whereby the things and relations of the objective world are erroneously transferred to the inner self, and once the not-self is distinguished from the self (ātman), to allow one's own identity with *Brahman* to become known. Such knowledge will consist not in the forceful annihilation of *avidyā,* but in the recognition that the content of *avidyā* simply does not exist.

The foregoing analysis of the aim of Vedānta makes it clear that since the *summum bonum* is the realization of what has always been one's own nature but has for a period been obscured by *avidyā,* the only means necessary for liberation is the removal of *avidyā,* by *vidyā.* Śaṅkara explicitly states: "Man's purpose is effected through knowledge."[117] Neither religion nor morality can serve as direct aids to *mokṣa.*

This description of Advaitic *mokṣa* as the knowledge of the identity of the *jīva* with *Brahman* brings into question the viability of ethics within such a metaphysical system.

An immediate reaction to the doctrine of unity of *Brahman* is that it seems to negate moral distinctions and makes the quest after the good life metaphysically redundant.

Responding to the first difficulty, namely, the metaphysical negation of moral distinction, there seems to be logic in the contention that if *Brahman* alone is real and the world is false, then all ethical distinctions within this unreal world must correspondingly be unreal. There can be no substance to the ethical enterprise because it takes place within a realm of shadows. One can hardly term the taking of life 'evil', or the saving of life 'good', when such categories are shaped only within a world of dreams. However, this logic breaks down when it is understood that though the world of moral experience is unreal in the sense that it has no existence apart from *Brahman,* this unreality does not make it illusory—it does have practical existence. Therefore, being related to *Brahman,* and not a mere illusion, the world of experience serves as a moral arena in which the soul is nurtured for the unitive experience of *Brahman.* Thus the world along with ethical activity within it is considered significant by Śaṅkara inasmuch as it leads to union with *Brahman.*

The second ethical difficulty arising out of the identity of the *jīva* with *Brahman* is whether there can be any room for the pursuit of virtue when the *jīva* and *Brahman* are one and the same. This difficulty disappears when we recognize that metaphysical oneness in the Advaita Vedānta is "a task as well as a fact," a "problem" as well as a "possession."[118] Oneness is always one's own innate character, but like the prince reared as a hunter from birth only later discovers his royalty,[119] we forget the fact of our true nature and are therefore confronted by the problem of having to discover what we already possess. Thus, as Radhakrishnan explains, " 'I am Brahman' does not mean direct identity of the active self with the Ultimate *Brahman* but only the identity of the real self when the false imposition is removed. The ethical problem arises, because there is the constant struggle between the infinite character of the soul and the finite dress in which it has clothed itself. While the natural condition of man is one of integrity, the present state of corruption is due to fall from it by the force of upādhis."[120]

Thus, the monistic philosophy of Advaita Vedānta does not preclude ethical considerations. To establish this claim concretely we shall now proceed to show the role of ethical and moral discipline in respect to *Brahma*-realization.

In view of the fact that *Brahma*-realization is its *summum bonum,* the

Vedānta defines 'good' and 'evil' in terms of whatever helps or hinders this realization. The personal embodiment of this ethical ideal is Īśvara who identifies himself with the cosmos and who acts in behalf of the needs of the whole world. Accordingly, the worshipper of Īśvara assumes a similar love toward everything in the world. He freely gives of himself to the needs of society, acting on its behalf in the spirit of humility and charity. In this way, the worship of Īśvara serves a moral purpose by extricating the soul from a narrow identification of itself with its own organism and thereby freeing it from egocentricity, possessiveness, and alienation from the outside world.

The most practical way in which the individual will is trained to rise to the level of the social will is by ascending the progressive steps of communal duties. The detailed description of these duties is found in the general framework of the *śāstra's* scheme of *Varṇāśrama dharma.*

The relevant passage dealing with *karman* as the means to knowledge is found in the third *adhyāya, pāda* four. Śaṅkara finds no contradiction between *sūtra* twenty-five which asserts that work enjoined on the different *āśramas* need not be observed because freedom is effected by knowledge, and *sūtra* twenty-six which states that "knowledge has regard for all works enjoined in the asramas and that there is no absolute non-regard." His explanation for the seeming contradiction between sūtras is as follows. "Knowledge having once sprung up requires no help towards the accomplishment of its fruit, but it does stand in need of something else with a view to its own origination."[121] Why is this so? "On account of the scripture statements of sacrifices and so on. For the passage, 'Him the Brahmanas seek to know by the study of the Veda, by sacrifice, by gifts, by penance, by fasting, declares that sacrifices and so on are means of knowledge, and as the text connects them with the 'seeking to know,' we conclude that they are, more especially, means of the origination of knowledge."[122]

Thus, as *smṛti* says, "works are the washing away of uncleanness but knowledge is the highest way. When the impurity has been removed, the knowledge begins to act."[123] But once knowledge has dawned, the needs for these pious works ceases.

In addition to these works in the form of Vedic study, sacrifice, alms, penance, and fasting which constitute the more 'remote' means to knowledge are the approximate means, comprising tranquility, self-restraint, renunciation, patience and concentration.[124] Basing his argument on the scriptural passage, "therefore he who knows this, having become calm, subdued, satisfied, patient and collected, sees Self in Self,"[125] Śaṅkara enjoins, "The seeker for knowledge must possess calmness of mind, must subdue his senses and so on."[126] While the remote or indirect means is discarded upon the gaining of knowledge, the approximate or direct means is continued for the knower.

Evaluating the functions of works as the means to knowledge, Deussen comments:

> The works named do not, strictly speaking, produce knowledge as their fruit, because knowledge is subject to no prescribed rule, and because its fruit (liberation) cannot be brought about by any means. These works are only auxiliaries (sahakarin) to the attainment of knowledge, in as much as the man who leads a life of holy works is not overpowered by affections (kleça) such as passion, etc. According to this their role in the scheme of salvation would be not so much meritorious as ascetic.[127]

Granted that works incumbent upon the *āśramas* are necessary auxiliaries to knowledge, are they indispensable? Śaṅkara replies in the negative. Persons not belonging to an *āśrama* are qualified for knowledge because the scriptures cite such persons as Raikva and the daughter of Vakanu who possessed the knowledge of *Brahman* without benefit of prescribed works. Śaṅkara points out:

> The favour of knowledge is possible through special acts of duty, such as praying, fasting, propitiation of divinities, etc., which are not opposed to their *āśrama*-less condition and may be performed by any man as such. The *Smriti* says, 'By mere prayer no doubt the *Brahmana* perfects himself. May he perform other works or not, the kindhearted one is called Brahmana' (Manu, Samh. 11.87), which passage shows that where the works of the *āśramas* are not possible prayer qualifies for knowledge. Moreover knowledge may be promoted by *āśrama* works performed in previous births. Thus *Smriti* also declares, 'Perfected by many births he finally goes the highest way' (Bha. Gītā VI, 45); which passage shows that the aggregate of the different purificatory ceremonies performed in former births promotes knowledge. Moreover knowledge—as having a seen result (viz. the removal of ignorance)—qualifies anyone who is desirous of it for learning and so on, through the absence of obstacles. Hence there is no contradiction in admitting qualification for knowledge on the part of widowers and the like.[128]

Even though it is conceded that knowledge is possible for those who pay no regard to the duties incumbent on the *āśramas,* nevertheless, the way of duties is preferable.

> A better means of knowledge is to stand within one of the *āśramas,* since this is confirmed by *Śruti* and *Smriti* for scripture supplies an indicatory mark in the passage, 'On that path goes whoever knows Brahman and who has done holy works (as prescribed for the *āśramas*) and obtained splendour (Bri. Up. V. 4.9); and *Smriti* in the passage, 'Let a Brāhmaṇa stay not one

day even outside the *āśrama*; having stayed outside for a year he goes to utter ruin'.[129]

It is now clear that works play a significant role in the scheme of salvation. It is all the more regrettable that along with works of a definite moral character are included a medley of ritualistic and ceremonial actions which have no relation to the *summun bonum* or anything in common with the qualifications necessary for the study of the Vedānta. These qualifications, in addition to the study of the Vedas, include the following requirements: (1) "Discerning between the eternal and non-eternal substance," (2) "Renunciation of the enjoyment of reward here and in the other world," (3) "the attainment of the six means"—tranquility, restraint, renunciation, resignation, concentration, belief, (4) and "the longing for liberation." It is a matter of some regret that several of the works included in the *Āśramadharma* have nothing in common with the elevated ethical spirit evident in these conditions preparatory for study. Yet, these nonethical works are deemed just as meritorious as the ethical ones in that all works effect an individual's *karman*, thereby determining the state of his future birth.

With these comments on Śaṅkara's attitude toward *Āśramadharma* as the means to *mokṣa,* we move on to a consideration of his assessment of the role of *Varṇadharma.* The subject is discussed in conjunction with his prescription for the external conditions for the study of the Vedānta.

After refuting the exclusive claims of men to knowledge, and having established the rights of gods and departed *ṛṣis* thereto, Śaṅkara raises the question about whether Śūdras are eligible for *Brahmavidyā.* His answer is a categorical 'No'.[130] The Śūdras' exclusion arises out of the fact that the study of Vedānta requires qualification in Vedic matters, "but a Sudra does not study the Veda *for* such a study demands as its antecedent the *upanayana*-ceremony, and that ceremony belongs to the three (higher) castes only."[131] The Śūdra may desire the knowledge of *Brahman,* but "the mere circumstance of being in a condition of desire does not furnish a reason for qualification, if capability is absent. Mere temporal capability again does not constitute a reason for qualification, spiritual capability being required in spiritual matters."[132] As it turns out, "spiritual capability" is nothing more than the caste right to study the Veda, reserved only for Brahmins, Kṣatriyas, and Vaiśyas. Thus "spiritual capability" has little to do with character, but much with caste.

Exceptions to this Vedic injunction are attacked with a good deal of intellectual 'swashbuckling'. Śaṅkara takes up the case of *saṁvargavidyā* which Raikva communicates to Gaṇaśruti. He argues that the *ṛṣi* could not have called Gaṇaśruti a Śūdra "because a (real) born Śūdra is not qualified (for the saṃvarga-vidyā)."[133] He suggests that the mention of 'Śūdra' should be understood etymologically and not traditionally. Interpreted etymologically: "because Janaśruti from sorrow *(cu-câ)* at the humiliating speech of the goose, had run *(dudrâ-va)* to Raikva, this Rishi, who, through supernatural knowledge, became aware of what happened, and wished to make this evident, called him a 'cû-dra' (!)".[134]

Further efforts to discount the Śūdra status of Gaṇaśruti are as laboured and artificial as the preceding. Because Gaṇaśruti is praised in the same *vidyā* with the Kṣatriya Abhipratarin, Śaṅkara takes this coincidence to mean that Gaṇaśruti must have also been a Kṣatriya—"for as a rule equals are mentioned together with equals."[135] Also, Gaṇaśruti must have been a Kṣatriya, because he had a doorkeeper and wielded authority belonging to a Kṣatriya. Grabbing for such straws in the winds, Śaṅkara concludes: "Śūdras are not qualified (for the knowledge of Brahman.)"[136]

A second apparent exception to the rule barring Śūdras from the knowledge of *Brahman* is the case of Satyakāma, the son of Jabālā. Śaṅkara's forced exegesis is as follows:

> The Śūdras are not qualified for that reason also that Gautama, having ascertained Jābāla not to be a Śūdra from his speaking the truth, proceeded to initiate and instruct him. "None who is not a Brāhmaṇa would thus speak out 'Go and fetch fuel, friend, I shall initiate you. You have not swerved from the truth' (Kh. Up. IV, 4, 5); which scriptural passage furnishes an inferential sign (of the Śūdras not being capable of initiation).[137]

An unbiased reader of the original story would see the case otherwise as a courageous breakthrough from caste rigidity. Though Jābāla's ancestry was dubious, Gautama initiated him because he thought the lad had the heart and mind of a Brahmin which was of more significance than biological descent.

Even had these cases been genuine exceptions to the Vedic rule excluding Śūdras from saving knowledge, they would carry little weight with Śaṅkara, because he argues that exceptions are exceptions of the rule and therefore do not contravene what is established.[138]

Śaṅkara finds the rule damning the Śūdra laid down unequivocally in the *smṛti,* and quotes it with authority.

> 'The ears of him who hears the Veda are to be filled with (molten) lead and lac', and 'For a Śūdra is (like) a cemetery, therefore (the Veda) is not to be read in the vicinity of a Śūdra'.
>
> 'His tongue [of the Śūdra studying the Veda] is to be slit if he pronounces it; his body is to be cut through if he preserves it'.[139]

However, the situation is different for Śūdras like Vidura who acquire knowledge in consequence of the moral productivity of former deeds. From these "the fruit of their knowledge cannot be withheld, since knowledge in all cases brings about its fruit."[140]

Moreover, even though the ordinary Śūdra is not qualified to hear the Veda, on the authority of *smṛti* he is "qualified for acquiring the knowledge of the *itihāsas* and the *purāṇas.*"[141]

The purpose of the ethical discipline as we have studied it within the general framework of *Varṇāśrama dharma* was to cultivate detachment and thereby assist *jñāna* toward the attainment of *mokṣa.* By cultivating the will and purifying the feelings, *jñāna* is enabled to remove *ajñāna,* and once the wrong notions of *ajñāna* are dispelled, the truth of the soul's identity with *Brahman* shines forth of itself. This is *mokṣa.* The realization of *mokṣa* in this life is known as *jīvanmukti.* It follows logically from the view that *mokṣa* is the essential nature of the soul and is, therefore, instantly realizable the moment the obstacles to this truth are removed by intuitive knowledge. Since the Vedāntic training leading directly to *jīvanmukti* is not within the realm of our study, we shall only mention its three steps: (1) *Śravaṇa*—study of Upaniṣads under the direction of an experienced teacher to discover saving truth. (2) *Manana* —analytical reflection to gain intellectual certainty, (3) *Nididhyāsana*—meditation on the unity of *Brahman* until *jñāna* arises.[142] At this final stage of Vedāntic training the aspirant is able to say from the depths of his own experience—*'Ahaṁ Brahmāsmi'* (I am Brahman).[143]. This is *mokṣa.*

As *summum bonum, mokṣa* is both the *raison d'être* and consummation of ethical conduct. By the aid of *dharma* the unreflective life of passion is raised to the level of reason and responsibility. But this, the moral level, cannot be an end in itself but only an intermediary training ground, pointing to a higher level on which the conflicts and coercions of the moral life finally cease. On this level, moral consciousness is fulfilled and transcended by spiritual consciousness.

With such a monistic crown, ethical existence is shown to possess a grounding in reality. Referring to the ethical significance of the "finale of perfect selfhood" within the state of *mokṣa,* Prof. S. K. Das says:

> An ideal fails to furnish the dynamic of moral life unless it is known to have been realised *in toto* in some integral experience. Not *doing* but *being* in an ultimate reference—that should in all conceivability be the ideal of ethical conduct, and it is only Saṅkara-Vedānta that has the sufficiency to envisage fully the ideal of perfection and pursue, with vertical consistency to its logical conclusion, the implications of the injunction: 'Be ye perfect'.[144]

The life of the *jīvanmukta* is characterised by inwardness,[145] cosmic consciousness,[146] and disinterested activity.[147] We shall examine these characteristics in some detail.

On the moral level the individual was bound by prohibitions and permissions because he erroneously connected the self with the body. But for the *jīvanmukta* who sees the self to be one only, there is no pressure of obligation to be virtuous, because obligations are externally imposed in respect to things to be grasped or given up.

> How then should he, who sees nothing, either to be wished or avoided, beyond the universal self, stand under any obligation? The self certainly cannot be enjoined on the self. Should it be said that injunctions and prohibitions apply to all those who discern that the soul is something different from the body (and therefore also to him who possess perfect knowledge) we reply that (such an assertion is too wide, since) obligation depends on man's imagining his self to be (actually) connected with the body. It is true that obligation exists for him only who views the soul as something different from the body; but fundamentally all obligation is an erroneous imagination existing in the case of him only who does not see that his self is no more connected with a body than the ether is with the jars and the like. For him, on the other hand, who does not see that connection no obligation exists, much less, therefore, for him who discerns the unity of the self.[148]

It is thus plain that moral obligation is meaningless for the *jīvanmukta*. However, enlightenment does not lead to the abandonment of virtue. *Mokṣa* is only the demise of moralistic individualism, not of morality *per se*. Addressing himself to this source of grave misunderstanding, Hiriyanna says:

> The jīvanmukta, having transcended the stage of strife, is spontaneously virtuous. Impulse and desire become one in him. He is not then realizing virtue but is revealing it. 'In one that has awakened to a knowledge of the self, virtues like kindness imply no conscious effort whatsoever. They are second nature with him.' (Naiṣkarmya-siddhi, iv. 69).[149]

An immediate consequence of the *jīvanmukta's* discovery of the Upaniṣadic teaching, 'That thou art', is the development of a sense of cosmic consciousness or the feeling of universal belonging. The sense of being one with all creation is expressed ethically in the Golden Rule. The connection between the command, "Love thy neighbor as thyself," and the Vedāntic principle of cosmic oneness is expressed well in this verse from the Bhagavadgītā:

> This highest Godhead hath his seat in every being, and liveth though they die; who seeth him, is seeing, and he who everywhere this highest God hath found, will not wound self with self.[150]

The spirit of universal love is expressed through disinterested activity in the service of the world *(lokasaṅgrahārtham)*. Prior to knowledge, all activity is motivated by desire. The fruit of desire keeps the individual bound to the cycle of *saṁsāra*. Upon gaining *jīvanmukti*, actions are performed through unselfish wisdom which, therefore, have no binding effect. Śaṅkara says: "To one who knows, no work will cling even if one performs works during his whole life—thanks to the greatness of knowledge."[151] Thus, renunciation, not retirement, is Śaṅkara's ideal for the *jīvanmukta*. His own life of selfless labour is the best illustration of dispassionate action for the good of society. Through his doctrine as well as deeds, Śaṅkara asks us "to suppress our selfishness, and, if that requires solitude and retirement, these are advised as means to an end. One who has completely shaken himself free from selfishness is at liberty to take upon himself the task of the world. His attitude will not be world-seeking or world-fleeing, but world-saving."[152]

The composite picture of the *jīvanmukta* is that of one who is in a "childlike state." By this is meant the absence of such evils as guile and pride. The *jīvanmukta* does not manifest himself by a "display of knowledge, learning, and virtuousness, just as a child whose sensual powers have not yet developed themselves does not strive to make a display of himself before others."[153] In agreement with this portrait, *smṛti* writers have said:

> He whom nobody knows either as a noble or ignoble, as ignorant or learned, as well-conducted or ill-conducted, he is a Brāhmaṇa. Quietly devoted to his duty, let the wise man pass through life unknown; let him step on this earth as if he were blind, unconscious, deaf.[154]

Thus, in Śaṅkara's perfectionist ethic we have witnessed a happy blending of moral perfection and metaphysical insight. Though the two have been sharply distinguished when considered separately, the former being auxiliary to the latter; within the state of *mokṣa* the two are also shown to be integrally related. This is because of the word *'jñāna'*. In English usage, 'knowledge' is restrictively intellectual, but in Śaṅkara's usage it is the complete expansion of the inner life. Here, knowledge is only the external symbol of an internal experience which encompasses the entire gamut of one's thinking, feeling, and willing.

Had *jñāna* been limited to thinking, it would have been possible to gain *mokṣa* by intellectually accepting the logic of the Vedānta's thesis. But this constricted notion of knowledge certainly would be considered inadequate by Śaṅkara. For him, knowledge also involves the will—the seat of ethical activity. Just as *ajñāna* which destroys *jñāna* is itself a total living experience involving cognitive error, the affective response to this error *(kāma),* and the expression of feeling through action *(karman),* so also, *jñāna* involves the total immersion of the self. It is within the context of this holistic experience that *ajñāna* is fully destroyed, and not by some one-sided effort of abstract intelligence. If the latter were true, one would only have to be a logician to say: *'Ahaṁ Brahmāsmi'.* Rather, to know *Brahman* fully one has to become *Brahman*—and this is being in its richest, truest, and highest mode. It is nothing short of perfection. It is perfection!

This realization of our rootedness in *Brahman* is a permanent part of our being. It is essentially a state of freedom—including freedom from moralistic individualism, though not freedom from morality. When death finally comes, only name and form are destroyed, never to be reborn. But *Brahman* remains *Brahman*—pure existence *(sat),* consciousness *(cit),* and bliss *(ānanda).* This is the state of *videhamukti.*

B. Viśiṣṭādvaita

The *summum bonum* in Rāmānuja's philosophical ethics is the "intuitive knowledge of Brahman," which is of the nature of supreme unsurpassable bliss. "He who knows Brahman attains the Highest."[155] The goal of life, therefore, is much more than the nonliability of the freed-self to births and death; it is the attainment of "God who in his form of perfect bliss is most dear to his worshipper."[156]

To understand and appreciate Rāmānuja's ethical ideal, we must first inquire into the nature of *Brahman,* the nature of the *ātman,* and the relationship between the two.

Rāmānuja's philosophy of Reality is monistic. All is *Brahman.* There is no reality other than Him, either of a similar or dissimilar nature. *Brahman* is the Absolute One. At the same time, the One is many. Within the unity of *Brahman* exist distinct but inseparable realities called *cit* (self) and *acit* (matter). These elements are mutually distinguishable from one another and from *Brahman.* They are without an absolute beginning and shall have no absolute ending.[157] Thus, the philosophy of Rāmānuja is actually a qualified monism *(Viśiṣṭādvaita).*

The analogy on which the relation between *Brahman* and the universe is conceived is the soul-body relation *śariri-sarīrasambandha).* The *ācārya* declares:

> All sentient and non-sentient beings together constitute the body of the Supreme Person, for they are completely controlled and supported by him for his own ends, and are absolutely subordinate to him. Texts which speak of the highest Self as 'bodiless among bodies' only mean to deny of the Self a body due to karman; for as we have seen, Scripture declares that the Universe *is* his body.[158]

The ethical implication of the soul-body relation is that inasmuch as the *ātman* is controlled, supported, and directed by the Supreme Person for his own ends, the *ātman* must, therefore, discover the meaning, value, and purpose of its existence to its Inner Ruler. The nature of goodness is inextricably bound up with the nature of godliness. To discover the former, we must delve into the nature of the latter.

Brahman is described as having characteristics of a double kind.[159] On the one hand he is free from all imperfections; on the other, he is a "treasure-house of all blessed qualities."[160]

Brahman abides in the soul as its Inner Ruler, but because it is "not subject to the influence of *karman,* is free from all imperfections."[161] Rāmānuja quotes the scripture as saying "that the Supreme Person is free from evil, free from old age, free from death, free from grief, free from hunger and thirst; that all his wishes realise themselves, that all its purposes realise themselves."[162] Since it is devoid of all evil characteristics common to *Prakṛti, Brahman* can be called *nirguṇa.*

Nirguṇa Brahman is simultaneously *saguṇa* because he possesses all good characteristics. Rāmānuja quotes *smṛti:* "He comprises within himself all blessed qualities, by a particle of his power the whole mass of beings is supported. In him there are combined energy, strength, might, wisdom, valour, and all other noble qualities."[163]

This brief description of the nature of *Brahman* as at once *nirguṇa* and *saguṇa* shows that Rāmānuja conceived of *Brahman,* the *Śarīrin,* not only in metaphysical and aesthetic terms, but in moral terms as well. "Reality and value are one, and the highest values of life like truth, goodness and beauty are intrinsic and eternal and are conserved in the absolute Self as its essential nature."[164]

The ethical import of viewing the nature of Īśvara in this way is such as to make holiness and righteousness—the moral predicates of the *śarīrin*—normative for ethical conduct on the part of the *śarīra.* Man ought to be compassionate, just, generous, and so on, because these are the qualities of the Inner Ruler. Thus the standard for ethical conduct is shifted from the little 'I' of *ahaṁkāra* (egoism) to the Absolute 'I' of the *śarīrin.*

Rāmānuja also conceived of the *ātman,* like Īśvara, as an ethical personality. It is not "the phenomenalised mode of pṛakrti," nor is it "the depersonalised instrument of divinity."[165]

The *ātman's* moral autonomy is first of all maintained by categorically differentiating it from the body in which it dwells.

> This body, though it may be put in *sāmānādhikaraṇya* with the experiencing-ātman, e.g. in the proposition "I am lean," etc. is different from the latter. Sages who possess exact knowledge of the body call it the expe-

riencing-ātman's field of experience. A person who knows this body and, because of this very knowledge, must be different from his body which is the object of his knowledge, is called *kṣetrajña* by these sages. That person may, when perceiving entities different from the body, consider his knowing ātman to be in a relation of *sāmānādhikaraṇya* to his body, for instance, in the proposition: "I who am a man know this jug"; still, when he perceives his body he will know that it is an entity different from his ātman and of the same order as a jug, because being an object of the ātman's knowledge it is of the same order as other objects of knowledge, so that now the proposition runs: "I know his body too, in the same way as I know a jug."[166]

By drawing this sharp distinction between the *ātman* and the body which particularises it, Rāmānuja preserves the freedom of the *ātman* against all naturalistic views of morals which, by identifying the *ātman* with *prakṛti,* would subject it to nature's causal necessity.

In the second place, the *ātman's* ethical personality is maintained against the possibility of its being conceived of as a depersonalised instrument of God. This danger arises out of Rāmānuja's view of God as Controller *(Niyantṛ)* and man as the controlled *(niyama).* As an instrument in the hands of God, the *ātman* is described as being dependent, controlled, and employed by God for the achievement of his own purposes.

This dependency relationship of the *ātman* on Īśvara could have become as damaging to the *ātman's* moral integrity as its assimilation within the natural process. Whether a cog within the machinery of nature or a helpless instrument in the hands of God, the *ātman* is in either case depersonalised and deprived of its power to choose.

Rāmānuja is aware of this second threat to the *ātman's* moral freedom as he is of the first. He cites several scriptural passages which seem to support the teaching that "the activity of the individual soul proceeds from the highest Self as its cause."[167] For instance, the Gītā says: "The Lord, O Arjuna, dwells in the heart of all creatures, whirling by his mysterious power, all creatures as if mounted on a machine."[168] Rāmānuja argues that if such scriptures were denials of the individual's freedom because of its dependence on Īśvara, then "the whole body of scriptural injunctions and prohibitions would be unmeaning."[169] The reason is straightforward. "Commandments can be addressed to such agents only as are capable of entering on action or refraining from action, according to their own thought and will."[170]

Rāmānuja tries to reconcile divine sovereignty and human responsibility by making the free activity of the individual contingent upon the will of God. He explains:

> The inwardly ruling highest Self promotes action in so far as it regards in the case of any action the volitional effort made by the individual soul, and then aids the effort by granting it favour or permission (anumati); action is not possible without permission on the part of the highest Self. In this way (i.e. since the action primarily depends on the volitional effort of the soul) injunctions and prohibitions are not devoid of meaning. The 'and the rest' of the Sutra is meant to suggest the grace and punishments awarded by the Lord. The case is analogous to that of property of which two men are joint owners. If one of these wishes to transfer that property to a third person he cannot do so without the permission of his partner but that that permission is given is after all his own doing, and hence the fruit of the action (reward or anything) properly belongs to him only.[171]

Thus, human freedom is preserved because men are free to choose without divine interference; but since this freedom is permitted by God, ultimately, it is He who is the subject of all actions. "Thus the Lord himself says, 'I am the origin of all, everything proceeds from me; knowing this the wise worship me with love. To them ever devoted, worshipping me in love, I give that means of wisdom by which they attain to me. In mercy only to them, dwelling in their hearts, do I destroy the darkness born of ignorance, with the brilliant light of knowledge."[172]

Though the *ātman* has affinity with God and is distinct from *prakṛti,* it ignorantly identifies itself with the body in which it resides. This ignorance is the source of all sin and suffering in the world. It binds the *ātman* to the body and makes it the slave of pain and pleasure arising from the body. It breeds a selfish attitude toward others and obscures the *ātman's* dependence on God.[173]

Since all acts have their inevitable consequences, an individual's past acts, freely chosen, determine his future existence. In this way he gets caught in the wheel of rebirth and death. The *ātman* itself does not die, nor is it reborn. These changes only belong to the bodies with which the *ātman* is associated. Though it is immortal, because of its false identification with the body, it appears to be mortal. Thus, through *karman* and *avidyā,* the *ātman* remains in the bondage of *saṁsāra.*

How can the *ātman* be delivered from this life of endless suffering?

Since activity motivated by the hope for reward binds the *ātman* to *prakṛti,* the first thing the *ātman* must do to escape this bondage is to eliminate all desire for results, including the desire for heaven which is the reward for virtuosity. This is accomplished by *karmayoga. Karmayoga,* followed by *jñānayoga* and *bhaktiyoga,* constitutes the first of successive levels reaching up to communion with God. These are not separate paths but separate stages, integrally related to one another. Rāmānuja considered them essential elements of Gītā doctrine.

Karmayoga is the primary stage of moral discipline. It is a *via media* between excessively activistic and ascetic moral perspectives. Its ideal of conduct is *niṣkāmakarma*—the performance of necessary actions without any egoistic desires. It advocates renunciation in action rather than renunciation of action.

Commenting on the important role of *karmayoga* within the moral life, Rāmānuja expands upon Gītā 3.19:

> No activity in executing a means is required if a person does no longer depend on a means for his contemplation of the *ātman*. When, however, such activity is still required, then *karmayoga* is the best means to execute, because it is easy to execute, does not cause a person to be negligent about it, implies true knowledge of the ātman and because even a *jñānayogin* is compelled to be active in order to exist; therefore one should perform acts disinterestedly until one has attained the *ātman*. That *karmayoga* is indeed the best means even for a *jñānayogin* is proved by the fact that the *rājarṣis,* who were the first of the *jñānins,* have also availed themselves of *karmayoga* to attain the *ātman.*[174]

The preceding passage makes it abundantly clear that Rāmānuja considered the ethics of duty for duty's sake of great importance.[175] The duties included those pertaining to the *varṇas* and *āśramas.*[176] They enable the aspirant to distinguish between the immortal *ātman* and perishable *prakṛti.* They help "purify the worshipping aspirant of his previous *karman* which is incompatible with his worship."[177] Along with the destruction of past accretions of *karman,* duties performed in the spirit of dedication to God, strengthen the sattvic nature of the *ātman* and enable it to behold the truth of things.[178]

The character of the man of duty reflects poise and equanimity. He neither gloats over success nor groans under failure.[179] At all times and in all places he remains calm, subdued, patient, satisfied, and collected.[180] Having freed his spirit of *rāga* and *kāma,* his work itself becomes worship.[181]

Karmayoga prepares the way for *jñānayoga.* Selfless acts destroy the cumulative effects of bad *karman* and thereby expand the *ātman's* capacity for knowledge. The true knowledge that is acquired by *jñāna-yoga* consists in constantly realising that "the *ātman* is a different entity from *prakṛti*;"[182] that God is our Inner Self; and that as modes of his substance we are dependent upon him.

The precise relation between *karmayoga* and *jñānayoga* is difficult to determine. Several passages conflict with one another.[183] Van Buitenen's conclusion on the subject is worth noting. He says:

> It seems to me that Rāmānuja attempted to reconcile both methods of the Gītā, and starting from the emphatically preferable *Karma Yoga* tried to

> reinterpret *jñāna yoga.* By introducing an element of jñāna into *karma yoga* itself, both disciplines could be stated in the terms of a continuity: *jñāna yoga* is now no longer a separate way—as such it is repeatedly condemned—but an advanced stage of *karma yoga.* From Rāmānuja's point of view *karma yoga* has two 'aspects', knowledge and action. That knowledge is originally the mediate, more or less 'abstract' knowledge of the *ātman,* corresponding with the *sāṃkhye buddhiḥ* of the Gītā. This knowledge is acted upon: interested action becomes disinterested action. Gradually (the process may take several lives) knowledge and action interact more directly; knowledge becoming more and more integrated in action, is concretized, action is spiritualized and interiorized, until at last both culminate in yoga where the *ātman* is recognized, *karma yoga* terminates in *jñāna yoga* and mediate, abstract knowledge is completely concretized in immediate intuitive perception *(sākṣātkāra).*[184]

Thus the integrated efforts of *karmayoga* and *jñānayoga* lead the aspirant to *yoga* which is the recognition of the *ātman* in himself and in others. Rāmānuja states that there are four degrees at the highest stage of development.

a) The *ātmans* of all creatures are equal when their proper form is separated from *prakṛti,* for all of them have one and the same form, knowledge; inequality is of *prakṛti.* This proves that a person who has brought his *ātman* into *yoga* will see similarity in all *ātmans* when separated from *prakṛti;* he will see that his own *ātman* is in all beings and that all beings are in his own *ātman;* in other words he will see that his own *ātman* has the same form as the *ātmans* of all other beings and contrariwise, so that he has seen all that is *ātman* when he has seen one *ātman.*
b) A man who has reached the highest stage of development and in the said manner views the equality of God and an *ātman* when the latter exists in its proper form beyond good and evil, will view God in all *ātmans* and all *ātmans* in God; in virtue of their mutual equality he will see by the one what is the other. That man indeed views the proper form of the *ātman* and God is equal to that form of the *ātman;* nor will man vanish out of the sight of God who views in him Himself, when in virtue of his equality to God he views his *ātman* as the equal of God.
c) At which stage will *yoga* develop into full maturity? When a yogin views his *ātman* in all beings becomes one with them because all have the same form of unrestricted knowledge, and when he renounces the differences of the *prakṛti* and devotes himself steadfastly to God, then—whatever condition he is in, even at the moment of awaking from *yoga*—he will always view his equality to God in his own *ātman* and in all beings.
d) He reaches the summit when he no longer perceives any difference between happiness and suffering of his own *ātman* and those of their *ātmans* inasmuch as his *ātman* and the *ātmans* of other beings are mutually comparable and as all *ātmans* are equal and have no relations.[185]

It is clearly manifest from this quotation that the ethics of interpersonal relationships has a solid foundation in *jñānayoga*. It asserts that all *ātmans* are similar, possessing common qualities. Distinctions of caste are at best relevant to the body, and have nothing to do with the essential nature of the *ātman*. Furthermore, *ātmans* are not simply equal but sacredly equal, being similar to God. An enlightened man cannot, therefore, love God and hate his fellows. Conversely, when he serves his fellows he worships God.[186] Moreover, it is not enough to contemplate such equalitarian thoughts in *yoga;* they must be habitually practised in everyday life. The highest stage is reached when one acts upon this knowledge by never again distinguishing between one's own *ātman* and the *ātmans* of others.

Jñānayoga leads to *bhaktiyoga*. "*Bhakti* or devotion is a vague term extending from the lowest form of worship to the highest life of realisation. It has a continuous history in India from the time of the Ṛg Veda to the present day."[187] For Rāmānuja, *bhakti* stands for the steady contemplation of the mind on God "because one loves God so dearly that one is unable to exist separated from his being, qualities, acts and dominion."[188] Rāmānuja explains the proper form of *bhakti* thus:

> One must focus one's mind constantly on God in all his glory. When focusing one's mind on God one must be animated by the most ardent love for God and perform sacrifices for the glory of God because one recognizes Him as the incomparably adorable One. But one must not stop at merely exerting oneself in this manner; one must resolve to prostrate oneself before God who is one's inner ātman. Then, when one has found one's sole support on God and in virtue of boundless and unsurpassed love enabled one's mind to experience Him, one should attain Him.[189]

Thus *bhaktiyoga* culminates in an intuitive realisation of God "who in his form of perfect bliss is most dear to his worshipper."[190] *Bhakti* is everlasting, "for once a man has attained God he will lose it never more."[191]

Now let us examine some of the ethical facets of *bhaktiyoga*.

First of all, the elaborate preparation for *bhakti* brings out its moral structure. The Śrībhāṣya states: "The highest self can be apprehended only by the mind purified by meditation on that Self."[192] This meditation is assisted by seven means: abstention *(viveka)*, freeness of mind *(vimoka)*, repetition *(abhyāsa)*, works *(kriyā)*, virtuous conduct *(kalyāṇa)*, freedom from dejection *(anavasāda)*, abstention from exultation *(anuddharṣa)*.[193] The moral elements of this discipline require some exposition.

Abstention refers to discrimination of food. "As a man eats, so becomes his mind," warns the Chāndogya Upaniṣad.[194] The *psyche* must be supported by the *soma*.[195]

"Freeness of mind" means the absence of attachment to desires. The desires to be eliminated are sexual passion, anger, vanity, jealousy, acquisitiveness.[196]

"Repetition" means the continuous focusing of the mind on God. As a man thinks, so he becomes, and there is no better object of thought than God.[197]

By "works" is understood "the performance, according to one's ability, of the five great sacrifices." In addition to sacred study and the offering of oblations to the gods and the manes, it includes hospitality to guests and the offering of food to the lowliest of animals.[198]

Virtuous conduct means the practice of "truthfulness, honesty, kindness, liberality, gentleness, and the absence of covetousness."[199]

Freedom from dejection means one is unaffected by "that lowness of spirit of want of cheerfulness which results from unfavourable conditions of place or time and the remembrance of causes of sorrow."[200]

By abstention from exultation is meant the possession of such character that one is not swept off his feet by the elation of joy and allurements.[201]

These seven means to the development of *bhakti* show that morality is an essential content of *bhakti.* "Bhakti is not mere emotionalism, but includes the training of the will as well as the intellect. It is knowledge of God as well as obedience to his will."[202]

A second ethical facet of *bhaktiyoga* lies in its activism. For all its emphasis on *prasāda* (grace), the importance of the devotee's personal efforts is never minimized.[203] Love, prayer, devotion, and dedication are all human efforts which serve as indirect means to attaining God. "Man's active life becomes thus dedicated to the One from whom he derives his acting power."[204] Of course, despite all of his own efforts, the devotee can never be confident that he loves God sufficiently, and, therefore, beseeches God for the grace to know him and love him.

Acts are important in man's progress to God but so are intentions. The outer life is integrated with the inner life, and the latter determines the consequences of the former. Rāmāñuja exclaims:

> How wondrous is this difference that, though devoting themselves to one and the same act, some partake of a very small reward and then fall back by nature and others partake of reward which means the attainment of God—that is perfect boundless bliss—, for the mere reason that both differ in their intentions![205]

Commenting on the Gītā text Rāmānuja goes on to show the importance of the worshipper's intentions.

> Those who intend worshipping Indra etc. will go to the gods; those who intend worshipping the deceased ancestors will go to them; those who intend

worshipping ghosts will go to them. Those, however, who worship God while uttering the intention: Let us worship by these same sacrifices the Supreme Ātman himself, the Lord Vāsudeva whose body is constituted by gods, deceased ancestors and ghosts,—those will go to God and never return.[206]

Worshippers of God are also distinguished according to their intentions. Quoting the Mahābhārata, Rāmānuja points out:

> There are votaries who lovingly offer God a leaf, a flower, a fruit or water, things which are available to anyone. If someone offers God such a leaf etc. with pious intention, this offering being his sole object because his uncommon love for God urges him on to make this offering, then God will even accept this leaf etc. and partake of them because He will hold them dear, although He can never have experience of anything but Himself and although this leaf etc. are foreign to his desire.[207]

A fourth moral facet of *bhaktiyoga* lies in its universality. All beings are equal for God. Rāmānuja says:

> Being a refuge for all God is the same toward all atmans of gods, men, animals, and immovables, which, according to their class, configuration, nature and knowledge, exists in an infinite plurality of forms, from the highest to the lowest. No one who has resorted to God will be abandoned by God because his humble class, configuration, nature and knowledge is odious to Him, and no one who has resorted to God together with a humbler votary is more beloved of God because of his more exalted class etc. All beings who worship God by bhakti—whether they be an exalted or humble class—will at their desire foregather in God as if they share his virtues, and God himself will dwell in them as if they are more exalted than He.[208]

Even the man who has transgressed the rules of class to which he belongs, should he be exclusively devoted to God, has the right to be "regarded as a leading Vaisnava" and esteemed highly.[209]

Bhaktiyoga and its two nonseparable auxiliaries, *jñānayoga* and *karmayoga,* constitute one path to salvation. An alternate means is found in *prapatti.* In the Śrībhāṣya, Rāmānuja allows for options between several meditations "on account of the non-difference of result."[210] *Prapatti* is accepted as a second means, because it, too, issues in the intuitive knowledge of *Brahman.*

Rāmānuja is silent on this doctrine in the Gītābhāṣya and Śrībhāṣya. He treats of it in his Gadyatraya, and apologizes for its earlier omission:

> I bow down to that doctrine of refuge which was concealed by me even in the Sribhasya, but which is brought to light in the Gadyatraya.[211]

The path of salvation represented by *karmayoga, jñānayoga* and *bhaktiyoga* is not accessible to whomsoever would desire it. Study of the scriptures, pilgrimages, building temples, rigorous disciplines, and a host of other details take their toll in terms of learning, money, concentration, and hard work which the majority of people can ill afford. Does this mean that the doors of salvation are only open to the elite among men? Surely not! Those who find the path of *bhakti* too difficult to follow can choose *prapatti.*

Prapatti is the absolute surrender of one's individuality to God. This attitude of self-surrender is present also in *bhakti,* but while the attitude is the same the method is different. "*Prapatti* method is simple in the sense that here the devotee is not in need of any external *'sādhana'* to purify his outer organs. A single moment of serious and sincere offering of oneself to God is considered "enough; and as it is immediate and non-laborious, it is regarded as superior to *bhaktiyoga.*"[212]

Prapatti is distinguished by six elements. They are harmonising one's will with the divine will; renouncing behaviour displeasing to God; confidence in divine protection; choosing God as Saviour of all; feeling hopelessly inadequate to pursue the path of *bhaktiyoga*; and resigning oneself wholly to God. The last factor is coterminus with *prapatti*; the five earlier ones are contributive to it.

When the heart of the devotee has been purified by *prapatti,* a certain character emerges as its logical and ethical consequence, marked by freedom from egoistic impulses, immortal bliss, and charity for all beings.

CHAPTER 4

Summary and Critical Résumé of Hindu Ethics

The *summum bonum* in Hinduism is to break the ties of individuality which bind one to this world and to realize oneness with *Brahman.* Man must strive toward this spiritual ideal by cultivating a life of contemplation and progressive resignation from the world. Looked at purely from this philosophical ideal, it seems that ethics, which defines man's active role in the world, is of little significance in Hinduism; that it is only a temporary detour from the royal road of philosophy, a shift in direction that is necessitated by man's involvement with the phenomenal world.

There is no denying the fact that in Hinduism, the philosophical ideal does indeed transcend the ethical ideal, but, like the rungs of a ladder, the higher and lower are intrinsically connected so that you cannot get to the one without the other. The philosophical ideal is higher than the ethical, but the ethical is the staging ground for the philosophical, and, as such, cannot be underestimated. Thus, while Hinduism draws a sharp distinction between the spiritual and material, the eternal and temporal, these dimensions of existence are not polarised but correlated within the concept of *dharma. Dharma* is "a unique joint product of the speculative and practical wisdom of the Hindus."[1]

The unity between philosophical wisdom and ethical excellence is clearly illustrated in the doctrine of *adhikāra.* This doctrine teaches that before a disciple can aspire after knowledge, he must first be morally qualified. The Upaniṣads are replete with references correlating *prajñāna* or saving knowledge with moral practice.

> Who has not ceased from evil ways,
> Who is untranquil, unprepared,

Or whose mind is not at peace,
By knowledge cannot win to him.[2]

Commenting on this verse, Rāmānuja explains it "teaches that meditation, which should become more perfect day by day, cannot be accomplished without the devotee having broken with all evil. This is the indispensable condition of pleasing the Lord and winning His grace."[3]

The truth of the *adhikāra* doctrine lies in the fact that rationality cannot be divorced from morality. Just as a sound mind requires a sound body, a sound philosophy requires a sound ethics. Prof. S. K. Saksena points out:

> If we analyze the behaviour of a truly rational man, we are sure to find a number of qualities in him which will prove to be moral. To be rational, for instance, is not to be partisan, or to have prejudices, or to be swayed by passions or self-interest, or to falsify truth, or to have double standards, but it is to stand for truth under all conditions, etc. These are moral qualities. In fact, to be rational is to be moral, and to be completely rational is to be completely moral. The moral and spiritual qualification of a philosopher is, therefore, a condition of his philosophizing properly. Passion or ethical failings cannot but distort the vision of even a philosopher. In fact, what is called intuition is not so much an independent faculty as a purity of the moral being of the knower which itself constitutes enlightenment.[4]

The moral discipline which Hinduism enjoins upon the seeker after philosophical truth springs from a comprehensive ethic. Hindu ethics is a systematic progression from the objective level to the subjective level, culminating on the super-ethical level. The first is the stage of social ethics; the second that of personal ethics; and the third is the ultimate end which is "the life absolute and transcendental."[5]

In its objective aspect, Hindu *dharma* is tridimensional. Social duties are classified as: (1) *Āśramadharma,* (2) *Varṇadharma,* (3) *Sādhāraṇadharma.*

The *Āśrama* scheme provides the framework within which an individual may express the total needs of his personality. These needs are incorporated within the doctrine of the four ends of life or *puruṣārthas,* and are identified as: *kāma, artha, dharma,* and *mokṣa.* The *puruṣārtha* doctrine constitutes the psychomoral basis of *Āśramadharma.*

The theory of the four *puruṣārthas* perceives human personality as a complex organism. It recognizes an empirical side to life, represented by the first three *puruṣārthas,* having natural desires and social aims. Man is conceived as naturally craving for sex, and feeling the need for wealth, power, and the realization of the common good. It also recognizes a spiritual side to life marked by otherworldly hungers. Moreover, both these sides are integrated within a holistic view of man. Thus, the *puruṣārtha* doctrine allows for no schism between desire and aspiration, or between the demands of the kingdom of earth and of heaven. Both are good when viewed relationally. True, the earth perishes while heaven abides, but to treat the perishable as nonexisting is to invite ruin. As the Upaniṣad states it: "In darkness are they who worship only the world, but in greater darkness they who worship the infinite alone. He who accepts both saves himself from death by the knowledge of the former and attains immortality by the knowledge of the latter."

The first ideal which every normal, intelligent person should strive to fulfil is that of *kāma.* This value refers to any pleasure derived through the five senses, and is under the control of the mind. *Kāma* includes sensuous enjoyments found in art, music, literature, and in sexual activity.

Sexual pleasure was deemed the best form of legitimate pleasure. Prof. A. L. Basham reminds us that Hindu religious and secular literature is replete with sexual allusions, symbolism, and undisguised eroticism.[6] In the Middle Ages the sex act was divinized to illustrate the process of creation, and figures of couples in close embrace were elaborately carved on temple walls. The celebration of sex reached its most exaggerated form with the introduction of ritual intercourse by certain religious sects. But this extreme form of sexual religiosity in the later Middle Ages was "only an expression of the vigorous sexuality which was to be found in Indian social life at all times."[7] Westerners who fault Hinduism for creating an ethos of asceticism must find this somewhat difficult to reconcile with Hindu India's population explosion!

The second need of human personality is *artha.* This value is cognisant of the economic and political needs of man. Property and power are productive means for developing personality. Through numerous passages, wealth is praised not only for its contribution to the physical well-being of personality, but also for its potency in bringing about a sense of social significance and political prestige. Wealth is said to transform a man of low social status into one of high status. He who possesses it can overcome all obstacles. No kith or kin can do for one what wealth can do. Contrary to the adage, "money is the root of all evil," Hinduism teaches that "all the virtues attach themselves to gold."

A paramount virtue connected with wealth is liberality. "Let the rich satisfy the poor; and keep in view the long pathway. Riches come now to one, now to another, and like the wheels of cars are ever turning."

Artha was deemed especially important for the king. "Let him be the Lord of endless treasures; let him as king be the master of the people. Grant him great power and strength; let his enemies be deprived of strength and vigor."[8]

Such prayers are found not only in the literature of the early Vedic period, but also in the contemplative literature of the Upaniṣads. The following is a typical Upaniṣadic prayer: "May I become glorious among men! Hail! May *I* be better than the very rich! Hail!"[9] Contrary to the popular notion that *artha* is downgraded in the Upaniṣadic literature, it must be recalled that all the teachers of the major Upaniṣads were property holders. Of course, there was Yājñavalkya, the most eminent of them all, who renounced the world and its riches—but only after he had enjoyed domestic bliss in the company of two wives.

While it is good for man to possess, it is evil when the possessor becomes the possessed. As long as *artha* is guided by *dharma* it is a blessing; but *artha* without *dharma* is a bane. Even when controlled by *dharma,* the value of *artha* is limited. This brings us to the third *puruṣārtha—dharma. Dharma* is one of the oldest philosophical concepts. Its roots go deep into Vedic soil, germinating in the idea of *ṛta.* The long history of this concept shows that Hindu anthropology has been morally conceived from earliest times. Prof. K. N. Upadhyaya states:

> The persistence and intensity with which the inquiry into *dharma* has been pursued in India is mainly on account of the firm conviction of the Indian people that *dharma* constitutes the differentia of man, whereby he is distinguished from brutes, just as in the West, following Aristotle, rationality is regarded as the distinguishing mark of man. This approach at once reveals . . . that what is most vital to man's life is not his mental, but his moral and spiritual nature.[10]

Dharma is formed from the root *'dhṛ',* to hold, and connotes what upholds a thing and supports it in being. In its broadest sense, *dharma* represents the ethical laws of the universe which regulate the moral life in the same way as the laws of nature govern the physical world. The universe is moral because it is divine. "The world of inorganic and organic nature is not just an evolution of an unconscious material power or force creating and expressing itself in a world of greater complexity and heterogeneity by its own unconscious dialectic. It is a world of divine and spiritual immanence with the fullest reality of moral values and forces flowing from *Śakti,* or the power of God."[11]

Since life in the universe is morally structured, a man must bring all of his warring passions under this principle of righteousness, both for his own good and for the good of society. This brings us close to the meaning of *dharma* in the context of a *puruṣārtha.* Here it refers to the performance of right action out of a consciousness of moral law. The effects of virtuous actions are conserved as merit which bears good fruit in the future.

We have already mentioned that *kāma* and *artha* are to be regulated by *dharma*. The rationale for this hierarchy of values is that whereas *kāma* is born or *tamas guṇa* (inertia), and *artha* is born of *rajas guṇa* (energy), the source of *dharma* is *sattva guṇa* (purity)—the highest of the three fundamental qualities of nature. On the basis of this criterion, Manu states that "wealth and happiness, which are repugnant to righteousness, must be discarded."[12]

Knowledge of one's own *dharma* or *'svadharma'* as the Bhagavadgītā puts it, is possible for the common man through a fourfold guide: (1) the Vedas, (2) the *smṛtis* which are the expositions of Vedic wisdom, (3) the conduct of righteous men, and (4) your own conscience.[13]

The three *puruṣārthas* studied thus far represent the ideals of empirical existence. They recognize and provide for the balanced satisfaction of all human desires for worldly pleasures. It is to be regretted that these Hindu values are not emphasised sufficiently, especially in view of their "formative influence on the everyday life" of the Indian people reaching back into ancient times.[14]

However, higher than the desires of the empirical self are the aspirations of the spiritual self. When Naciketas was given the opportunity to receive pleasures here or in the hereafter, he exclaims:

> Ephemeral things! That which is a mortal's, O End-maker,
> Even the vigor *(tejas)* of all the powers, they wear away.
> Even a whole life is slight indeed.
> Thine be the vehicles *(vaha)*! Thine be the dance and song![15]

In the same spirit, Maitreyī asks Yājñavalkya when he was about to leave her: "If now, sir, this whole earth filled with wealth were mine, would I be immortal thereby?" Her sage husband replies in the negative: "As the life of the rich, even so would your life be. Of immortality, however, there is no hope through wealth."[16]

Immortality or *mokṣa* constitutes the fourth and highest *puruṣārtha*. It is the state of liberation wherein the spiritual self comes into its own. When correctly pursued, *kāma, artha,* and *dharma* lead to *mokṣa*. *Mokṣa* is not the denial of these values but their fulfilment.

Thus, on the basis of our study of the doctrine of the four *puruṣārthas* we find that Hindu ethics is a rich compendium of elements in life which less imaginative systems have deemed exclusive and antagonistic. Its complex anthropology permits it to blend activism with renunciation, and the empirical with the spiritual. Its view of man is not only holistic but optimistic. As in the case of the *Āśramadharmas* and *Varṇadharmas,* the *puruṣārthas* are based on "the principle of the progressive realization of the spirit."[17]

The structure of existence defined by the *puruṣārthas* calls for a correlative social structure through which human nature in all of its variegated forms is actualised. This is supplied in the *Āśrama* scheme. Not only does this scheme channel the individual's natural inclinations, it is a practical outlet for his sense of social obligations formalised in the great ethical concept of the 'Three Debts' *(ṛṇas).*

Before a person qualifies for *mokṣa,* he must pay off vital obligations incurred as a member of the family of man. There is the debt to the *ṛṣis (ṛṣi-ṛṇa)* who have served as the revealers of truth contained in the Vedas. This is repaid by passing through the *Brahmacarya āśrama* in which the Vedas are studied according to the prescribed rules *(vidhivat).* Then there is the debt to the ancestors *(pitṛ-ṛṇa).* This is repaid by passing through the *Gārhasthya āśrama.* The householder procreates many sons in accordance with *dharma (dharmataḥ)* and thereby ensures the perpetuation of his own family and that of the human race.[18] The third debt is to the deities *(deva-ṛṇa).* It is reciprocated by performing the sacrificial duties of the *Vānaprasthya āśrama* according to one's ability *(saktitaḥ).*

Like the *puruṣārthas,* the *ṛṇas* also bespeak an affirmative approach to life. Both doctrines demonstrate the necessity for accepting and appreciating that which is given in nature and in society as good. But the *ṛṇas* insist that it is more blessed to give than to receive! This goodwill is motivated by a grateful sense of being involved in mankind—the complete opposite of isolation and retreat with which Hinduism is so often maligned. In the spirit of the *ṛṇas,* a Hindu sage could well have uttered the words of John Donne: ". . . any man's death diminishes me . . . and therefore never send to know for whom the bell tolls; It tolls for thee."[19]

Having explored the 'Four Ends of Life' and examined the three springs of social obligation, we are now prepared to investigate the ethical organization in which the *puruṣārthas* are realized and the *ṛṇas* redeemed. The Hindu philosophers, unlike their Western counterparts, were not content with theorizing about life. They were practical enough to organize the life of the individual in such a way that he would have ample scope to fulfil himself. This organization for the individual life is known as *Āśramadharma.*

Āśramadharma enjoins that each individual pass through four stages in the quest after his true self. These stages are: *Brahmacarya,* the stage of studentship; *gārhasthya,* the period of the householder; *Vānaprasthya,* the stage as a forest-dweller; and *Saṁnyāsa,* the stage of complete renunciation. As the term *āśrama* suggests, each of these stages is looked upon as a resting place as well as a training ground.

During the formative period of eight to twelve years, the student attaches himself to a teacher who is now looked upon as a spiritual parent.

His objectives are threefold: to acquire knowledge (sacred and secular), to develop character, and to learn to assume social responsibility. He progresses at his own pace and pursues learning as an end in itself and not as a means for material gain. He submits to an austere discipline aimed at helping him conserve his energy and build a strong mind and body. Upon completion of studies, the *brahmacārin* takes a bath, symbolic of his graduation, and thereby becomes a *snātaka* or one who has taken a bath. The Taittirīya Upaniṣad is famous for its "Convocation Address" which we repeat here because it provides a clear description of the ethical teachings which characterized Hindu education from ancient times:

> Speak the truth.
> Practise virtue *(dharma)*.
> Neglect not study [of the Vedas].
> Having brought an acceptable gift to the teacher, cut not off the line of progeny.
> One should not be negligent of truth.
> One should not be negligent of virtue.
> One should not be negligent of welfare.
> One should not be negligent of prosperity.
> One should not be negligent of study and teaching.
> One should not be negligent of duties to the gods and to the fathers.
> Be one to whom a mother is a god.
> Be one to whom a father is a god.
> Be one to whom a teacher is a god.
> Those acts which are irreproachable should be practised, and no others.
> Those things which among us are good deeds should be revered by you, and no others.
> Whatever Brahmans *(brāhmaṇa)* are superior to us, for them refreshment with a seat should be procured by you.
> One should give with faith *(śraddhā)*.
> One should not give without faith.
> One should give with plenty *(śrī)*.
> One should give with modesty.
> One should give with fear.
> One should give with sympathy *(sam-vid)*.
> Now, if you should have doubt concerning an act, or doubt concerning conduct, if there should be there Brahmans competent to judge, apt, devoted, not harsh, lovers of virtue *(dharma)*—as they may behave themselves in such a case, so should you behave yourself in such a case.[20]

The young man is now at the stage when he must take unto himself a wife and begin living the life of a householder. Marriage binds couples with sacramental ties and sets them on a journey of righteous living. In the Śāntiparva, the Mahābhārata emphasises the place of highest honour ascribed to the *Gārhasthya āśrama*. Manu is equally emphatic upon the pivotal significance of *Gārhasthya āśrama* within the body politic. Rāmānuja only admitted those candidates into the monastic life who had first passed through the householder stage. But there was always room for exceptions, as in the case of Śaṅkara who renounced the householder's life in favour of a life of knowledge.

The householder engages in *artha* and *kāma* within the limits set by *dharma*. Daily, he recites the Vedas, offers water to the ancestors, sacrifices to the gods, offers sustenance to all beings, and exercises the proverbial hospitality of the Indians. He undertakes these sacrifices out of a respect for learning, pride of family solidarity, dependence on the divine, and a thankful spirit that wants him share the good things in life with man and beast. Thus, the characteristic mark of the *gṛhastha* is that of *dāna* or giving.

Dāna is also a virtue of the householder's wife, especially in her roles of wife and mother. Śaṅkara says, "A bad son may be born, but there never is a bad mother." The mother of a home is loved and revered as a presiding deity. Her honour is higher than that of father or teacher. Without her, a man is not a man, and a home is not a home. The functions of a woman are quite different to that of a man, but unfortunately the difference is mistaken for inferiority. At the same time, it should be admitted that women are restricted by certain religious and social regulations. Most of these restrictions were later developments, and were the consequences of females from backward cultures being assimilated into Āryan society. Men then began to think of women as weak, emotional, and unstable, and, therefore, in need of constant protection by the "stronger sex."

When the householder finds his hair grown grey, his skin wrinkled, and he is a grandfather, it is time for him to leave his family and village, and seek retirement in the forest *(vāna)*. His wife may accompany him if she cares. *Gārhasthya āśrama* is not an end in itself. It is the matrix in which all one's capacities are moralised and socialised, but beyond the social good is a higher value. As one passage states it: "For the family sacrifice the individual; for the community the family; for the country the community; and for the soul the whole world." At the *Vānaprasthya* stage the individual begins sacrificing all of his earlier responsibilities and pleasures in the interests of his soul. He now wants to be alone with the Alone. He knows: "the last part of life's road has to be walked in single file."[21]

To develop spiritual awareness, the *Vānaprastha* espouses a life of rigorous austerity. All avenues of sensuous excitement are kept under tight control. He lives as a strict celibate, eating fruits and vegetables only, and dwelling under the trees. Through penances *(tapas)* he curbs his bodily appetites and strengthens the power of his soul. Studying the scriptures and performing religious sacrifices with undisturbed attention not possible as a householder, he advances in knowledge and acquires merit. His compassion reaches out to all men and to all creatures. Should he die in this stage, he goes to the region of *Brahmā.*[22]

The *Vānaprasthya* stage is probationary to the final stage of *Saṁnyāsa*. The *sannyāsin* completely renounces the world. His sole purpose is to realize spiritual freedom and to become one with the divine. Surrendering the world, he essentially surrenders his consciousness of "I." Without the sense of "mineness," the *Sannyāsin* develops an evenness of temper and calmness of mind. No more is he impatient, touchy, or hateful. Circumstances may change around him, but inwardly he is above all vicissitudes. He extinguishes all desires, wanting neither life nor death. Mystically united with the Absolute, the *Sannyāsin* treats all life as sacred. He sees everything and everybody through cosmic eyes. "These *sannyāsins* do not serve our policies that make the world unsafe for human life, do not promote our industries that mechanize persons, and do not support our national egoisms that provoke wars. Patriotism is not enough for these fine souls. Life, and not India's life or England's life, demands their devotion. They look upon all men and all groups as equal *(samatā sarvasmin)*."[23]

The preceding description should not suggest that the *Sannyāsin* makes no contribution to the society which he has renounced. To the contrary, he is a living proof that spiritual freedom is possible, that man can perfect himself in this world, and that, though the masses live on the level of selfishness and chauvinism, the brotherhood of man is not an impossible dream. Thus, the *Sannyāsin* is the embodiment of the essential humanity of the people, its ground for hope, and its promise for fulfilment. "When the wick is ablaze at its tip, the whole lamp is said to be burning."[24]

Having described the ethical organization of the individual life, what do we consider to be some of its strengths and weaknesses? First, the institution of *Āśramadharma* is a unique contribution of Hindu religion and philosophy to human ideals. Perhaps the only parallel to this type of scheme is found in Plato's *Republic.* Second, unlike other traditional systems of ethics that legislate uniformity with only token deference to individual plurality, the discipline *Āśramadharma* is genetically oriented. It is adapted to the progressive development of a person's body, mind, and spirit, and defines responsibility in terms of the relation of duty to capacity. Third, its holistic view of man recognizes congeries of human needs, and systematically brings them to fruition on successsive levels of maturation, corresponding to youth, adulthood, and retirement. A person is considered *right* for a particular stage when he is *ripe* for that stage. Here, ethics is not only seen to be connected with philosophy and theology, but also with biology and psychology. Fourth, *Āśramadharma* is to be commended for its faith in human dignity and capacity. Contrary to ethical theories that claim to be realistic, assuming the depravity of man, *Āśramadharma* assumes that given the proper nurture, every man has the inner ability to meet all his debts to nature, God, and man, and to advance through progressive nonattachment to a state of spiritual freedom.

Today, *Āśramadharma* is restricted to the two stages of *Gārhasthya* and *Saṁnyāsa,* but all the ideals of the fourfold plan still influence Hindu culture. Unfortunately, instead of genuine monks coming out of households in which they have led full, responsible, and productive lives, the majority of India's holy men have donned saffron garbs to escape the harsh realities of life. The common people, grown accustomed to the ideal of freely supplying the material needs of persons who have taken up the life of holiness, unwittingly lend aid and comfort to charlatans in sadhu's clothing. Bemoaning the degradation of so noble an ideal, Prof. S. K. Saksena comments on how cheats can thrive on charity. "People are expected to see that no holy man is ever in need of shelter or his daily ration of food. This explains why millions of persons in India even without requisite moral or spiritual qualifications are still flourishing today under the titles of swami and sadhu. In no other culture or religion, could we have found so many millions of human beings living with perfect respectability or prestige without working for their livelihood."[25]

Happily, efforts have been made to offset this exploitative and unproductive image of the Hindu holy man. In modern times, Swami Vivekananda (1863–1902), applying the teachings of his Master Sri Ramakrishna (1836–1886) to the practical demands of national life, made the order of *Sannyāsins* exemplary for society, not just in terms of religious devotion and spiritual achievement, but in social service and relief work for the suffering and downtrodden.

We now move from the ethical organization of the individual represented by *Āśramadharma,* to the ethical organization of society represented by *Varṇadharma.* Both *dharmas* are coordinated, forming a composite system. Whereas the organization of *Āśramadharma* approaches life from the side of nurture *(śrama),* training it through successive stages, the organization of *Varṇadharma* approaches life from the side of nature *(guṇa),* defining the role of the individual in society by virtue of natural tendencies and innate dispositions.

The Sanskrit word *'varṇa'* literally means 'colour'. Originally, it was connected with the class structure of the Vedic Āryan tribesmen. It is scientifically inaccurate to apply the meaning of 'caste' to *varṇa*. Prof. A. L. Basham clarifies the confusion:

> There are only four *varṇas*. There never have been less than four or more than four. It is said that at the present time there are 3000 castes, and the number of castes is known to have risen, and perhaps has sometimes fallen, over the past 2000 years. Caste and *varṇa* are quite different institutions, different in origin, different in purpose, and different in function.[26]

Originally, the class structure was devised to promote a functional harmony between the various segments of society. Society was conceived of as constituting four distinct types. The Brahmins belonged to the first type. They were the priest-teachers. Due to the prevalence of *sattva guṇas* in their nature, they were capable of living on an exalted plane of intellect and purity. The Kṣatriyas belonged to the second type. They were the warrior-kings. Possessing a large portion of *rajas guṇa,* they demonstrated uncommon virility, and were primarily men of action. The Vaiśyas belonged to the third type. They were traders and craftsmen. The dominance of *tamas guṇas* made them into men of feeling. The Śūdras belonged to the fourth type. They were manual labourers. Their professions reflected the fact that none of the aforementioned traits were significantly developed in them.

Modern Hindus consider the reasoning behind the original classification of society valid for all times. Realistically speaking, all men are not created equal. There is no democracy in nature. Some men are naturally endowed to become scholars, teachers, rulers and administrators; others are martially equipped to serve as protectors of the nation; others seem to have a yen for commercial enterprises; and a great many lack the gifts and graces to do anything special on their own, and therefore, must, serve the preceding. Describing the natural orientation of *Varṇadharma,* Mahatma Gandhi has said: "It is a law of spiritual economics and has nothing to do with superiority and inferiority."[27]

However, it was not long before the "law of spiritual economics" was displaced by the law of heredity, and an iron-clad caste system took on all the marks and trappings of superiority and inferiority in respect to food, clothing, language, ceremonials, social intercourse, marriage, and occupation. Just as *Āśramadharma* degenerated to the point where mendacious monks received the highest honour of society, *Varṇadharma* degenerated into the caste system based on heredity.

The evils of the caste or *jāti* system are too well known to bear repetition or reproach. But this should not detract from its lesser-known merits. After all, if *jāti* has survived the centuries, it must have had some survival value.

It is safe to say that an individual's social position should not be fixed by heredity, but Western critics may question whether their system of an aristocracy of wealth is any more defensible than the Indian's system of an aristocracy of birth.

One merit of the caste system is that it has provided the individual with the sense of belonging. By contrast, in Western cities today, loneliness is an omnipotent and painful threat to an increasing number of persons. These individuals describe their predicament as that of being "on the outside" and isolated. The more educated among them describe their situation as one of alienation. In Hinduism the sense of community has traditionally been so strong that the feeling of being uprooted and dislocated is quite foreign. Wherever the individual travels, the eyes of his community are upon him, watching his conduct and having an interest in his affairs. Even in an urban setting he maintains a closeness of relationship which the atomistic Westerner can only expect in some rural habitat.

Second, caste supplies the Hindu with economic security. It eliminates the aggressive "dog-eat-dog" philosophy of a competitive society, and, like a trade union, protects the "little guy" from being exploited by the moguls of business. The preservation of jobs has also meant the survival of several Indian arts and crafts which, in a competitive society, would have become economically extinct.

Third, the caste system has helped preserve Indian culture. Dr. Thomas Welty observes that amid extended periods of chaos and disorganization, the caste system helped Indian civilization survive by supplying it with the lifeblood of stability and continuity. "No matter under what alien king or conqueror the Indian was forced to live, he maintained his loyalty and devotion to the caste and in this way preserved Indian culture."[28]

However, all of these social, economic, and cultural assets of the caste system were purchased at a great price—the loss of freedom and the sacrifice of social progress. Freedom was lost because the individual had to submit himself totally to the system, and social progress was sacrificed because the principle of heredity was the sole determinant of one's role in life. The doctrine of *karman* could explain one's present position in relation to the past and even provide incentive to perform good deeds, with a view to meriting a higher caste in a future existence, but too often this doctrine was only a moral rationalization of social inequities.

The impression should not be given that Hindus only became embarrased by the caste system upon contact with Western ideals of liberty, fraternity, and equality. Actually there has always been a countermovement, questioning and controverting the rigidity and inviolability of the principle of heredity.

In the Chāndogya Upaniṣad there is the celebrated story of Satyakāma who, though born out of wedlock and ignorant of his father's lineage, was considered a Brahmin because he was unashamed to speak the truth.[29] Manu, himself a lawgiver, says: "A twice-born man who, not having studied the Veda, applies himself to other (and worldly study), soon falls even while living, to the condition of a Sudra and his descendants (after him)."[30] In the Mahābhārata, Yudhiṣṭhira teaches: "Truth, charity, fortitude, good conduct, gentleness, austerity, and compassion—he in whom these are observed is a *brāhmaṇa*. If these marks exist in a *śūdra* and are not found in a twice-born, the *śūdra* is not a *śūdra,* nor the *brāhmaṇa* a *brāhmaṇa*."[31] The Bhagavadgītā accepts the caste ideal on religious, biological and sociological grounds, but, as Professor K. N. Upadhyaya has shown, the Gītā universalises the orthodox concept of salvation to make it accessible to all men; and further, it refuses to categorise moral acts by hierarchical standards.[32]

Some Hindu sects, such as Śaivas and Vaiṣṇavas, made no rule of caste distinctions. In the same spirit, reform movements have discarded caste practices. Rām Mohun Roy (1772–1833), founder of the Brāhmo Samāj which is a school of rational theism based on the Upaniṣads, fought against caste, calling it a departure from true Hinduism. The Ārya Samāj founded by Swami Dayānanda (1824–1883), denounced caste as a later development, having no support in the Vedas on which the movement took its stand. Mahatma Gandhi (1869–1948) believed in *Varṇadharma* as "the law of life," but crusaded against caste as alien to Hinduism. He was especially burdened for the Untouchables—India's outcastes—and gave them a new designation: *Harijans* or sons of God.

Thus it was when India became a democratic republic in 1947, the abrogation of caste by her constitution was in no conflict with the original spirit of Hindu social ethics.

In addition to *viśeṣa* or 'specific' duties, objective ethics includes *sāmānya* or 'generic' duties. Whereas the one is relative and conditional, the other is common and unconditional. The common duties or *Sādhāraṇadharmas* are common in the sense of being independent of caste and station in life, and are binding upon man as man—not as a member of a community.

Since human rights precede communal rights, *Sādhāraṇadharmas* provide the basis for *Varṇāśramadharmas* and also define their boundaries. For instance, a Brahmin wanting to make a sacrificial offering is not at liberty to acquire the object of sacrifice by stealth, for *asteya* or nonstealing is a universal duty. *Sādhāraṇadharmas* are thus the preconditions and foundations of *Varṇāśramadharmas.* They perform the role of watchdog over parochial and provincial egoism, evaluating communal rights within the larger ethical framework of human rights.

Prof. S. K. Maitra has pointed out that within the humanitarian scheme of *Sādhāraṇadharma* even the lowly Śūdra was granted more civic status than the barbarian and helot could have expected within the Platonic scheme of justice.

> For Plato the barbarian is without any moral standing: there are not only no duties to be fulfilled by him but also no duties to be fulfilled *in respect* of him. The Hindu, however, in spite of the social degradation of the Shudra, does not exclude him altogether from moral protection, but shelters him from persecution through a code of universal duties which are obligatory on man as man. These duties are to be observed by all alike, being the duties obligatory on everybody in his dealings with everybody else. They are thus to be observed not merely by the Shudras but also by members of the higher caste.[33]

The motivation behind *Sādhāraṇadharmas* is twofold: the sacredness of life, and gratitude for life. The unity of man is deeper than his diversity, and out of this unity is born the sense of sacredness. We are not Brahmacārins or Brahmins; not Sannyāsins or Śūdras who happen to be people; but people who happen to occupy this particular station or that particular caste, both of which are relative and changing.

Second, there is the same sense of gratitude operant in *Sādhāraṇadharmas* as in *Āśramadharmas.* Man is indebted to his community and therefore sacrifices; but even more so is he culturally and experientially indebted to humanity and must therefore serve the universal good.

What are these universal duties? Following Manu, the *Sādhāraṇadharmas,* like the laws of Moses, are ten in number:

1. Steadfastness *(Dhairya)*
2. Forgiveness *(Kṣamā)*
3. Application *(Dama)*
4. Nonappropriation *(Cauryābhāva)*
5. Cleanliness *(Śauca)*
6. Repression of the sensuous appetites *(Indriyanigraha)*
7. Wisdom *(Dhī)*
8. Learning *(Vidyā)*
9. Veracity *(Satya)*
10. Restraint of anger *(Akrodha)*

It is quite obvious that the virtues listed are largely ascetical (steadfastness, application, repression), and dianoetic (wisdom, learning, veracity). Their purport is self-culture, constituting an ethics of self-autonomy. This is in harmony with the moral law of *karman* which states that a man rises or falls by virtue of his own deeds. The emphasis on self-sufficiency is well made, but we miss any reference to social service.

The element lacking in Manu's list is partially compensated for in Praśastapāda's list of generic or *sāmānya* duties. The humanitarian ideal of life is brought out more strongly by the inclusion of such duties as *ahiṁsā* (refraining from injury to living beings), and *bhūtahitatva* (seeking the good of creatures).

Our description of *Varṇāśramadharmas* and *Sādhāraṇadharmas* requires one final qualification. The duties and obligations outlined are those done under normal conditions. At the same time, the Epics and Dharma Śāstras allow for emergency conditions in which the conventional must be superseded in favour of the prudential. For instance, while it is customarily good to speak the truth, under extenuating circumstances when the truth could cause the death of the innocent, it is prudentially expedient to tell lies. In such cases the end justifies the means.

Thus, Hindu ethics is not absolutist and unbending but is reflective and contextual in its approach to ethical problems. To safeguard this situationalism from degenerating into privatism, the *smṛtis* make it plain that exceptions are only to be made for the sake of others, not for one's own private advantage.

Objective Ethics constitutes the first stage of Hindu *Dharma.* On this stage morality is represented by social codes demanding external conformity. Psychologically understood, this is the stage of socialization and introjection. The voice of conscience is the interiorized voice of the group. The essence of conscience is a "must." The feel of conscience is that of fear of punishment for duties not done.

Hindu *Dharma* further teaches that one should progress from the 'must-consciousness' to the 'ought-consciousness'. This transformation comes out of a deepened self-awareness. Looking into the self, one becomes concerned with inner purity and acts of free will. This is the subjective stage known as *Cittaśuddhi* or purification of the mind.

Subjective Ethics is an advance over Objective Ethics because "virtues are superior to duties." Whereas duty represents external sanctions, virtue represents internal sanctions. Duties are related to experiences of prohibition and fear, but virtues arise from experiences of preference and the feeling of self-respect. Duty denotes tribalistic morality; virtue denotes individualistic morality. Duty is *ad hoc* and specific; virtue is generic and dynamic. Summarily stated, while Objective Ethics springs from a sense of duty, usually entailing an element of coercion, Subjective Ethics springs from virtue which is always a labour of love. This love is either the product of a theistic consciousness that views all life as the handiwork of God and hence sacred, or the perception of a philosophic consciousness which envisions all forms of life as essentially one and therefore always worthy of one's best.

Capacity to love is dependent on the individual's degree of freedom. The loving individual is a free agent. This is precisely what the word 'individual' means. Dr. Kalidas Bhattacharya defines an individual as "a human being who is not entirely an item of Nature, accepting unquestioningly what Nature offers and submitting blindly to its forces, but one who often resists it and initiates new actions, one, in other words, who is as much above Nature as in it. This over-natural status of man is called 'freedom'."[34]

Freedom is the *sine qua non* of any system of ethics. Hindu ethics is constantly being attacked on this central issue on the grounds of two doctrines which critics claim are denials of individual freedom. The first is the doctrine of *guṇas,* the other the doctrine of *karman.*

Hindu ethics classifies actions as *tāmasika, rājasika,* and *sāttvika. Tāmasika* movements are biological, and, therefore, uncontrollable and unfree. *Rājasika* movements are propelled by strong passions of love *(rāga)* or hate *(dveṣa)* and are therefore also unfree even though the person knows these actions to be his own.

However, while *tāmasika* and *rājasika* actions provide no room for volition, voluntaristic activity is possible on the *sāttvika* level. Here, actions are characterized by *vairāgya* or detachment. Detachment is believed to undo the consequences of the law of *karman. Vairāgya* admits of degrees. "Short of absolute detachment, it lends to actions which are socio-moral *(dharma)* at the lower stage and spiritual *(ādhyātmika)* at a higher."[35]

The second doctrine critics claim is the negation of freedom is the law of *karman.* The West knows this doctrine well but comprehends it little. The doctrine is very ancient and is to be seminally found in the Vedic concept of *ṛta.* It postulates a universe governed by law. The same immutable law which charts the course of the sun and moon across the sky operates in the rational and ethical realms with equal exactitude. There is nothing sown that is not reaped, and there is nothing reaped that is not sown. Action and retribution are the two sides of *karman.* This alternation is empirically verifiable, signifying the inherent justice of the universe.

Since the universe is morally structured, it must be assumed that an action without retribution is still in the process of maturation, and that eventually in some future life what has been sown will be reaped. Thus, by inference, the theory of *saṁsāra* or rebirth is deduced from the law of *karman.*

There are three areas in which the moral deserts of past lives determine the present. They are one's psychophysical constitution, family, and caste; one's span of life; and one's activities. By linking the present with the past, the law of *karman* attempts to explicate the mysteries behind individual inequalities, and the problem of suffering. This shows that *karman* is not a strange, extraneous force which determines what shall happen to the individual. Rather, *karman* is the individual himself, formed by his own past.

Since the individual is the author of the story of his life, *karman* leaves no room for fatalism. Fate (*fatum,* 'that which has been said') signifies a contradiction of freedom, but *karman* signifies a polar correlation. *Karman* is not the opposite of freedom, but points to the conditions and limits of freedom. *Karman* is the ground of freedom; and freedom participates in moulding *karman*.

This dynamic relationship between *karman* and freedom becomes apparent in the twofold results of every action. First, there are the direct results over which one has no control. As stated earlier, one's physical and mental makeup, family and caste are all predetermined and one has absolutely no option but to accept the given. However, past actions also produce indirect results which form an individual's natural inclinations. Propensities may prod but do not push the individual in a given direction. Whereas direct results precipitate action, indirect results leave room for reaction. The reaction is a free act, but it is performed within the limits set by nature. This means that the future is conditioned, but it is not determined. The difference between the conditioned state of man and the determined state of animals is the presence of spirit in man. Man, as Radhakrishnan states, is more than a complicated piece of machinery.

> The spirit in him can triumph over the automatic forces that try to enslave him. The *Bhagavadgītā* asks us to raise the self by the self. We can use the material with which we are endowed to promote our ideals. The cards in the game of life are given to us. We do not select them. They are traced to our past Karma, but we can call as we please, lead what suit we will, and as we play, we gain or lose. And there is freedom.[36]

Thus, on the moral and spiritual levels of existence, the law of *karman* is not opposed to freedom. This conclusion reconciles the operation of *karman* with the spirit of freedom implicit in the scriptures. The scriptures are full of prescriptions and prohibitions, but, as Rāmānuja has pointed out, "commandments can be addressed to such agents only as are capable of entering on action or refraining from action, according to their own thought and will."[37]

The claim for the freedom of moral and spiritual actions is also supported by the theory that the merits or demerits of actions get depleted in their consequences which are experienced as rewards or punishments. In this way justice is maintained. But if the results of former acts were themselves the seed for some future harvest in this world or the next, that would contradict the whole idea of justice that the law of *karman* is supposed to uphold. It would be tantamount to rewarding or punishing the individual eternally. This possibility is ruled out by the central tenet of the theory that merits or demerits are dissipated in their results.

Next, what is the quality of a moral and spiritual deed which is free? It is characterised by *vairāgya* or detachment. The theory of detached action is known as *niṣkāmakarma*. Whereas *karman* binds the actor to the fruit of his actions through feelings of attraction or repulsion, *niṣkāmakarma* frees him from bondage because *karman* without *kāma* has no potency for rebirth. The practical appeal of this quality of action resides in the fact that it is calling not for renunciation *of* action but renunciation *in* action. The Gītā arrives at this formula by combining the essential elements of two ideals; *pravṛtti* or 'active life', and *nivṛtti* or 'quietism'.

In the spirit of *vairāgya* the unattached individual lives the life of virtue. According to Vātsyāyana, *dharma* or virtue has three forms, namely:

1. Virtues of the body—charity, helping the needy, social service
2. Virtues of speech—truthfulness, benevolence, gentleness, recitation of scriptures
3. Virtues of the mind—kindness, unworldliness, piety

Like *dharma, adharma* is also threefold:

1. Vices of the body—cruelty, theft, sexual indulgence
2. Vices of speech—falsehood, harshness, scandal
3. Vices of the mind—hatred, covetousness, disbelief

The Western student of Hindu ethics quickly perceives that far greater importance is attached to Subjective Ethics than to Objective Ethics. Concern for social welfare is minor as compared to concern for individual perfection. How may we account for this disproportion of interest?

First, Hindu philosophers reasoned in a fashion common to preindustrial thinking that to change society one must start with the individual. The whole is made up of parts, and when the parts are healthy, the whole is healthy. This reasoning was adequate for its times, but today Indian society cannot afford to continue to place personal ethics above social ethics. In modern urban life it is society that makes the individual and not the individual who makes society.

Furthermore, in ancient India, common people could be relied upon to play the role of the 'Good Samaritan' by following their own *dharma*. But those were times when religion was vigorous and the country was prosperous. Today, the religion is alive but tired because of an impoverished environment, and unless something drastic is done to change the socioeconomic environment, *dharma* will lose its present appeal to the people. *Artha* without *dharma* is blind, but *dharma* without *artha* is empty.

On the Objective level the ethical character of the individual was disciplined by codes of duties specifying right and wrong actions. This discipline was preparatory to the higher level of Subjective Ethics. The task on this second level was purification of the mind or *Cittaśuddhi.* By the inwardisation of objective morality, duty was transformed into virtue. However, even Subjective Ethics is not the highest level of spirituality. Like social ethics, personal ethics is not an end in itself but a means toward the ultimate end which is "the life absolute and transcendental."

> Here sociality as well as subjective morality must be merged in the end and thereby either to be annulled and transcended or to re-appear in a new light and charged with absolute significance. This is the underlying intent of Patanjali's Scheme of Yoga, Shankara's view of Moksha, Rāmānuja's doctrine of Bhakti and the Buddhist theory of Nirvāna. All these agree in recognizing the transcendental as the limit of the empirical life, the timeless as the truth of all that is in time. This timeless, transcendental life is therefore the culminating stage of the spirit, the sphere of its consummation and fruition.[38]

The transcendental life is not a new acquisition. Just as the first three *puruṣārthas* were organically related to one's empirical being, *mokṣa,* the fourth *puruṣārtha,* is intrinsically related to one's essential being. The self is already perfect, immortal, and free; only its true nature is concealed by *māyā* or cosmic ignorance. Under the spell of *māyā,* all one can see is the chrysalis, but when knowledge penetrates ignorance, the chrysalis is transformed into a butterfly! This transformation is a total experience, involving both a change of intellectual understanding and a change of heart. A whole new consciousness floods the liberated self, pointing to the essential nature of the soul as pure existence *(sat),* pure consciousness *(cit),* and pure bliss *(ānanda).*

The transcendental level of life is a postethical plane of being. Ethics is only significant as long as one finds multiplicity in the world, but on the higher plane of supramundane unity, ethics loses its substance. On this level, all empirical contradictions are transcended—cold and heat, pleasure and pain, praise and blame, but also, good and evil, right and wrong!

The transcendence of ethics in *mokṣa* has led to gross misunderstanding with accusations that Hindu ethics is ultimately antinomian. It must be clearly stated, therefore, that though Hindu philosophy teaches that the metaphysical ideal is higher than the ethical ideal, nevertheless, the two are synthetically related. The person who has achieved the mystical state of *mokṣa* does not consciously follow the ethical path, but neither can he deviate from it. The path of an enlightened man is paved with virtue. The Bhagavadgītā declares:

> The holy men whose sins are destroyed, whose doubts (dualities) are cut asunder, whose minds are disciplined and who rejoice in (doing) good to all creatures, attain to the beatitude of God.[39]

Thus, love and compassion to all creatures are the spontaneous products of wisdom. This kind of knowledge helps one overcome the world, but since through it one sees the Divine in all beings, one cannot become otherworldly. Social responsibilities are taken all the more seriously. Śaṅkara is a case in point. He is well known as an eminent philosopher. But the philosopher was also a great humanitarian; and that, not in spite of his philosophy, but because of his philosophy!

The unitive view of reality underlying the *mokṣa* doctrine has contemporary relevance for several problems besetting American society, but we shall single out the problem of ecology for special focus. In the remaining section of this chapter we shall first try to show the relationship between ethics and ecology, and then proceed to indicate how Hindu philosophy can provide the basis for an environmental ethic.

Ecology presupposes ethics. We must view the environmental crisis not only as a physical and technical problem, or one that raises fundamental political and economic questions about private and public planning, but also as a problem rooted within the value dimensions of our culture.

Our problem is not that we lack the money, scientific expertise, or legislation that is necessary to overcome the crisis. Americans are the world's experts in all of these areas. We can spend billions of dollars on antipollution programmes, we can tax polluters, we can punish violators, and the president can promote endless roadshows to express executive alarm; but none of these is sufficient to solve the problem. Something more is needed if we are going to recover and preserve our natural environment. This is precisely the one thing money cannot buy, which lawmakers cannot legislate, and which programmes and presidents cannot promote. This is a *reverence* for nature.

To attain a right relationship with nature, modern man must assume vital obligations for the web of life in which his own life is wonderfully woven. Furthermore, if this sense of obligation is to be meaningful, it must become a matter of conscience. This is not to indict the West for thus far not having had a conscience. The problem is, its conscience has been predominantly social, whereas the situation in which we find ourselves demands, in additon to a social conscience, an ecological conscience. The ecological conscience views the natural world as a series of interrelated systems which are in a state of dynamic equilibrium, and within which man must play his part as a responsible spectator and participant. In the balance of ecology, the responsibility or irresponsibility of an act is defined by its ability either to preserve or to destroy the integrity of the biotic community.

This means, if we are going to be scientific in our approach, we cannot speak of man *and* nature, but of man *in* nature. The first view is anthropocentric; the second is biocentric. The first view has characterised Western man's approach to nature; the second has been more characteristic of the Hindu perspective.

The outlook on life underlying the *summum bonum* of Hindu ethics is fundamentally cosmic. The essential self in man is not only identified with the group, or society, or the nation, or even the whole human race, but it is inclusive of all these and much more! If the nature of the self ended with human identity, we could only expect Hinduism to provide a social conscience, as do the Western religions. But the nature of the self in Hinduism includes all lesser forms of existence, and, therefore, it also has an ecological conscience. The cosmic view of the self is found in such passages as:

> The essential self or the vital essence in man is the same as that in a gnat, the same as that in an elephant, the same as that in these three worlds, indeed the same as that in the whole universe.[40]

The general idea behind this text is that the individual *ātman* is one with the universal *Brahman*. *Brahman* literally means 'the growing or increasing force' *(bṛh)*. This *Brahman* force is manifest uniformly in the divinities of heaven, and in human and animal and plant life on earth. All of these entities live an apparently independent existence, but they all emanate from *Brahman* and are finally reabsorbed into it. *Brahman* itself is infinite and is, therefore, greater than the sum of all its manifestations, past, present, and future.

This belief in *Brahman* provides the philosophic basis for the Hindu's veneration of the natural world. The natural world is not a commodity which man possesses but a community to which he belongs. The universe appears to be material, but it is the universal consciousness or *Brahman*. Since all is one, the conquest of nature cannot be true to reality, and our sense of separateness, isolation, and egotism is the product of ignorance.

Man cannot act ethically toward nature as long as he is ignorant of himself. Lacking his own sense of identity, he cannot identify with the trees and the mountains, nor can he feel empathy for the beasts of the fields. Nature is empty because he is empty. He manipulates nature because he manipulates himself. As psychologist Rollo May puts it, "the loss of the relation to nature goes hand in hand with the loss of one's own self."[41] William Wordsworth perceived this correlation between our inner world and the outer world, and expressed it in a sonnet.

> The world is too much with us; late and soon,
> Getting and spending, we lay waste our powers;
> Little we see in Nature that is ours;
> We have given our hearts away, a sordid boon!
> This Sea that bares her bosom to the moon,
> The winds that will be howling at all hours,
> And are up-gathered now like sleeping flowers.
> For this for everything, we are out of tune.[42]

The basic message of Hindu ethics, rooted in the ancient idea of *ṛta,* is that harmony is already here; that we do not have to create it—only discover it! Since *Brahman* and Nature are one, we must see the Supreme Being in the whole world, and the whole world in Him!

Notes

INTRODUCTION

1. L. M. Joshi, *Brahmanism, Buddhism and Hinduism* (Kandy: Buddhist Publication Society, 1970), p. 32.
2. P. Deussen, *The Philosophy of the Upanishads,* 1st rev. ed. (New York: Dover Publications, 1966), p. 324ff.
3. W. N. Brown, *Man in the Universe* (Berkeley and Los Angeles, California: University of California Press, 1970), p. 8.
4. Muṇḍaka Upaniṣad 3.1.5., in R. E. Hume, trans., *Thirteen Principal Upanishads,* 2d rev. ed. (London: Oxford University Press, 1971), p. 374.

CHAPTER 1

1. H. Zimmer, *Philosophies of India,* 8th ed. (New York: The World Publishing Co., 1964), p. 9.
2. A. A. Macdonell, *A History of Sanskrit Literature* (London: D. Appleton and Co., 1900), p. 8.
3. A. L. Basham, *The Wonder that Was India* (New York: Grove Press, 1954), p. 236.
4. RV. X.XXX.1.2. in R. T. H. Griffith, trans., *The Hymns of the Rigveda,* 3d ed., vol. 2 (Benares: Lazarus and Co., 1926), p. 425. All quotations are taken from this source.
5. Ibid., I.XXXII.1-5.
6. S. Radhakrishnan, *Indian Philosophy,* vol. 1 (London: Allen and Unwin, 1966), p. 106.
7. R. C. Majumdar, *Ancient India* (Delhi: Motilal Banarsidass, 1964), p. 51.
8. Ibid.
9. RV. II.XXIV.20
10. A. C. Bose, *Hymns from the Vedas* (Bombay: Asia Publishing House, 1966), p. 21.

11. Majumdar, loc. cit.
12. Radhakrishnan, loc. cit.
13. Ibid.
14. E. W. Hopkins, *Ethics of India* (New Haven, Connecticut: Yale University Press, 1924), p. 2.
15. RV. X.XLIII.I.
16. RV. I.XXXI.10.
17. Ibid. I.1.8.
18. Ibid., I.CLVI.3.
19. Ibid.
20. Ibid., II.XXIII.17.
21. Ibid., I.XXIII.5.
22. Ibid., VIII.XLI.7–10.
23. Ibid., X.X.2,8.
24. Ibid. VII.LXXXVI.1–8.
25. Ibid. VII.LXXXVI.5.
26. Ibid.
27. Ibid., vs. 6.
28. Bose, op. cit., p. 14.
29. RV. I.CXLVII.5.
30. Ibid., VII.CIV.8.
31. Ibid., X.CVII.8.
32. Ibid., X.CXVII.
33. Ibid., X.CXVII.1.
34. Ibid.
35. Ibid., X.CXVII.3.
36. Ibid., X.CXVII.5.
37. Ibid., X.CXVII.9.
38. Ibid., X.LXXXV.36–39.
39. Ibid., X.CXVII.10.
40. Atharva Veda III.30.
41. RV. I.9.
42. Ibid., X.L.XIII.15.
43. *Vide* S. R. Shastri, *Women in the Vedic Age* (Bombay: Bharatiya Vidya Bhawan, 1954), p. 2.
44. RV. I.CXIII.2.
45. *The Cultural Heritage of India,* 2d ed., vol. 1 (Calcutta: Rama Krishna Institute of Culture, 1958), p. 222.
46. RV. V.XXVIII.
47. Ibid., VIII.LXXX; X.CLXXIX; VII.1; X.XXXIX; X.LXXXVI.
48. *Cultural Heritage,* op. cit., p. 223.
49. RV. X.XXVII.12.
50. Ibid., I.CXIII; X.LXXXVI.
51. Ibid., X.LXXXV.26.
52. Yajur Veda, vs. 36.18., in Bose, op. cit., p. 11.
53. RV. X.CXXXVI.2,3.
54. Ibid., III.XXXIV.9; II.XII.4.
55. Ibid., X.XC.11–12.
56. R. C. Dutt, *The Early Hindu Civilization* (Calcutta: Punthi Pustak, 1963), p. 57.

57. RV.VIII.XXXV.16–18.
58. Dutt, loc. cit.
59. RV. IX.CXII.3.
60. Ibid., III.XLIII.5.
61. *Cultural Heritage,* op. cit., p. 226.
62. RV.II.XLIII.2.
63. P. H. Prabhu, *Hindu Social Organization* (Bombay: Popular Prakashan, 1963), p. 288.
64. TS. VII. 1.8.2; TS. 1.6.8.1; MS. 1.4.10.
65. ŚB. III.2.1.18–23.
66. Ibid., XI.2.3.6; X.4.3.3–8.
67. Ibid., I.7.4.6–8.
68. Ibid.
69. Ibid., I.7.3.19.
70. Ibid., VI.2.1.37.
71. J. Eggeling, trans., *Śatapatha Brāhmaṇa* in Sacred Books of the East, F. M. Müller, ed. (Oxford: Clarendon Press), 11.2.2.6. All quotations are taken from this source.
72. ŚB. X11.8.7.1–22; TS. II.
73. Keith, *infra,* p. 463.
74. Ait. B. I.25.
75. Ibid., I.26. In J. McKenzie, *Hindu Ethics* (Oxford: Oxford University Press, 1922), p. 30.
76. ŚB. XIV.1.1.3.
77. Ibid., I.1.6.
78. Ibid., I.1.9.
79. JB. I.98.
80. ŚB. X.4.3.9.
81. Ibid., I.7.4.1.
82. Ibid XIV.1.1.4.
83. Ibid., I.8.1.1–10.
84. TS. VII.1.8.2.
85. ŚB. III.4.2.8.
86. A. B. Keith, *Religion and Philosophy of the Veda,* vol. 32, Harvard Oriental Series, C. R. Lanman, ed. (Cambridge: Harvard Oriental Press, 1925), p. 477.
87. ŚB. III.1.2.10.
88. Ibid., III.1.3.18.
89. Ibid XI.6.1.4.
90. Ibid., XI.6.1.5.
91. Ibid XI.6.1.8–13.
92. Ibid., IV.4.5.23.
93. Ibid., IV.1.2.4.
94. Keith, op. cit., p. 478.
95. Hopkins, op. cit., p. 50.
96. ŚB. I.1.1.4.
97. Ibid., I.1.1.5.
98. Hopkins, op. cit., p. 62.
99. R. K. Mookerji, *Ancient Indian Education* (Delhi: Motilal Banarsidass. 1960), p. 85.
100. ŚB. XIII.2.6.10; X.3.5.16; Ait. B. IV.11.6–9; Taitt. B. III.8.13.1.

101. ŚB. II.3.1.31; Taitt. B. II.7.1.1.
102. ŚB. XI.5.6.3.
103. Ibid., XI.5.7.1.
104. Ibid., I.6.2.4.
105. S. P. Kanal, *Dialogues on Indian Culture* (Delhi: Panchal Press, 1955), p. 81.
106. ŚB. XI.5.4.17.
107. Mookerji, op. cit., p. 101.
108. ŚB. XI.3.3.2.
109. Ibid., XI.3.3.5.
110. Ibid., XI.3.3.4; XI.5.4.5.
111. Ibid., III.6.2.15.
112. Mookerji, op.cit., p. 96.
113. Kanal, op. cit., p. 74.
114. Ait. B. II.19.
115. Pañc. B. XIV.6.6.
116. TS. VII.4.19.
117. Ibid., V.6.8.3., in Dutt, op. cit., p. 95.
118. ŚB. II.5.2.20.
119. Dutt, op. cit., p. 100.
120. Keith, op. cit., p. 475.
121. Ait. B. VIII.13–18., in Dutt, op. cit., p. 103.
122. Atharva Veda VI.11.
123. ŚB. XIV.1.1.31.
124. Ibid., I.3.1.13.
125. Ibid., I.3.1.12.
126. Ibid., I.3.1.9.
127. Dutt, op. cit., p. 102.
128. ŚB. V.2.1.10.
129. Ibid., I.1.4.13.
130. Ibid., XIII.2.6.7.
131. Mait. S. III.6.3.
132. TS. VI.5.8.2.
133. ŚB. III.2.4.6.
134. Mait. S. IV.7.4.
135. ŚB. X.5.2.9.
136. Ibid., IV.4.2.13.
137. Keith, op. cit., p. 475.
138. ŚB. V.2.1.10.
139. Ait. B. III.12; TS. VI.6.4.
140. Dutt, op. cit., p. 105.
141. Shastri, op. cit., p. 80.
142. Maitri Up. IV. 1–3.
143. Dutt, op. cit., p. 109.
144. Radhakrishnan, op. cit., p. 132.
145. ŚB. V.4.4.19.
146. Ibid., XIII.8.3.11.
147. Ibid. XII.4.4.6.
148. TS. II.5.12.
149. Ait. B. VIII.24.
150. ŚB. XI.6.2.10.

151. Dutt, op. cit., p. 75.
152. Ait. B. VIII. 27.
153. ŚB. VI.4.4.13.
154. Ibid., I.1.3.12.
155. Ibid. III.1.1.10.
156. Pañc. B. VI.1.11.
157. ŚB. I.1.4.11.
158. Bṛh. Up. I.3.28.
159. S. Dasgupta, *A History of Indian Philosophy,* vol. 1 (Cambridge University Press, 1969), p. 42.
160. Bṛh. Up. IV.4.22, in Hume, op. cit., p. 143.
161. *Vide* Tait. 2.8; 3.10.4; Maitri. 6.17; 7.7; Bṛh. 5.15; Iśā 16.
162. M. Hiriyanna, *Outlines of Indian Philosophy* (London: Allen and Unwin, 1970), p. 55.
163. Chānd. Up. 6.1.2.
164. Ibid., vs. 3.
165. Ibid., 6.2.3.
166. Ibid., 6.9.7.
167. Kaṭha Up. 5.11.
168. Ibid., 6.14.
169. Swami Nikhilananda, *The Upanishads* (New York: Harper and Row, 1964), p. 63.
170. Chānd. Up. 8.3.2.
171. Bṛh. Up. 4.4.23.
172. K. N. Upadhyaya, *Early Indian Buddhism and the Bhagavadgītā* (Delhi: Motilal Banarsidass, 1971), p. 85.
173. Chānd. Up. 8.7.3.
174. Muṇḍ. Up. 3.1.5.
175. Kaṭha Up. 2.7.8.
176. Muṇḍ. Up. I.2.12.
177. Chānd. Up. 8.7.2.
178. Muṇḍ. Up. I.3.12; Praśna Up. I.1.
179. Kaṭha Up. 3.3-11.
180. Ibid., 2.1-5.
181. Prayer of invocation in Praśna Up.
182. Chānd. Up. 7.26.2.
183. Muṇḍ. Up. 3.2.3.
184. Kena Up. 4.33.
185. Taitt. Up. I.11.1.
186. *Vide* Muṇḍ. Up. 3.1.6.
187. Chānd. Up. 6.12.3.
188. Taitt. Up. I.11.1.
189. Chānd. Up. 2.23.1. See Prof. Mukhopadhyaya's commentary, *infra,* p. 152ff.
190. Taitt. Up. I.9.
191. Ibid., I.11.3.
192. G. Mukhopadhyaya, *Studies in the Upaniṣads* (Calcutta: Calcutta Oriental Press, 1960), p. 157.
193. Chānd. Up. 3.16.1.
194. Ibid., 3.17.4.
195. Bṛh. Up. 5.2.1.

196. Taitt. Up. I.11.1.
197. Bṛh. Up. I.4.17.
198. Kaṭha Up. I.8.
199. Ibid., I.10–13.
200. Taitt. Up. I.4.3
201. Shastri, op. cit., p. 81.
202. Ait. Up. II.1.
203. Bṛh. Up. 3.6.
204. Ibid., 6.4.17.
205. Ibid., 6.4.3.
206. Ibid., vs. 6.
207. Ibid., vs. 8.
208. Chānd. Up. 4.4.4.
209. Ibid., vs. 5.
210. Muṇḍ. Up. I.2.7.
211. Bṛh. Up. 6.2.3.
212. Ibid., vs. 4.
213. Chānd. Up. 5.5.7.
214. Bṛh. Up. 4.4.23.
215. Muṇḍ. Up. 2.2.2; 3.2.7; Praśna Up. 4.9.10.
216. Bṛh. Up. 4.3.22.
217. Ibid. 4.4.22.
218. Hume, op. cit., p. 60.
219. Kaṭha Up. 2.10.
220. Kaṭha Up. 3.7–8; Muṇḍ. Up. 3.1.5,8; 3.2.3; Bṛh. Up. 4.4.23; Taitt, Up. 1.4; Chānd Up. 8.4.3.
221. Kaṭha Up. 2.7.
222. Chānd. Up. 5.10.7.
223. Ibid.
224. Bṛh. Up. 4.4.5.
225. Chānd. Up. 5.11.5.

CHAPTER 2

1. V. Raghavan, "Introduction to Hindu Scriptures," *The Religion of the Hindus*, ed. K. W. Morgan (New York: Ronald Press, 1953), p. 271.
2. S. Radhakrishnan, *The Hindu View of Life* (New York: Macmillan, 1965), p. 56.
3. Tr. G. Bühler, *The Laws of Manu* in the Sacred Books of the East, ed. F. Max Müller (Oxford: Clarendon Press, 1886), 11.6.12. All quotations taken from this source.
4. Manu I.87.
5. Ibid.
6. Ibid., I.98.
7. Ibid., I.88.
8. Ibid., I.93.
9. Ibid., I.95.
10. Ibid.
11. Ibid., I.98.
12. Ibid., XI.238.
13. Ibid., III.109.
14. Ibid., II.162.

15. Ibid., II.126.
16. Ibid., II.159.
17. Ibid., I.107.
18. Gaut. XII.17.
19. Mbh. 12, 268, 15. Also, Manu VIII.336.
20. Trans. G. Bühler, *Aspastamba and Gautama* in the Sacred Books of the East, ed. F. Max Müller (Oxford: Clarendon Press, 1879), vol. II, Gaut. XII.1-6.
21. Trans. Julius Jolly, *The Institutes of Viṣṇu* in the Sacred Books of the East, ed. F. Max Müller (Oxford: Clarendon Press, 1880), vol. VII. LXXXII.1-2.
22. Ibid.
23. Ibid., XXXII.17.
24. Āpas. II.5.11.
25. Ibid., I.11.31.24.
26. Hiraṇyakeśin Śrauta Sūtra VI.4.
27. Āpas. II.2.4.24-27.
28. Ibid., II.6.15.12.
29. Viṣṇu III.81.
30. Gaut. VIII.13.
31. Ibid., XII.8-13.
32. Ibid., VIII.1,4,7.
33. Baud. 1,5,10.26. *Vide* Dutt, op. cit., p. 135.
34. Āpas. I.6.18.19; Artha IX.2.
35. Manu VII.35.
36. A. L. Basham, *Aspects of Ancient Indian Culture* (New York: Asia Publishing House, 1970), p. 5.
37. Ibid., p. 14.
38. Mbh. XII.67.
39. Ibid., XII.59.
40. Gaut. X.32.
41. Manu VII.20,21,22.
42. Artha VI.
43. Manu VII.
44. Basham, *Aspects,* op. cit., pp. 22, 23.
45. Artha I.16.
46. *Vide,* Basham, *Wonder,* op. cit., ch. IV.
47. Artha 41.
48. Trans. T. N. Ramaswamy, *Essentials of Indian Statecraft: Kautilya's Artha-śāstra for Contemporary Readers* (Bombay: Asia Publishing House, 1962), ch. 41.
49. Mbh. XII. 97,25.
50. Āpas. II.5.10.11.
51. Gaut. X.17.18.
52. Baud. I.10.18.
53. Manu VII. 90-93.
54. Viṣṇu III.47,48,49.
55. Baud. I.5.10.24.
56. Gaut. V.41-42.
57. Ibid., V.45.
58. Ibid., X.51.
59. Ibid., vs. 52.

60. Ibid., vs. 65.
61. Ibid., vs. 56.
62. Ibid., vs. 60.
63. Ibid., vs. 61.
64. Ibid., vs. 63.
65. Gaut. XII.1-7.
66. Manu I.31,87.
67. Trans. E. Deutsch, *The Bhagavadgītā* (New York: Holt, Rinehart and Winston, 1968), pp. 1, 40–42, 34.
68. Trans. S. C. Vidyarnava, *Yājñavalkya Smriti* in the Sacred Books of the Hindus (Allahabad: The Panini Office, 1918), vol. XXI.1.1.14. All quotations are taken from this source.
69. Āśv. G. S. I. 19ff.
70. Āpas. I.1.20.
71. Āśv. G. S. I.21.7.
72. Āpas. I.1.1.13–17.
73. Ibid., I.1.2.20ff.
74. Āpas. I.2.8.25–28.
75. Manu II.97.
76. Ibid., II.118.
77. Ibid. II.96.
78. Yāj. I.11.28.
79. Āpas. II.16.
80. Mahā. Sabhā. 5.112.
81. Manu III.1.
82. Yāj. I.11.40–46.
83. Dutt, op. cit., p. 182.
84. Ibid.
85. Gaut. III.3; also, Manu III.78.
86. Yāj. 1.V.115; also, Gaut. IX.46.
87. Yāj. 1.97–116, *passim,* in *Sources of Indian Tradition,* ed. W. T. De Bary (New York: Columbia University Press, 1966), vol. 1, pp. 226, 227.
88. Manu IV.92. Contrast with Yāj. I.115.
89. Mbh. XIII.104.16.
90. Yāj. I.111.78–81.
91. Āpas. I.9.24.5.; Gaut. XXII.17.
92. Manu IX.17,18.
93. Mbh. XIII.40.12–13.
94. Mahā. Anu. 38–39.
95. Vas. V.1.
96. Baud. II.2.3.45.
97. Manu IX.3.
98. Yāj. I.111.71.
99. Mahā. Śānti. 266,38,40.
100. Manu III.55–62.
101. Mbh. IX.46.
102. Dutt, op. cit., p. 46.
103. Āpas. I.10.28.9.
104. Viṣṇu XXXI.1–2.
105. Gaut. II.50,51.

106. Trans. G. Bühler, *Vasiṣṭha and Baudhāyana* in the Sacred Books of the East, ed. F. Max Müller (Oxford: Clarendon Press, 1882), vol. XIV, Vas. XIII.48.
107. Trans. C. Rajagopalchari, *Rāmāyaṇa* (Bombay: Bharatiya Vidya Bhavan, 1962), pp. 72, 73.
108. Āśv. G. S. I.5.1-3.
109. Manu III.27-34.
110. Āpas. II.5.11.17-20.
111. Yāj. I.111.52.
112. Manu VI. 2-8.
113. Ibid., VI.33.
114. Manu VI. 46-48.
115. Ibid., 85.
116. K. Motwani, *Manu Dharma Śāstra* (Madras: Ganesh and Co., 1958), p. 61.
117. Āpas. I.9.23.5-6.
118. Gaut. VIII.22,23.
119. Vas. X.30.
120. Manu X.63.
121. Yāj. I.V.122.
122. Compare J. McKenzie, op. cit., p. 41.
123. Vas. VI.2-4.
124. Gaut. VIII.23.
125. Ibid., vss. 24,25.
126. Hopkins, op. cit., p. 91.
127. Vas. XXX.1.
128. Hiriyanna, *Outlines,* p. 109.
129. BG. VIII.15.
130. Ibid., IX.3. in Deutsch, op. cit. All quotations are from this source unless otherwise noted.
131. Ibid., XIV.20.
132. BG. V.24.
133. Ibid., VIII.8.
134. Upadhyaya, op. cit., p. 408.
135. BG. I.29-35.
136. Ibid., II.2,3.
137. Ibid., III.34.
138. Ibid., IV.21,22.
139. Ibid., IV.24.
140. Hiriyanna, *Outlines,* op. cit., p. 121.
141. BG. II.47.
142. Hiriyanna, loc. cit.
143. BG. II.48.
144. Ibid., VI.1.
145. Ibid., V.11.
146. Ibid., III.25-26; VI.3.
147. Ibid., IX.27.
148. Ibid. IX.31.
149. Ibid., XVIII.5.
150. Ibid., III.31,32.
151. Ibid., IV.15.
152. Ibid. XVIII.41-44.

153. Ibid., II.31.
154. Ibid., II.32,33.
155. Ibid., I.40–42.
156. Upadhyaya, op. cit., p. 507.
157. BG. IX.32.
158. Ibid., XVIII.45.
159. Ibid., II.7.
160. Trans. S. Radhakrishnan, *The Bhagavadgītā* (London: Allen and Unwin, 1948), p. 101.
161. BG. I.45;II.8.
162. Ibid., I.46.
163. Ibid., I.47.
164. Ibid., I.31; I.38, 39; I.36; II.7; III.2.
165. Ibid., II.11.
166. Ibid., II.18.
167. Ibid., II.27.
168. Ibid., II.20.
169. Ibid.
170. Ibid., II.22.
171. Ibid., II.21.
172. Ibid., II.23.
173. Ibid., II.28.
174. Upadhyaya, op. cit., p. 422.
175. BG. II.31.
176. Ibid., II.32.
177. Ibid., II.33.
178. Ibid., II.34–36.
179. Ibid., II.37.
180. Ibid., II.32,33.
181. Ibid., XVIII.60.
182. Ibid., VI.41–43.
183. Ibid., III.33.
184. Ibid., II.60.
185. Ibid., III.42.
186. Compare J. P. Sartre's *Existentialism and Human Emotions,* and B. F. Skinner's *Beyond Freedom and Destiny.*
187. BG. XIV.22–25.
188. Ibid., XVIII.53.

CHAPTER 3

1. S. Radhakrishnan and C. Moore, eds., *A Sourcebook in Indian Philosophy* (Princeton, New Jersey: Princeton University Press, 1967), p. 349.
2. H. Zimmer, *Philosophies of India* (New York: World Publishing House, 1964), p. 605.
3. Hiriyanna, *Outlines,* op. cit., p. 177.
4. S. Dasgupta, op. cit., p. 75.
5. F. Max Müller, *Six Systems of Indian Philosophy* (London: Longmans, 1928), p. x.
6. Radhakrishnan and Moore, op. cit., p. 354.
7. B. Keith, *Indian Logic and Atomism* (Oxford: Clarendon Press, 1921), p. 3.

8. Ibid.
9. NS. I.1.1; VS. I.1.2.
10. NS. I.1.21.
11. NS. I.1.2. in S. C. Vidyabhusana, trans., *The Nyāya Sūtras of Gotama* in Sacred Books of the Hindus, ed. B. D. Basu (Allahabad: Panini Office, 1930), vol. VIII.
12. NB. I.1.2. in G. Jha, trans., *Gautama's Nyāyasūtras (with Vātsyāyana bhāṣya)* in Poona Oriental Series (Poona: Oriental Book Agency, 1939) no. 59.
13. NS. IV.1.3.
14. NB. IV.1.3.
15. NB. I.1.2.
16. Ibid.
17. Ibid.
18. NS. I.1.21.
19. VS. I.1.1. in N. Sinha, trans., *The Vaiśeṣika Sūtras of Kaṇāda* in the Sacred Books of the Hindus, ed. B. B. Basu (Allahabad: Panini Office, 1923), vol. 6.
20. VS. I.1.2.
21. NB. I.1.22.
22. NS. 4.2.47 in Jha, op. cit.
23. NB. 4.2.46.
24. NS. 4.2.46.
25. NB. 4.2.46.
26. Trans. G. Jha, *Padārthadharmasaṃgraha of Praśastapāda* (Allahabad: E. J. Lazarus and Co., 1916), VI 133.
27. Ibid.
28. PP. VI.134.
29. Ibid., VI. 134.
30. Ibid., VI. 135.
31. Ibid., VI. 136.
32. R. Garbe, *Sankhya,* in *Encyclopaedia of Religion and Ethics,* ed. J. Hastings (New York: Scribners, 1925), vol. XI, p. 189.
33. S. Radhakrishnan, *Indian Philosophy* (London: Allen and Unwin, 1951), vol. 2, p. 309.
34. Kārikā XI in G. Jha, trans., *The Tattva-Kaumudī,* 2d ed. (Poona: The Oriental Book Agency, 1934), p. 42.
35. SK. IX.
36. Ibid., XV.
37. Ibid., XI.
38. Ibid., XII, XIII.
39. *Tattva-Kaumudī,* op. cit., p. 49.
40. SK. XXI.
41. Ibid., XXII.
42. Ibid., XXV.
43. Ibid., LVII.
44. M. Hiriyanna, *The Essentials of Indian Philosophy* (London: Allen and Unwin, 1967), p. 119.
45. Radhakrishnan, *Indian Philosophy,* op. cit., p. 310.
46. Compare F. Max Müller, op. cit., p. 255.
47. Saṁkhya Pravacana Sūtra, I.82,85.
48. SK. XL.

49. SPS. I.19.
50. SK. XVII.
51. Tat. Sam. I.149.
52. SPS I.19.
53. SPB. I.58.
54. SK. LIX in Jha, trans., op. cit.
55. Ibid. LXVII.
56. SPS. III.30.
57. VB. III.74.
58. SK. I.
59. *Tattva-Kaumudī,* op. cit., p. 6.
60. J. Ghosh, *Sāṁkhya and Modern Thought* (Calcutta: The Book Company, 1930), pp. 97, 98.
61. *The Yoga Sūtras of Patañjali* in the Sacred Books of the Hindus, ed. B. D. Basu (Allahabad: Panini Office, 1924), I.15.
62. YB. I.15.
63. YS. I.16.
64. Ibid., II.29ff.
65. Ibid., II.29.
66. Ibid., II.30.
67. Ibid., II.35.
68. Ibid., II.31.
69. YB. II.31.
70. YS. II.32.
71. Ibid., II.40–45.
72. Ibid., II.34.
73. YB. II.34.
74. YS. I.15.
75. Hiriyanna, *Outlines,* op. cit., p. 296.
76. YS. I.34.
77. *'svargakāmo yajeta.'*
78. Mīmāṃsā Sūtras of Jaimini in N. V. Thadani, trans., *Mimansa: The Secret of the Sacred Books of the Hindus* (Delhi: Bharati Research Institute, 1952), XII.IV.38–47. See also pp. xxx, xxxi, xlv, xlviii, lxxiv, xci, xcii, clv, clxxvii, cxxi, clxxxix.
79. *Vide* G. Jha, *Pūrva-mīmāṃsa in its Sources* (Benares: Benares Hindu University Press, 1942), p. 26 for Śabara's views; p. 28 for Prabhākara's views; and p. 32 for Kumārila's views.
80. Compare Ślokavārttika, Ātmavāda, Śāstradīpikā.
81. Mīmāṃsā Sūtra I.1.1. in *Mīmāṃsa Sūtra,* trans. G. Jha (Baroda: Oriental Institute, 1936).
82. Ibid., I.1.2.
83. Kumārila Bhāṭṭa, *Ślokavārttika,* trans. G. Jha (Calcutta: Asiatic Society of Bengal, 1909), 15, p. 555.
84. Ibid., 13–14.
85. Ibid., 16.
86. S. C. Chatterjee and D. M. Datta, *An Introduction to Indian Philosophy* (Calcutta: Calcutta University Press, 1968), p. 339.
87. Ibid.
88. *Tantravārtika,* pp. 368–372 (Benares edition).

89. Radhakrishnan, *Indian Philosophy,* vol. 2, op. cit., p. 124.
90. *Vide* Pārthasārathi's *Śāstra-Dīpikā* (Bombay: Nirṇaya Sagar, 1915), p. 80; Śalikanātha's *Prakaraṇa-Pañcikā* (Benares: Chowkhamba, 1903), pp. 184–95; Śabara-bhāṣya, II.1.5.
91. *Tantra-Vārtika,* I.111.2.
92. *Prakaraṇa-Pañcikā,* op. cit., pp. 185, 186.
93. Ibid., pp. 154–160.
94. Ibid., VIII., pp. 152–153.
95. *Śāstra-Dīpikā,* op. cit., pp. 126–127.
96. *Mānameyodaya,* 2.26.
97. *Mīmāṃsā Sūtra* VI.1.26 in Jha, trans., op. cit.
98. *Vide* Thadani, op. cit., pp. 416–420.
99. MS. VI.1.39 in Thadani, trans.
100. Thadani, op. cit., footnote, pp. 121, 122.
101. MS. VI.1.6–9 in Thadani, trans.
102. Ibid., VI.1.12–24.
103. I. C. Sharma, *Ethical Philosophies of India* (Nebraska: Johnsen Publishing Co., 1965), p. 217.
104. Chatterjee and Datta, op. cit., p. 339.
105. BG. V.11; 111.20; IX.27.
106. Sharma, op. cit., p. 229.
107. MS. I.1.26 in Thadani, trans.
108. *Vide* Radhakrishnan, *Indian Philosophy,* vol. 2, op. cit. p. 419.
109. *Tantrarahasya,* p. 66.
110. Trans. G. Thibaut, *The Vedānta-Sūtras with Śaṅkara's Commentary* in Sacred Books of the East, ed. F. Max Müller (Oxford: Clarendon Press, 1890), vol. XXXIV, p. 9.
111. *Brahma satyam jagan mithya jīvo Brahmaiva nāparaḥ,* in Madhavananda, *Vivekachūḍāmaṇi of Śaṅkarāchārya* (Almora: Advaita Ashram, 1944), vs. 20, p. 8.
112. VED. S., op. cit., pp. 3, 4.
113. Ibid., p. 5.
114. Ibid., p. 7.
115. Ibid., pp. 7, 8.
116. Ibid., p. 8.
117. Ibid., III.4.25.
118. S. K. Das, *A Study of the Vedānta* (Calcutta: Calcutta University Press, 1937), p. 339.
119. Bṛh. Up., II.1.20.
120. S. Radhakrishnan, *The Vedānta* (London: Allen and Unwin, 1928), p. 188.
121. VED. S. III.4.26.
122. Ibid.
123. Ibid.
124. Ibid., III.4.27.
125. Bṛh. Up. IV.4.23.
126. VED. S. III.4.27, op. cit., vol. XXXVIII.
127. Paul Deussen, *The System of The Vedānta* (Chicago: Open Court, 1912), pp. 411, 412.
128. VED. S. III.4.38, op. cit.
129. Ibid., III.4.39.

130. VED. S. I.3.34.
131. Ibid.
132. Ibid.
133. Ibid., I.3.34.
134. Deussen, op. cit., p. 63.
135. VED. S. I.3.35.
136. Ibid.
137. Ibid. I.3.37.
138. Ibid., I.3.34.
139. Ibid., I.3.38.
140. Ibid.
141. Ibid.
142. Ibid., IV.1.1-2.
143. Ibid.
144. Das, op. cit., p. 341.
145. Trans. Swami Gambhirananda, *Eight Upaniṣads* (Calcutta: Advaita Ashram, 1957), p. 231ff.
146. VED. S. IV.1.13.
147. SBG. IV.19.
148. VED. S. II.3.48.
149. Hiriyanna, *Outlines,* op. cit., pp. 381, 382.
150. BG. XIII.27-28.
151. VED. S. III.4.14.
152. Radhakrishnan, *Vedānta,* op. cit., p. 199.
153. VED. S. III.4.50.
154. Ibid.
155. Trans. G. Thibaut, *Vedānta-Sūtras (with Rāmānuja's Commentary)* in Sacred Books of the East, ed. F. Max Mūller (Delhi: Motilal Banarsidass, 1962), Vol. XLVIII, III.3.57.
156. Gītābhāṣya 9.2. in J. A. B. van Buitenen, *Rāmānuja on the Bhagavadgītā* (Delhi: Motilal Banarsidass, 1968), p. 113.
157. Śrībhāṣya III.2.28.
158. Ibid., II.1.9.
159. Ibid., III.2.1.
160. Ibid., III.2.11.
161. Ibid., III.2.1.
162. Ibid.
163. Ibid., III.2.11.
164. P. N. Srinivasachari, *The Philosophy of Vishistadvaita* (Madras: Vasanta Press, 1943), p. 94.
165. Ibid., p. 147.
166. Gītābhāṣya 13.1.
167. Śrībhāṣya II.3.40.
168. BG. XVIII.61.
169. Śrībhāṣya II.3.40.
170. Ibid.
171. Ibid., II.3.41.
172. Ibid.
173. Gītābhāṣya 18.13.
174. Ibid., 3.9.20.

175. BG. III.19.
176. Śrībhāṣya 3.4.12.
177. Gītābhāṣya 18.5.
178. Ibid. 18.56.
179. Ibid., II.48,68.
180. Brahma-Sūtra 3.4.27.
181. Gītābhāṣya 18.46; Śrībhāṣya 4.4.22.
182. Ibid., 6.8.
183. Compare, ibid., 2.54–58; 2.72; 3.1ff; 4.8; 4.17ff; 3.34; 3.37; 4.18; 5.1ff; 5.27–28.
184. Van Buitenen, op. cit., p. 21.
185. Gītābhāṣya 6.29, 32.
186. Ibid., 18.46.
187. Radhakrishnan, *Indian Philosophy,* vol. 2, p. 704.
188. Gītābhāṣya 7.1.
189. Ibid., 9.34.
190. Ibid., 9.32.
191. Ibid.
192. Śrībhāṣya I.2.2.
193. Ibid., I.1.1.
194. Chānd. Up. 6.6.5; 7.16.2.
195. Śrībhāṣya I.1.1.
196. Ibid.
197. Ibid.
198. Ibid.
199. Ibid.
200. Ibid.
201. Ibid.
202. Radhakrishnan, *Indian Philosophy,* pp. 704, 705.
203. Śrībhāṣya 4.4.22.
204. Van Buitenen, op. cit. p. 23.
205. Gītābhāṣya 9.25.
206. Ibid.
207. Ibid., 9.26.
208. Ibid., 9.29.
209. Ibid., 9.30.
210. Śrībhāṣya 3.3.57.
211. Gadyatraya, quoted in K. D. Bharadwaj, *The Philosophy of Rāmānuja* (New Delhi: Sir Shankar Lall Charitable Trust Society, 1958), p. 202.
212. A. S. Gupta, *A Critical Study of the Philosophy of Rāmānuja* (Benares: Chowkhamba, 1967), p. 151.

CHAPTER 4

1. R. N. Dandekar, "The Role of Man in Hinduism," in Morgan, op. cit., p. 134.
2. Kaṭha Up. II.24 in J. Rawson, trans., *The Kaṭha Upaniṣad* (London: Oxford University Press, 1934), p. 115.
3. Śrībhāṣya IV.1.13.
4. S. K. Saksena, "The Philosophical Theories and the Affairs of Men," *The Indian Mind,* ed. C. E. Moore (Honolulu: East-West Center Press, 1967), pp. 33, 34.
5. S. K. Maitra, *The Ethics of the Hindus* (Calcutta: Calcutta University Press, 1925), p. 1.

6. Basham, *Wonder,* op. cit., p. 170.
7. Ibid., p. 171.
8. RV. X.CXVII.5.
9. Taitt. Up. I.4.3.
10. K. N. Upadhyaya, "Dharma as a Regulative Principle," p. 1 (unpublished paper).
11. S. K. Saksena, *Essays on Indian Philosophy* (Honolulu: University of Hawaii Press, 1970), p. 40.
12. Manu IV.176 in Upadhyaya trans., op. cit.
13. Manu II.12.
14. Basham, *Aspects,* op. cit., p. 10.
15. Kaṭha Up. I.26.
16. Bṛh. Up. 2.4.1-3.
17. D. S. Sharma, "The Nature and History of Hinduism," Morgan, op. cit., p. 21.
18. Manu VI.36.
19. John Donne, "Devotions."
20. Taitt. Up. I.11.1-4.
21. Radhakrishnan, *Hindu View,* op. cit., p. 64.
22. Manu VI.32.
23. Radhakrishnan, *Hindu View,* op. cit., p. 65.
24. Ibid., p. 66.
25. Saksena, op. cit., p. 48.
26. Basham, *Aspects,* op. cit., p. 6.
27. M. Gandhi, *Young India,* September 22, 1927.
28. T. Welty, *The Asians: Their Heritage and Destiny* (Philadelphia: Lippincott, 1963), pp. 90, 91.
29. Chānd. Up. IV.4.
30. Manu II.168.
31. Mbh. III.CLXXX.2,25.
32. Upadhyaya, *Early Buddhism,* op. cit., p. 507.
33. Maitra, op. cit., p. 18.
34. K. Bhattacharya, "The Status of the Individual in Indian Metaphysics," *Indian Mind,* op. cit., p. 300.
35. Ibid., p. 301.
36. Radhakrishnan, *Indian View,* op. cit., p. 54.
37. Śrībhāṣya, II.3.40.
38. Maitra, op. cit., p. 5.
39. BG. V.25 in Radhakrishnan, trans.
40. Bṛh. Up. I.3.22.
41. Rollo May, *Man's Search for Himself* (New York: Norton, 1953), p. 75.
42. William Wordsworth in *The Golden Treasury,* ed. P. T. Palgrave (London: Nelson and Sons, n.d.), p. 310.

Bibliography

Books Cited

Basham, A. L.

Aspects of Ancient Indian Culture. New York: Asia Publishing House, 1970.

The Wonder That Was India. New York: Grove Press, 1954.

Bharadwaj, K. D.

The Philosophy of Rāmānuja. New Delhi: Sir Shanker Lal Charitable Trust Society, 1958.

Bose, A. C.

Hymns from the Vedas. Bombay: Asia Publishing House, 1966.

Brown, W. N.

Man in the Universe. Berkeley and Los Angeles, California: University of California Press, 1970.

Bühler, G.

Trans., *The Laws of Manu,* in *Sacred Books of the East,* Vol. XXV, F. M. Müller, ed. Oxford: Clarendon Press, 1886.

Trans., *Vāsiṣṭha and Baudhāyana,* in *Sacred Books of the East,* Vol. XIV, F. M. Müller, ed. Oxford: Clarendon Press, 1882.

Trans., *Āpastamba and Gautama,* in *Sacred Books of the East,* Vol. II, F. M. Müller, ed. Oxford: Clarendon Press, 1879.

Chatterjee, S. C. and Datta, D. M.

An Introduction to Indian Philosophy. Calcutta University Press, 1968.

Das, S. K.

A Study of the Vedānta. Calcutta: Calcutta University Press, 1937.

Dasgupta, S.

A History of Indian Philosophy. Vol. 1. Cambridge: Cambridge University Press, 1969.

De Bary, W. T., ed.
Sources of Indian Tradition. Vol. 1. New York: Columbia University Press, 1966.
Deussen, P.
The System of the Vedānta. Chicago, Illinois: Open Court, 1912.
The Philosophy of the Upanishads. 1st ed. New York: Dover Publications, 1966.
Deutsch, E.
Trans., *The Bhagavadgītā*. New York: Holt, Rinehart and Wilson, 1968.
Dutta, R. C.
The Early Hindu Civilization. Calcutta: Punthi Pustak, 1963.
Eggeling, J.
Trans., *Śatapatha Brāhmaṇa,* in *Sacred Books of the East,* Vols. XII, XXVI, XLI, XLIII, XLIV. F. M. Müller, ed. Oxford Clarendon Press.
Gambhirananda, Swami,
Trans., *Eight Upaniṣads*. Calcutta: Advaita Ashrama, 1957.
Garbe, R.
Sāṅkhya, in *Encyclopaedia of Religion and Ethics*. Vol. 11. New York: Scribners, 1925.
Ghosh, J.
Sāṃkhya and Modern Thought. Calcutta: The Book Company, 1930.
Griffith, R. T. H.
The Hymns of the Ṛgveda. Vols. I and II. 3d ed. Benares: Lazarus and Co., 1926.
Gupta, A. S.
A Critical Study of the Philosophy of Rāmānuja. Benares: Chowkhamba, 1967.
Hiriyanna, M.
Outlines of Indian Philosophy. London: Allen and Unwin, 1970.
The Essentials of Indian Philosophy. London: Allen and Unwin, 1967.
Hopkins, E. W.
Ethics of India. New Haven, Connecticut: Yale University Press 1924.
Hume, R. E.
Trans., *The Thirteen Principal Upanishads*. 3d ed. Oxford: Oxford University Press, 1971.
Jha, G.
Trans., *Gautama's Nyāyasūtras (with Vātsyāyana's Bhāṣya),* in Poona Oriental Series, 59. Poona: Poona Book Agency, 1939.
Padārthadharmasaṃgraha of Praśastapāda. Allahabad: E. J. Lazarus and Co., 1916.
The Tattva-Kaumudī. 2d ed. Poona: Oriental Book Agency, 1934.
The Tattva-Kaumudī (Vācaspati Miśra's Commentary on the Sāṁkhya-Kārikā. 2d rev. ed. Poona: Oriental Book Agency, 1934.
Pūrva-Mīmāṃsā in its Sources. Benares: Hindu University Press, 1942.
Mīmāṃsā Sutra. Baroda: Oriental Institute, 1936.
Ślokavārtika by Kumārila Bhāṭṭa. Calcutta: Asiatic Society of Bengal, 1909.

Jolly, J.
Trans., *The Institutes of Vishṇu* in the *Sacred Books of the East,* Vol. VII. F. M. Müller, ed. Oxford: Clarendon Press, 1880.
Joshi, L. M.
Brahmanism, Buddhism and Hinduism. Kandy: Buddhist Publication Society, 1970.
Kanal, S. P.
Dialogues on Indian Culture. Delhi: Panchal Press Publications, 1955.
Keith, A. B.
Indian Logic and Atomism. Oxford: Clarendon Press, 1921.
The Religion and Philosophy of the Vedas and Upanishads, in *Harvard Oriental Series.* Vol. XXXII. C. R. Lanman, ed. Cambridge, Massachusetts: Harvard University Press, 1925.
Macdonell, A. A.
A History of Sanskrit Literature. London: 1900.
Madhavananda,
Vivekachūḍāmaṇi of Śaṅkarācharya. Almora: Advaita Ashrama, 1944.
Majumdar, R. C.
Ancient India. Delhi: Motilal Banarsidass, 1964.
McKenzie, J.
Hindu Ethics. London: Oxford University Press, 1922.
Mookerji, R. K.
Ancient Indian Education. Delhi: Motilal Banarsidass, 1960.
Motwani, K.
Manu Dharma Śāstra. Madras: Ganesh and Co., 1958.
Mukhopadhyaya, G.
Studies in the Upaniṣads. Calcutta: Sanskrit College Series, 1960.
Müller, F. M.
Six Systems of Indian Philosophy. London: Longmans, 1928.
Nikhilananda, Swami,
The Upanishads. New York: Harper and Row, 1964.
Prabhu, P. H.
Hindu Social Organization. Bombay: Popular Prakashan, 1963.
Prasada, R.,
Trans., *Yoga Sūtras of Patañjali,* in *Sacred Books of the Hindus (With the Commentary of Vyāsa and the Gloss of Vāchaspati Miśra).* Vol. IV. B. D. Basu, ed. Allahabad: Panini Office, 1924.
Pārthasārathi
Śāstra-dīpikā. Bombay: Nirnaya Sagar, 1915.
Radhakrishnan, S.
The Vedānta. London: Allen and Unwin, 1928.
Indian Philosophy, Vol. I. London: Allen and Unwin, 1966.
Indian Philosophy, Vol. II. London: Allen and Unwin, 1951.
The Hindu View of Life. New York: Macmillan, 1965.
Trans., *The Brahma Sūtra.* London: Allen and Unwin, 1960.
Trans., *The Bhagavadgītā.* London: Allen and Unwin, 1948.

Radhakrishnan, and C. Moore, Eds. *A Sourcebook in Ind*
Princeton, New Jersey: Princeton University Press, 1967.
Rajagopalachari, C.
Trans., *Rāmāyaṇa*. Bombay: Bharatiya Vidya Bhavan, 1962.
Ramaswamy, T. N.
Trans., *Essentials of Indian Statecraft. Kautilya's Arthasastra for Conten rary Readers.* Bombay: Asia Publishing House, 1962.
Sartre, J. P.
Existentialism and Human Emotions. New York: The Wisdom Library, 1957.
Śālikanātha
Prakaraṇa-pañcikā. Benares: Chowkhamba, 1903.
Sharma, I. C.
Ethical Philosophies of India. Nebraska: Johnsen Publishing House, 1965.
Sinha, N.
Trans., *The Vaiśeṣika Sūtras of Kaṇāda,* in *Sacred Books of the Hindus.* Vol. VI. B. D. Basu, ed. Allahabad: The Panini Office, 1923.
Skinner, B. F.
Beyond Freedom and Destiny.
Srinivaschari, P. N.
The Philosophy of Vishishtadvita. Madras: Vasanta Press, 1943.
Thadani, N.
Trans., *Mimansa: The Secret of the Sacred Books of the Hindus.* Delhi: Bharati Research Institute, 1952.
Thibaut, G.
Trans., *Vedānta-Sūtras (with Rāmānuja's Commentary)* in *Sacred Books of the East.* Vol. XLVIII. Delhi: Motilal Banarsidass, 1962.
Trans., *The Vedānta-Sūtras With Śaṅkara's Commentary,* in *Sacred Books of the East.* Vol. XXXIV. Oxford: Clarendon Press, 1890.
The Cultural Heritage of India. 2d ed. Vol. 1. Calcutta: Ramakrishna Mission, Inst. of Culture, 1958.
Upadhyaya, K. N.
The Bhagavadgītā and Early Buddhism. Delhi: Motilal Banarsidass, 1971.
Van Buitenen, J. A. B.
Rāmānuja on the Bhagavadgītā. Delhi: Motilal Banarsidass, 1968.
Vidyabhusana, S. C.
Trans., *The Nyāya Sūtras of Gotama* in *Sacred Books of the Hindus.* Vol. VII. B. D. Basu, ed. Allahabad: The Panini Office, 1930.
Zimmer, H.
Philosophies of India. 8th ed. New York: The World Publishing Company, 1964.

Index

S. Cromwell Crawford, born in India, grew up in a Hindu ethos, experiencing directly the values about which he writes. His academic background includes: B.D. from Serampore University, India; M.A.T. from Indiana University; and Th.D. from Pacific School of Religion, Berkeley, California. He is also a Fellow of the Royal Asiatic Society of Great Britain and Ireland. He is currently Professor of Religion at the University of Hawaii—with teaching responsibilities in Asian and Western ethics.

Asian Studies at Hawaii

No. 1 *Bibliography of English Language Sources on Human Ecology, Eastern Malaysia and Brunei.* Compiled by Conrad P. Cotter with the assistance of Shiro Saito. September 1965. Two parts. (Available only from Paragon Book Gallery, New York.)

No. 2 *Economic Factors in Southeast Asian Social Change.* Edited by Robert Van Niel. May 1968. Out of print.

No. 3 *East Asian Occasional Papers (1).* Edited by Harry J. Lamley. May 1969.

No. 4 *East Asian Occasional Papers (2).* Edited by Harry J. Lamley. July 1970.

No. 5 *A Survey of Historical Source Materials in Java and Manila.* Robert Van Niel. February 1971.

No. 6 *Educational Theory in the People's Republic of China: The Report of Ch'ien Chung-Jui.* Translated by John N. Hawkins. May 1971. Out of print.

No. 7 *Hai Jui Dismissed from Office.* Wu Han. Translated by C. C. Huang. June 1972.

No. 8 *Aspects of Vietnamese History.* Edited by Walter F. Vella. March 1973.

No. 9 *Southeast Asian Literatures in Translation: A Preliminary Bibliography.* Philip N. Jenner. March 1973.

No. 10 *Textiles of the Indonesian Archipelago.* Garrett and Bronwen Solyom. October 1973. Out of print.

No. 11 *British Policy and the Nationalist Movement in Burma, 1917–1937.* Albert D. Moscotti. February 1974.

No. 12 *Aspects of Bengali History and Society.* Edited by Rachel Van M. Baumer. December 1975.

No. 13 *Nanyang Perspective: Chinese Students in Multiracial Singapore.* Andrew W. Lind. June 1974.

No. 14 *Political Change in the Philippines: Studies of Local Politics preceding Martial Law.* Edited by Benedict J. Kerkvliet. November 1974.

No. 15 *Essays on South India.* Edited by Burton Stein. February 1976.

No. 16 *The* Caurāsī Pad *of Śrī Hit Harivaṁś.* Charles S. J. White. 1977.

No. 17 *An American Teacher in Early Meiji Japan.* Edward R. Beauchamp. June 1976.

No. 18 *Buddhist and Taoist Studies I.* Edited by Michael Saso and David W. Chappell. 1977.

No. 19 *Sumatran Contributions to the Development of Indonesian Literature, 1920–1942.* Alberta Joy Freidus. 1977.

No. 20 *Insulinde: Selected Translations from Dutch Writers of Three Centuries on the Indonesian Archipelago.* Edited by Cornelia N. Moore, 1978.

No. 21 *Regents, Reformers, and Revolutionaries: Indonesian Voices of Colonial Days, Selected Historical Readings, 1899–1949.* Translated, edited, and annotated by Greta O. Wilson, 1978.

No. 22 *The Politics of Inequality: Competition and Control in an Indian Village.* Miriam Sharma. October 1978.

No. 23 *Brokers of Morality: Thai Ethnic Adaptation in a Rural Malaysian Setting.* Louis Golomb. February 1979.

No. 24 *Tales of Japanese Justice.* Ihara Saikaku. Translated by Thomas M. Kondo and Alfred H. Marks. January 1980.

No. 25 *Mandarins, Gunboats, and Power Politics: Owen Nickerson Denny and the International Rivalries in Korea.* Robert R. Swartout, Jr. March 1980.

No. 26 *Nichiren: Selected Writings.* Laurel Rasplica Rodd. 1980.

No. 27 *Ethnic Groups and Social Change in a Chinese Market Town.* C. Fred Blake. 1980.

No. 28 *The Evolution of Hindu Ethical Ideals.* S. Cromwell Crawford. 1982.

Orders for Asian Studies at Hawaii publications should be directed to The University Press of Hawaii, 2840 Kolowalu Street, Honolulu, Hawaii 96822. Present standing orders will continue to be filled without special notification.